THE EARLY DOORS

THE EARLY DOORS

ORIGINS OF THE MUSIC HALL

HAROLD SCOTT

EP Publishing Limited
1977

First published by Ivor Nicholson &
Watson Ltd., London, 1946

Republished 1977 by
EP Publishing Limited
East Ardsley, Wakefield
West Yorkshire, England

ISBN 0 7158 1219 X

British Library Cataloguing in Publication Data

Scott, Harold
The early doors.
1. Music-halls (Variety-theaters, cabarets, etc.) – Great Britain – History
I. Title
792.7'0941 PN1968.G7
ISBN 0-7158-1219-X

Please address all enquiries to EP Publishing Limited
(address as above)

Printed in Great Britain by
The Scolar Press Limited
Ilkley, West Yorkshire

By courtesy of British Museum

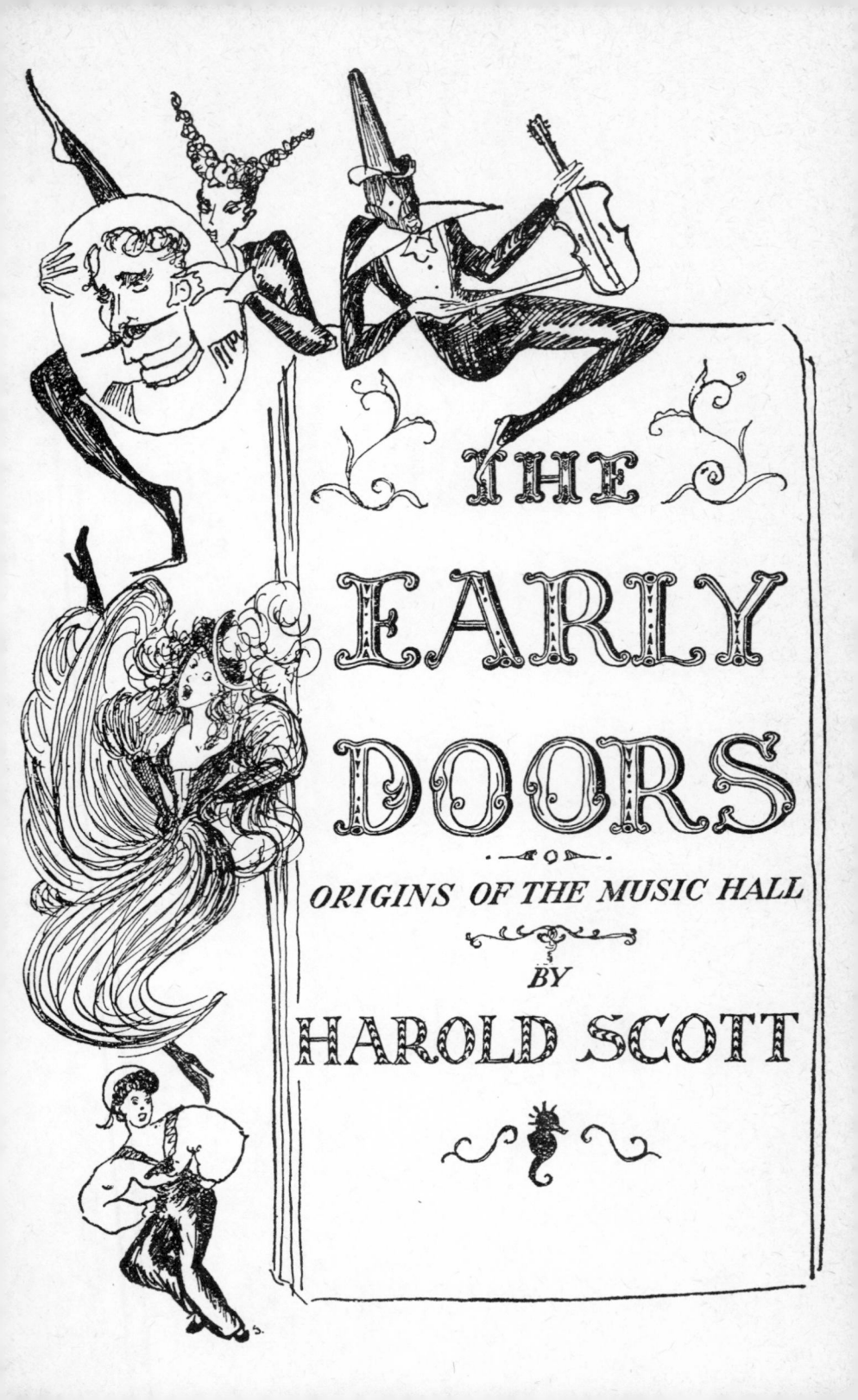

THE EARLY DOORS

ORIGINS OF THE MUSIC HALL

BY

HAROLD SCOTT

TO
BARBARA
WITH
LOVE

CONTENTS

FOREWORD

I HAVE given no particulars of the Music Hall of a later date than the nineteen-twenties, except in the case of the note on managers which is written as applying to the year 1935, a year which closely preceded the death of some famous figures, such as Sir Oswald Stoll, who died in 1942. My very grateful thanks are given to Miss Enid Brett for her assistance in compiling references ; to the officials of the Music Departments at the British Museum for their help in tracing obscure songs ; and to Mr. W. L. Hanchant, who opened for me his remarkable store of nineteenth-century scholarship.

THE EARLY DOORS

CHAPTER I

Introductory

THE ACHIEVEMENTS of the Music Hall in the 'eighties and 'nineties revealed its significance even to the world of culture, to whose self-conscious influence it owed, by that time, very little. Poets and painters found their way to it, in the company of Max Beerbohm and Havelock Ellis. The most level-headed among these critics and enthusiasts was Max himself. He found that the Music Hall sought to hold up to ridicule a life even more sordid than that forced upon the majority of its audiences; and further pronounced "without mitigation or remorse of voice" that its laughter was based upon "a delight in suffering and a contempt for the unfamiliar." But he also showed, in his studies of the greater artists, how subtle was the transmutation of these elements—how, in the work of Dan Leno and Marie Lloyd, for instance, the selfish cackle developed into a good-humoured roar. There is no gradual process of evolution to be discerned in this, it is simply that their gifts and sensitivity were of a high order and that in the Music Hall they found a place in which to become articulate.

The subject-matter was the same as always, the jokes the oldest jokes in the world. (Or, more accurately, as Beerbohm points out, not of necessity "the same old jokes but jokes on the same old subjects.") He has listed them; it is not a long list but it is comprehensive and it squares with his analysis of Music Hall humour. Oddly, however, his list does not contain the joke about red noses—"through what wild centuries . . ." !

In all such matters there is no beginning to the story and it is difficult to make a start in telling it. Of equally ancient origin, for example, is the other side of Max Beerbohm's picture: the Music Halls' contribution to the art of make-believe, the attempt to give the puzzle-picture of life a richly romantic and glossy surface. This aspect of the Music Hall, for which it borrowed

material from outside sources, supplies an excuse for some of the excursions into adjacent territory which are made in this book.

If one were not searching for origins and for a point of view, it would be fairly logical to begin with Charles Morton and his Canterbury Music Hall (his admirers called him "The Father of the Halls"). But I hope it will be of interest to readers to try for something more; and to give some attention to the historical background of miscellaneous entertainment.

Enquiry into Music Hall origins has not often been made with much enthusiasm; historians have identified that world of rogues and vagabonds with its economic and social limitations.

In most periods the type of performer associated with variety entertainment has been forced to follow his profession under a cloud of disapproval; he has sometimes been denied a place in the community. This attitude has never become completely obsolete and it is older than the Christian Church. In mediæval England it was certainly weakened by custom but it broke out again during the Commonwealth. Secular legislation reflected the religious attitude as early as the fourteenth century.

At the Renaissance, cultural prejudices replaced the religious ones and the eighteenth century added social barriers.

In the nineteenth century, however, on the wave of the mania for popular education in the form of "instructional entertainment," an extraordinary thing happened. Variety performances began to range themselves with this movement and it was in this connection, as we shall see later, that Charles Morton seized his opportunity.

But Morton's Picture Gallery and Concert performances of Grand Opera at The Canterbury were soon shaken off when the Music Hall became firmly established. Simultaneously the comic song, which had wilted under a literary influence, came into its own. The comic song was the corner-stone of the genuine Music Hall. It called for a new type of performer and gave opportunities to men (and a little later to women) who could be funny though they might be completely uneducated. In genuinely democratic surroundings these songs and their singers created a tremendous vogue and men like George Leybourne became as famous as Henry Irving. This raciness is the vital element in Music Hall history. The popular voice had broken through; popular expression, thwarted at one time and another, found itself housed and recognized.

* * * *

During the Middle Ages there would appear to have been no popular theatre. There is a hint of the drama in various festivals and celebrations and, of course, the liturgical plays

performed in the churches or their precincts. But dramatic performances, it seems, were absent even from courtly life. There are, however, good grounds for assuming that in very early days there existed the practice of acting a kind of play on the platforms of booths at fairs or markets. These probably bore some resemblance to the "drolls" of which Francis Kirkham published examples in 1673. He called his book *The Wits: or Sport Upon Sport,* and the little pieces in it consisted mainly of incidents from plays popular before Cromwell closed the theatres. But three of them are of a different character. They are "jigs"; that is to say, they are dramatized songs or song playlets. These jigs had found their way into the theatre of Shakespeare and were performed by comedians such as Tarleton and Kempe. In one of his studies W. J. Lawrence has suggested that Tarleton may have been the inventor of the "jig," but it seems more likely that it was a popular, though unrecorded item of entertainment before his time.

The important Elizabethan theatres were built expressly for the performance of full-length plays. They were designed to house the developing drama, which grew within the space of fifty years from *Gammer Gurton's Needle* to *Romeo and Juliet.* But before the building of the regular theatres and co-existing with them were other places of entertainment, also known as Playhouses, of which there is practically no record. Historians have described these places as harbouring performances of "the lowest class." There is also mention of various "activities" such as fencing, acrobatics, feats of strength and the like, which would remind a contemporary audience of the modern "Variety Theatre." Here "jigs" would find a natural home, and their presence in the "literary" theatre would be accounted for as an interpolated popular feature. (The Dumb shows sometimes included in the plays quite possibly had a similar origin.)

The regular theatres themselves often lapsed into variety performances, just as did the Edwardian theatres before the outbreak of the 1914 war. The Swan, for instance, at first a lavishly equipped house devoted to important plays, was later used for those "activities" which we should to-day unhesitatingly call Music Hall performances. Bankside teemed with comic singers, rope dancers, animal trainers, musicians and the like, and when this theatre or the other declined, they surged in.

This early Music Hall did not develop; the scene was set but nothing much happened. Patronage was lacking and the age of capitalism had not yet arrived. Puppet shows, however, appear to have been successfully exploited in the theatre, for it is on record that at a performance at the Red Bull in 1599 a gallery gave way under the pressure of a crowded audience.

In the regular theatre the actors had not yet become specialized performers. There are many evidences of the astonishing versatility of the comedians.[1] The fact is that they were variety artists who, by accident, found themselves playing the comic parts in Shakespeare's plays. The comedians supplied the purely professional element in the public theatres. The actors of the tragedies were at first mostly recruited from the amateur or semi-amateur performers in the town plays and miracles. Most of Burbage's colleagues belonged also to other professions, in which they remained after they had become liveried servants of their aristocratic patrons.

The comedians influenced the plays they performed in and claimed scenes especially contrived for them. The liberties they were in the habit of taking with the text annoyed Shakespeare, who delivered a famous reproof in *Hamlet* which is familiar to all playgoers.

What type of men, one wants to know, were those interlopers from the taverns and fair grounds who gave a comic leaven to the Elizabethan drama? Among them the personality of Richard Tarleton has left the most vivid impression. If not exactly an innovator, he must have been a performer of great originality. His most celebrated talent was his ability to answer in extemporized rhyme any question or comment levelled at him by the audience. He probably took hints for some of his repertoire from the visiting Italian companies, who came to England in the fifteen-seventies, who were themselves experts in extemporization. Some of his performances were in line with the "sketches" and playlets of the *commedia del arte*. But this extemporizing in rhyme may very well have been his own idea. This is a feat which has remained to the present day in the catalogue of music hall accomplishments. In the early nineteenth century, Charles Sloman made himself famous with this trick at the Cider Cellars, and years ago I heard the same thing done in a cabaret performance at the Kit Kat Club. Tarleton excelled also in a form of lyrical one-man "jig," or "very long humorous song," as Halliwell-Philips calls it, differing in no important particular from the modern music hall song. An example of this type of

[1]As, for example, that company of comedians, mentioned by Chambers (*The Elizbethan Stage*, II, 272), who accompanied Leicester to Holland when he took command of the English forces in 1585, and who gave a show, half dramatic, half acrobatic, of the *Forces of Hercules*, at Utrecht on April 23rd, 1586. Similar demands would doubtless be made from the English actors introduced into Germany by Robert Browne, who spent considerable periods in that country from 1590-1620 and took with him "relays of actors, some of whom split off into independent associations, and account for most, although not all, of the groups of Englanders who became familiar figures at the Frankfort spring and autumn fairs, and even in out-of-the-way corners of northern Europe."

song is *Tarleton's Jigge of a Horse-loade of Fooles*, now held to be, at any rate partially, a forgery. To compensate us, however, there is the long jig printed over the initials R. T., called *The Crow sits on the Wall*, which may very well be the work of Richard Tarleton, who was possibly an author in his way. The first three verses are representative of the entire seventeen.

Please one and please all,
Be they great, be they small,
Be they little, be they lowe—
So pypeth the crowe,
Sitting upon a wall—
Please one and please all,
Please one and please all.

Be they white, be they black,
Haue they a smock on their back,
Or a kircher on their head,
Whether they spin silke or thred,
Whatsoeuer they them call—
Please one and please all,
Please one and please all.

Be they sluttish, be they gay,
Loue they worke, or loue they play,
Whatsoeuer be theyr cheere,
Drinke they ale, or drinke they beere,
Whether it be strong or small—
Please one and please all,
Please one and please all.[1]

Catch phrases of the time such as " Please one, please all " and " What d'ye lack ? " were undoubtedly characteristic of these songs, as they are of the modern comic song.

There are many stories extant about Tarleton, which, though possibly apocryphal, help us to build up a strong feeling of his personality. Essentially a funny *person*, " much of his merriment lay in his very looks and actions. The self-same words spoken by another would hardly force a sad soul to laughter." This fundamental quality was helped out by the little man's possession of a funny face. His nose was flattened, which gave his big eyes a chance to be more than usually expressive. He exploited this funniness by a trick of appearing suddenly between the stage

[1]The entire jig may be found in the Philobiblon Society's publication, *Ancient Ballads and Broadsides*, 1867, pp. 377 *et seq.*

curtains.[1] He often supplied his own musical accompaniment and made a point of entering the stage beating a drum. Allied to his supreme stage sense in the use of extemporized humour, his appeal seems always to have been to the good-natured and the human. There is a vivid story of Tarleton when he was performing at the Belle Sauvage visiting a neighbouring performance at which was exhibited Banks' Celebrated Trained Horse. On seeing Tarleton in the room, the trainer told the horse to pick out the " veriest fool in the company." The horse came straight to Tarleton and drew him towards the platform. " God 'a mercy, horse ! " said Tarleton, in such an inimitable manner that the exclamation became a cant phrase of the time.[2]

Such artists as Tarleton we may take to be the aristocracy of that miscellaneous crowd of performers who belong by tradition to the great wandering theatre of the open air. They find their places in the theatre by virtue of the fact that its *personnel* was dependent in certain cases upon these performers. We have seen that the actors of morality and tragedy were in early instances enthusiastic amateurs. " The japes, toys, marionettes and inventions " of the professional comedian were importations into the theatre of literature and often affected the structure of the play. Indeed, they became at times a thorn in the side of the author, and Shakespeare, as we have said, complained of " gagging " comedians in *Hamlet*.[3] Their material was handed down by tradition through performances at the fairs, in inn-yards, and such other places of assembly as baiting rings and halls hired for performances.

Of these the fairs provided perhaps the most important *venue* of the travelling actor. Hundreds of these existed up and down the country, necessary themselves as an integer in the life of a

[1]This trick of sudden appearance was later to be associated with Dan Leno and George Robey : the characteristic entrance of Leno is described by Harry Randall (*Harry Randall, Old Time Comedian*, by Himself, p. 147) : " a quick run down to the footlights, a roll like a drum with his feet, his leg raised, and brought down with a loud clap from the foot."

[2]Two further anecdotes are taken from the posthumous *Tarleton's Jests*. The first tells *How Tarleton deceives the watch in Fleet Street :* " Tarleton, having bin late at court, and comming homwards throw Fleet Street, he espied the watch, and not knowing how to passe them, hee went very fast, thinking by that meanes to goe unexamined. But the watchmen, perceiving that hee shunned them, stept to him and commanded him, in the Queene's name, to stand. Stand ! quoth Tarleton, let them stand that can : for I cannot. So falling downe as though he had been drunke, they helpt him up, and so let him passe."

The second occasion is that *Of Tarleton's wrongful accusation :* " Upon a time Tarleton was wrongfully accused for getting of a gentleman's maid with child, and for the same brought before a justice in Kent, which justice said as followeth : it is a mervaile, M. Tarleton, that you, being a gentleman of good qualitie, and one of her majestie's servants, would venture thus to get maides with child. Nay, rather quoth Tarlton, were it marvell, if a maid had gotten me with child."

" [3]And let those that play your clowns speak no more than is set down for them." *Hamlet* III, 2.

community lacking modern methods of transport. A brief survey of the entertainments at these fairs must suffice for our purpose. The most famous and, to modern readers, the most familiar, was that held in the vicinity of the Church and Priory of St. Bartholomew the Great in Smithfield. Rahere, its founder, was representative of the educated minstrels of the eleventh century. He joined the Church, became the first prior of St. Bartholomew and conceiving the idea of the fair, obtained grants as a means of exploiting it for the benefit of his Order. Here at a very early date were assembled, as in more recent times, all those elements of popular entertainment to which reference has been made. The fair is perhaps the most conservative institution in the country. At the present day a visit, for instance, to that assemblage of side-shows which annually surrounded the circus held at Olympia takes one straight back through all these centuries. Bartholomew Fair flourished, though its history was occasionally chequered, from the eleventh to the early nineteenth century, its demise being finally pronounced in the words of Augustus Sala, " by an assemblage of Victorian aldermen."[1]

The fair was the natural home of the puppet show—an entertainment of great antiquity and an instance of the Latin tradition. Records of puppets and marionettes indicate that they have always been used to reflect in miniature the larger stage of the human actor, and from their prevalence in the Middle Ages is to be adduced the probability of a knowledge of plays and dialogue throughout the period. Strictly, this cannot be taken as a final proof, for it is obviously possible to exhibit puppets spectacularly or in scenes of action without these additions. But it is known that these shows gave representations of the moralities and mysteries, performances of which type can sometimes be seen in the villages of France and Belgium.[2] The balance of probability is in favour of a complete continuity in dramatic performances on the puppet stage.

The exhibition in the nineteenth century of miniature figures worked by some form of mechanism belongs to the peep-show rather than to the puppet stage, and in the peep-show we see the precursor of the " diorama " and similar entertainments on a large scale. This type of show is also of great, though perhaps not such great antiquity as the puppet show. Their focus of interest is the setting and they may be said to have fostered among poorer folk the demand for theatrical display unobtainable

[1]The range of its performances is fully illustrated by the reproductions in Prof. Morley's *History of Bartholomew Fair* and, more recently, by the collection assembled by Mr. McKechnie in his *History of Popular Entertainment throughout the Ages :* animal impersonators, comic singers, and acrobats all figure in these delineations.

[2]An excellent description of one of these latter performances may be read in Aldous Huxley's story, *Little Mexican.*

by other means. For the aristocracy this instinct could always be satisfied by "disguisings," masques and the elaborate machinery of court revels ; in the peep-show one may sense a humble approach to such things. Later, towards the end of the eighteenth century, when the booths had acquired a wealthier standing, they borrowed all the tinsel grandeur of the contemporary stages ; the reaction was mutual, for these stages themselves must have owed not a little in their tricks and transformation scenes to the elaborations and performances of puppet shows which developed before the popular stage had aspired to any degree of magnificence. In the later Middle Ages—when the Church was producing vast miracle performances in their three-dimensional settings—some of that richness had reached the masses ; but in the early ecclesiastical theatre there was nothing to marvel at beyond the tableaux with their costly vestments placed in the churches at times of festival.[1] Some of the mechanical devices of the peep-show and certain forms of the puppet show derived directly from this practice and carried into the humblest surroundings that creation of illusion and the fantasy of a unreal world which is perhaps the basis of all popular entertainment and which was brought into the music hall by way of the ballet pantomimes and extravaganzas of the minor theatres and saloons. I have not been able to obtain particulars of the extent to which mechanical devices were used by early puppet or peep-shows, but one may assume that the type of show given by Powell, Flockton, and Pinketman in the early eighteenth century had been in existence centuries before their time. The spectacular element in these shows was very marked.[2]

It will readily be seen that the conception of the "diorama[3]" (introduced in the late eighteenth century and achieving a tremendous popular vogue in the early nineteenth century) has

[1]It may be pointed out that at the Commonwealth, a time when the Church had dispensed with all elements of theatrical display and every attempt was being made to suppress dramatic spectacle, the puppet-shows alone remained to satisfy these instincts.

[2]I have a recollection of a street peep-show. I saw as a child in London one which could have been of mediæval structure. It consisted of a large box, wheeled on a hand-cart. Shells were fixed to the exterior of the proscenium side of the box, forming a kind of grotto, and the scene depicted was the interior of a Cathedral, possibly Canterbury, in which a procession of choir boys and Church dignitaries moved erkily when the proprietor turned a handle.

[3] "A spectacular painting or connected series of paintings intended for exhibition to spectators in a darkened room, in a manner to produce by optical illusion an appearance of reality."—(*Chambers' Encyclopedia*). [Notes : p.1]

The diorama, then, was a variant of the panorama—a term also used to describe any large painting displayed in such a manner as to produce some illusion of reality. Dioramas usually consisted of a moving picture placed on rollers and lit in a number of cunning ways to produce a heightened effect. Sometimes, however, it was the audience which moved, the seats in this instance being placed on a revolving rostrum.

[0]See *infra*, page 73.

far more in common with those penny shows which sought to exhibit all the wonders of the world in silent pageantry, than with the pantomimic spectacles which base their origin on the masks of the Renaissance. On the other hand, the puppet show and the masque are themselves coeval and related institutions, the difference being chiefly one of magnitude. In the puppet show is the same approach to the marvellous, the same attempt to create an illusion of life in new forms; the elaborate machinery only is lacking.

It is probable that a good deal of mechanical elaboration in the peep-shows is of very early date. Here is the substance of an eighteenth-century play, clearly a mediæval survival, quoted by Strutt in *Sports and Pastimes*: "Noah and his family coming out of the Ark with all the beasts two and two, and all the fowls of the air seen in a prospect sitting upon trees . . . moreover, a multitude of angels will be seen in a double rank, which presents a double prospect, one for the sun, the other for a palace, where will be seen six Angels ringing of bells; Likewise Machines descend from above, double, and treble with Dives rising out of Hell, and Lazarus seen in Abraham's bosom."

The marionette shows had another and important function, that of being used on the booth parades as a means of drawing attention to the shows within. A famous illustration of this use is to be found in Ben Jonson's *Bartholomew Fair*. In addition to such performances, songs and dances, as well as snatches of dialogue, were all used for the same purpose.

The puppets and peep-shows have persisted through the centuries. In Mayhew's *London Labour and the London Poor* are to be found many entertaining particulars of the methods of the itinerant peep-show men of the nineteenth century. The proprietor of a peep-show was interviewed and spoke of the two types of show-case used. "There are two kinds of peep-shows, which we call 'back shows' and 'caravan shows.' The caravan-shows are much larger than the others, and are drawn by a horse or by a donkey. They have a green-baize curtain at the back, which shuts them out as don't pay. The showmen usually lives in these caravans with their families . . . these caravans mostly go into the country, and are seldom seen in town. They exhibit principally at fairs and feasts, or wakes, in country villages. . . . The scenes of them caravan shows is mostly upon recent battles and murders. Anything in that way, of late occurrence, suits them. Theatrical plays ain't no good for country towns, 'cause they don't understand such things there. People is werry fond of the battles in the country, but a murder wot is well known is worth more than all the fights. . . . The back shows are peep-shows that stand upon tressles, and are so small as to

admit of being carried on the back. The scenery is about eighteen inches to two foot in length, and about fifteen inches high. . . . The back shows generally exhibits plays of different kinds wot's been performed at the theayters lately."

* * * *

In earlier times the use of some form of variety entertainment was, particularly, a favourite device of the mountebank as a prologue to his harangue; itself developed with so much art as almost to be included in the same category. Kirkman, in his preface to *The Wits*, recommends his drolls to him for this purpose in the following words: "If the mountebank will but carry this book, and three or four young fellows to act what is here set down for them, it will most certainly draw in auditors enough." For the most part, as to-day, the rougher elements of entertainment predominated. In *The Walk to Smithfield, or A description of Bartholomew Fair*, 1701, the clown attached to a booth is described as exhibiting, on his arrival on the platform, "a singular instance of his cleverness by blowing his nose upon the people."

A year before this visit to the fair, the shows known as "the singing booths"—the nearest approach in the fair to a music hall entertainment—had been suppressed on the excuse of the alleged obscenity of the performances and the undesirable behaviour of their audiences. One of them, however, that managed by the celebrated Pinketman and known as "Pinketman's Medley," still remained for our visitor to describe; here were to be seen vaulting, ladder dances and a wheel-barrow dance. Ned Ward in the previous year also describes a visit to a music booth which Professor Morley assumes to have been the Turk's Head booth. He makes the following quotation from its advertisement: "You will see a Scaramouch dance, the Italian punch's dance, the quarterstaff, the antick, and the Merry Cuckholds of Hogsden, etc., etc." One may assume a complete variety entertainment in the singing booth from the fact that the dramatic booth was beginning to offer a fully fledged theatrical programme. Tom Dogget, a celebrated actor and a patentee of Drury Lane Theatre, was already associated with the King's Players' Booth, and Elkanah Settle, Dryden's rival, was at work at about the same time on the adaptations of his tragedies for the booth stage.

In 1699, the year before his pilgrimage to Smithfield, Ned Ward had paid a visit to the music house at Sadler's Wells. Here in this early example of an alfresco entertainment centre, a variety show was in full swing. There will be occasion later to speak of the tendency to take pleasure in public gardens, which slightly

predated the Restoration and probably derived from French and Italian sources. Sadler's Wells, being prettily situated on a slight eminence, in a village within easy walking distance of the centre of London, was at a spot conveniently placed for this form of diversion. Ward, in vigorous rhymed couplets, describes how, in holiday time he took a walk with a female acquaintance in the fields near the New River-head and with her turned into the recently opened grounds of Islington Spa. They did not find this visit altogether to their taste and their fancies, inclining to

> " some pretty Collation
> Of Cheesecakes, and Custards, and pidgeon-pye-puff,
> With Bottle-Ale, Cider and such sort of stuff,"

This visit was paid only a few years after the re-discovery of the mineral spring, known two hundred years before to the monks of the Priory of St. John, by whom it was apparently turned to some commercial advantage. The discovery does not mark the origin of the house and its garden as a pleasure centre ; it claimed legal status as such in the reign of Elizabeth. But the spring greatly enhanced the attraction of the place. Not only could it claim, on the most respectable authority, to have medicinal properties, but springs and waterfalls as an aid to amusement were becoming fashionable. The Spring Gardens at Charing Cross (on the site of the present Admiralty Arch), and the Mulberry Gardens (nearby where Buckingham Palace now stands), provided instances of this form of diversion. The former had the more elaborate arrangements ; in addition to a bathing pool, an archery ground, and bowling houses, there was a concealed spring which, upon the pressure of the foot, sprang they made their way into Sadler's " for the sake of the organ."[1]

[1]An interesting note on the presence of organs in taverns (including, of course, such houses as Sadler's Wells), is to be found in a seventeenth century *Character of England*, reprinted in the second volume of the *Harleian Miscellany*. The passage is as follows :

> " . . . . There are a meaner sort of Cabarets . . . and that nothing may be wanting to the height of luxury and impiety of this abomination, they have translated the organs out of the Churches, to set them up in Taverns : chanting their Dithyrhambis and bestial bacchanalias to the tune of those instruments which were wont to assist them in the celebration of God's praises, and regulate the voices of the worst singers in the world ; which are the English, and in their Churches at present."

Although in the pre-" talkie " days of the cinema orchestral or organ accompaniment was, for the most part, reserved for dramatic feature films and shorter films of the " to see much is to learn much " type, organ accompaniments to the comic films were occasionally to be heard. Perhaps a closer, relevant parallel between the cinema and the gardens occurs in the fact that owing to the small salaries of church organists then and now the eighteenth and nineteenth century gardens were able to attract the services of the church organists very much as the cinema did at a later date.

See Chapter III.

up and " wetted whoever was foolish or ignorant enough to tread upon it."

The Music House which was built in the latter part of the seventeenth century centralized the amusements at Sadler's Wells, though for a time performances were not confined to the interior of this building. The acrobats and contortionists still performed among the trees, and early in the eighteenth century Mrs. Pearson could be heard playing her dulcimer at the end of the Long Walk. Later, the whole show moved indoors, though dancing still took place on a circular platform derived from the threshing floors used for the same purpose in harvest-home celebrations. The habit persisted and was still in vogue at Cremorne, when it closed in 1877.

At this point we may return to Ned Ward and follow him into the Music House. There is a vivid description of the audience. Then Ward and his trull go up into the balcony, as in the nineteenth century the more exclusive part of the auditorium (a long quotation must be forgiven for the richness of the detail) :

" Thus having Refresh'd ourselves after our Walk,
We look'd o'er the Gallery like the rest of the Folk ;
Without-side of which, the Spectators to please,
Were Gods Painted roving in Clouds in Seas ; and

. . . . .

" Our Eyes being glutted with this pretty Sight,
We began to look down and examine the Pit,
Where Butchers and Bayliffs, and such sort of Fellows,
Were mix'd with a Vermin train'd up to the Gallows.

. . . . .

" And some with the Tapsters, were got in a Fray,
Who without Paying Reck'ning were stealing away,
Which made Lady Squab, with her Moonifi'd Face,
By the side of the Organ, resume her old Place,

With hands on her Belly, she open'd her Throat,
And silenc'd the Noise, with her Musical Note :
The Guests were all Hush, and Attention was given,
The listening Mob thought themselves in a Heaven ;
If the Ravishing Song which she sung, you wou'd know,
It was *Rub, rub, rub ; rub, rub, rub ; in and out ho.*

" As soon as her sweet, modest Ditty was done,
She withdrew from her Wicker, as Chaste as a Nun.
The Butchers so pleas'd with her warbling strains,
Both Knock'd her, and Clap'd her all round for her Pains.

Then up starts a Fiddler, in Scarlet, so fierce,
So unlike an *Orpheus*, he look'd like a *Mars*.
He runs up in Alt, with a Hey-diddle-diddle
To shew what a Fool he could make of a Fiddle ;
And has such an excellent hand at a Pinch,
He hits half a Note to a Quarter of an Inch.
Then in comes a Damsel drest up in her Tinsy,
Too Homely and Sluttish to tickle one's Fancy ;
By her Impudence sure, tho' she's Ag'd but Eleven,
She knew how to Sin by the time she was Seven ;
Arm'd *Amazon* like, with abundance of Rapiers,
Which she puts to her throat, as she Dances and Capers.
And further, the Mob's Admiration to kindle,
She turns on her Heel like a Wheel on a Spindle ;

. . . . .

" The next that appear'd, was a Young Babe of Grace,
With *Merc'ry* in's Heels, and a Gallows in's Face ;

. . . . .

" Then in a Clown's Dress comes my honest Friend *Thomas*,
Who looks by his Bulk to be Lord of the *Domus* ;
He cocks up his Hat, draws his Heels to his Arse,
And makes his own Person as good as a *Farce*."

The gallery at Sadler's Wells is clearly a heritage from the balcony of the Elizabethan theatre, which was the seated, and, therefore, the more expensive part of the auditorium. Indeed, in the earlier music houses the occupants of the ground space probably stood, as at the Globe or the Swan, for such an arrangement would facilitate indoor dancing. This system of pricing the house remained a feature of the music houses, though the change to modern methods was made in the regular theatre in the seventeenth century. In this respect, as in many others, the saloon theatres of the mid-Victorian period, such as the Britannia and the Grecian, are directly related to the Elizabethan houses.

Thus under the conditions I have endeavoured to outline, the scattered community of Bankside continued for centuries to practise its art. In spite of the severities it suffered from time to time, this miscellaneous entertainment continued to play its important part in the life of the people.

CHAPTER II

Before 1843

WITH the early days of the eighteenth century, the progress of miscellaneous entertainment developed into an invasion of the theatre. Then began the many interactions which, originating with the introduction of English pantomime, multiplied through an entire century, and blurred the dramatic outline.

In 1737 this tendency to confusion received a stimulus from the passing of the Licensing Act, which pronounced all forms of play-production illegal, except at those two theatres (Covent Garden and Drury Lane) holding the royal patents granted by Charles II.

I propose to deal in a later chapter with the history of the events leading up to this situation : for the moment, it is sufficient to note that the evasions of this law, under which dramatic performances were presented in a *quasi*-variety form, intensified the break-up of the regular drama which had been heralded by Rich's introduction of harliquinade at Covent Garden in 1717.

The minor theatres' very successful struggle for existence during which the nominal avoidance of illegality was reduced to a fine art, led to a kind of retaliation by retreat on the part of those who were upholding their sole right to perform the works of Shakespeare and Marlowe ; and early in the nineteenth century we hear, as a consequence, of troops of elephants at Covent Garden, and of water-tanks, freaks and giants at Drury Lane. Indeed, pantomime, which in its English form was a receptacle for many elements of variety, became universal, and even found its way into the repertory of David Garrick.

The confusion, worse confounded as time went on, might even have tended to obliterate any clear demarcation of theatrical form, had it not, by rendering the situation an almost complete *reductio ad absurdum*, led eventually to further legislation.

The Act of 1843 made it possible for all places of entertainment holding the strange " burletta licence," to present stage plays—

so long as they were willing to accept the embargo imposed upon them as to smoking and the sale of intoxicants.[1]

The visible effect of this legislation, however, was by no means immediate. The act of 1843 did nothing to restore a purely dramatic movement on the one hand, or to bring the music hall into being on the other.

For a number of years before 1843, the vogue for miscellaneous entertainment had made many of the tavern saloons ambitious to challenge the minor theatres on their own ground. Ballets, farces and extravaganzas were being performed wherever a hastily put together stage in the " long room " made it physically possible to do so, and the Act was passed at a moment when the minor theatres and the larger saloons were offering an almost identical type of performance. Indeed, the development of a distinct music hall form was, actually, a reluctant one, and in spite of the example set by Evans's Song and Supper Rooms, would not have been effected, but for the dominant factor of the new legislation prohibiting dramatic entertainment accompanied by eating and drinking in the auditorium. On this point, Government control, acting in the interest of those who had taken up the dramatic licence, was of the severest kind. It is easy to see how serious a handicap this enactment was to those places in which audiences had been trained to expect an entertainment which contained a dramatic element accompanied by refreshments. Managers who found it advisable to retain the undisputed right to produce plays, were naturally extremely jealous of any infringement of that right on the part of houses which chose the alcoholic privilege ; for, although drinking in the auditorium had been largely abandoned in the major theatres, it had been fully exploited at all the others. In the houses of an intermediate type—such as the Grecian—the sale of food and drink was an especially important feature. The Grecian was the leading saloon theatre of London ; by this phrase the reader will at once perceive the existence of a hybrid, half theatre and half tavern, at which the Act of 1843 aimed a blow. The rise of the saloon theatre reflects a hundred years' development of the lower middle class, and their special characteristics were brought into existence by that class's borrowed preference for alfresco pleasure haunts, for a characteristic of the saloon theatre was that it stood in its own pleasure grounds.

As we have seen from instances cited in the previous chapter, this movement was already well on foot at the Restoration ;

[1]Clement Scott, in his *Drama of Yesterday and Today*, claims to have remembered alcoholic drinking in the auditorium of Drury Lane in 1849. Here his memory must be at fault, but beer was probably drunk in the pit and gallery until the passing of the Act.

[2]*See* Chapter VII, page 116 *et seq.*

henceforward there was to be an overwhelming growth of the gardens and tavern grounds. That growth was rapidly brought to a high standard of development after the opening, on an enlarged plan, of the New Spring Gardens at Vauxhall in June 1732, by Jonathan Tyers. The success of this venture was so complete and instantaneous, that within a few years, imitations of Vauxhall—its attractions reproduced on a miniature scale—were to be found surrounding their parent taverns in all parts of London and its suburbs. Where ground was already available, or could be acquired, it was developed, and in all directions there is a tale of enlargement and reconstruction, though an unusual exception to this rule is to be found at the tavern and music house at Sadler's Wells. Here the garden and its medicinal spring were given no prominence beyond the early years of the eighteenth century, and this abandonment encouraged the characteristics which later gave the place a certain odium in the locality. As a spa, Sadler's Wells had always much to contend with, due to the severity of local competition set up by the miraculous discovery of healing waters all over the neighbourhood.

Except in the notable instance at Vauxhall, which at its inception was designed to attract an aristocratic patronage, these gardens became the background for a much broader type of entertainment than that which could easily be housed in a tavern room. At first, they probably concentrated more upon sport than upon the arts of entertainment. A quotation has already been made from Ned Ward which contains a reference to the gaming houses at Islington Spa. At the Haymarket Spring Gardens there were " a fair house and two bowling greens, made to entertain bowlers and gamesters," and, in addition, there was a tennis court. Mulberry Gardens had a bathing pool, and the simple sport of " pulling off cherries and, God knows what " in a " pretty contrived plantation " appeared, according to Pepys, in 1665, to have satisfied visitors to the rustic " Fox Hall." But a significant note is struck by another observation of the same chronicler:— " Here fiddles and there a harp, here a jew's trump."

The inquirer into the history of the early music hall will feel less a sense of strangeness from the innocent nature of these pleasures, on discovering that the Canterbury Arms opened its career in 1849 with glee-singing and that at the Strand Musick Hall, the appearance of the favourite comedian " Jolly " Nash alternated with evenings devoted to the Masque of *Comus*. For one must remember that nineteenth century entertainment was, in its earlier stages, coloured by the remembrance of times when a distorting mirror at one end of a banqueting

room, or the playing of Handel's music on Mr. Bridge's water organ, were considered equally amusing diversions.[1]

Of the early days of the gardens, few details of the variety and musical attractions are available, as programmes at the less important places were not printed. The day of the typical gardens song (the Chappell ballad of the period) was at hand, and soon in every form of publication the country was to be flooded with the interminable pastorals of James Hook. In the mid-eighteenth century a " favourite " ballad from the theatre, a duet for a lady and gentleman, and a song of bucolic humour, often set to a traditional tune, together with a performance on the organ, would be the ingredients of the musical programme. Out of doors, some tight or slack-rope dancing and tumbling, or Mr. Jones playing the fiddle as he danced. Also some fireworks when the hours of opening made this possible.

There is every evidence of the lower moral status of the " Wells," however, and there is no doubt that this is connected with the tendency to make the place solely an indoor affair. Its music house had actually been built on the site of an open-air " orchestra " erected by the original Sadler in 1683, a date which emphasizes the existence of outdoor concert performances before they were made fashionable by Tyers at Vauxhall. Indeed, before Miles erected his naughty music house at the end of the century, concerts, quite in the Vauxhall manner, had been given in this orchestra, and in addition there was alfresco dancing to the music of a piper seated, perhaps rather uncomfortably, on a shell-work rock. The institution of the music house brought trouble in its train. In 1712 a murder was committed " near the organ loft " (there was still an organ) and very uncomplimentary reports were made by the Middlesex magistrates, in July of that year, on the manners of its frequenters. The advent of Vauxhall, however, brought fresh inspiration, and when Rosoman took the place two years later, he swept and garnished it, set up horse patrols in the principal roads leading to town, and organized a variety entertainment, lacking the grosser elements of earlier performances, such as the devouring of a live fowl, " feathers and all."

Thus, as in the arenas of the Elizabethan period, sport enters first, but art is not far behind. Moreover, the tavern houses to which the grounds belonged, became enriched by the addition of music houses in which entertainment other than the collation of " tarts, salt meats, and Rhenish wine " solaced the fatigues of those who rambled among the groves, thickets and wildernesses

[1]The atmosphere indicated by these entertainments is often more of Victorian sedateness. At Bagnigge Wells, there were special seats on the Banks of the New River set aside for smokers among those who desired to fish.

surrounding them. In 1678, another important garden lying near the Bankside was opened, and was known later as Cuper's Gardens after the proprietor who made them famous and embellished them with marbles from Arundel House—a gift to him from its owner, when that mansion was pulled down.[1]

The Marylebone Gardens, known for their bowling greens, existed in a rudimentary form in the seventeenth century and are mentioned in an entry in Pepys' diary for 1668. The discovery of the chalybeate spring in Islington in 1684 which led to the establishment of a dancing room, walks, arbours, and gaming tables under the title of the New Tunbridge Wells, concludes the list of the more important precursors of Vauxhall. But although relatively few in number, they offered certain entertainment attractions before the year 1700.

Taverns are to be found at this time devoted to the milder traffic of the new non-alcholic beverages, or at any rate with these added as a special attraction. This was an outgrowth of middle-class family habits. The rage for tea drinking provided an objective for these journeys to the suburban villages. Unlike coffee, tea captured the imagination of the middle class, after a short reign in exclusively aristocratic circles ; perhaps because it is so much easier to make. At Islington Spa, by 1733, tea and coffee had completely replaced the sale of intoxicants. Here the tea-drinking gave elegance to the repast, which was heightened by the thinness of the bread and butter which accompanied it.

> "'Tis drinking Tea in summer afternoons
> At Baggnige Wells, with china and gilt spoons."

Respectability, an essay at tone, and moral innocuousness are the looked-for ingredients of the gardens once they passed into these worthy hands. Though in certain cases there might be an element of the questionable (Islington Spa only recovered its moral equilibrium with the tea drinking) the places which purveyed these refreshments, where entertainments began at five in the afternoon, and closed at 8 p.m., where sessions of dancing were held at eleven in the morning, were not likely to engender or to suffer laxity, and do something to account for the rather homely simplicity of the early nineteenth-century comedians nurtured in the succeeding saloon theatres, such as Glindon, Howell, and even Robson. It is, moreover, significant that in the earlier century no trace of a performer such as George Alexander

[1]In 1752 the licence for Cuper's Gardens was rescinded. The interest of the not very distant Vauxhall may have been a motive for this action. In 1741 a bill advertising the attractions of the place announced performances of the songs from Shakespeare's *As You Like It*, composed by " the ingenious Dr. Arne."

Stevens is to be found, and in the later one no comedian tainted, as was Tom Hudson, with the Regency licentiousness. This ingenuousness even survived at the midnight revels of Evans's Supper Rooms of the eighteen-fifties.

Amidst a growing taste for rational pleasure, Tyers in 1732 reopened the Spring Gardens with a *Ridotto Al Fresco*, and the scheme which he originated held place for over a century. He made use to the full of a prevalent and increasing feeling for a half-fantastic but pseudo-historical environment. Though the word Gothic might still be fairly regarded as a term of abuse, though Bishop Percy had not yet published his *Reliques of Ancient Poetry*, and Horace Walpole had not yet written his *Castle of Otranto*, there was in the air what has been called the " little " romantic movement, and this romanticism was to be seen in such adjuncts to landscape gardening as the construction of Merlin's Caverns (a device to be found among the Islington pleasure resorts), with their rocks, cascades and grottos. Virgilian retreats though some were intended to be, they actually differed but little in spirit from the artificial Gothic ruins which at a slightly later date in its history invaded Vauxhall Gardens and persisted there until its last days. These decorations had less severity, a greater sense of mystery and delicious secretiveness than the pretty but frigid devices of the seventeenth century.

The Gothic evoked was, of course, a Gothic still shrouded in heroic couplets and had no more of the actual spirit of the Middle Ages than the wells and fountains which preceded them had of the true Parnassus. Still, they were rather exciting, and the middle classes rapidly caught the fever. It must be remembered that they were drinking madness from the tinsel theatre of their time, a madness running through the make-believe of all popular expression, dimmed and silent as it is forced to be from time to time. At this moment the instinct surged up in the attempt to create fantasy in concrete images. And delight in such pastimes as singing, dancing and dressing up was enhanced by creating a picturesque background, and by pretending that life had a soothingly romantic and impossible surface. It was this instinct which produced the gardens, and the gardens the saloon theatres, which in their turn gave so much to the music hall. It is impossible to escape a sense of the connection which exists between the old-style acrobat of the music hall with his personal finery and painted back-cloth of some impossible Versailles, and those alfresco performances of the pleasure gardens.

Tyers lost no time in setting up his monster " orchestra," the focus of his gay scene, relics of which survived to be sold by auction when the gardens at last closed in 1859. He increased the number and luxuriance of the shaded walks, placing

triumphal arches over them, and decorating their terminals with painted perspectives, which carried them to an illusory horizon. Side-shows such as the " tin cascade," as it was rather unkindly called, and a Rotunda, in the rococo manner, were added ; and later came the marble statue of Handel, by Roubiliac (now to be seen on the staircase landing of Messrs. Novello's premises in Wardour Street), and other marvels. He decorated the supper boxes (which formed an arc of a circle round the lawn facing the orchestra) with pictures by Hayman, after designs by Hogarth, who took a great interest in the place, and he even brought visitors by river, in a painted barge.

The orchestra was at first Vauxhall's only music hall ; for a year or two, instrumental music alone was provided, and then were added singers from the theatres, among whom were famous artists. As has been said, the songs for the most part were of the " Daphne and Strephon " type, but there were not entirely lacking the more racy lyrics and tunes of the kind that Tom d'Urfey had sung at court in the preceding century, and such songs at Vauxhall provided a link with genuine popular music. The list of varieties was not, in the eighteenth century, a large one, but in the nineteenth century it became enormously increased. Vauxhall, in this respect, lagged behind the other gardens, and with an eye on aristocratic patronage, held aloof ; even displays of fireworks are not recorded here before 1798. It did, however, set the pace for magnificence and was imitated everywhere in this respect. Cuper's Gardens, which stood on a site through which the Waterloo Road now runs, was, for a time, its nearest approach to a rival.

Bagnigge Wells (whose site is now marked by a tavern in the King's Cross Road) had meantime developed a number of attractive features. The " Long Room," a common term of the time, which survived among the Victorian taverns, was the centre of attraction, and here concerts were held. It was seventy-eight feet long and, of course, contained an organ. (Dickens, describing a concert at the Eagle Tavern, states that the organ there was used as an accompaniment to the comic singer !) Sunday concerts were attempted here, but the same Observance Act which is now an enemy to the cinema, silenced these. In the Baggnigge Wells Long Room, by the early days of the nineteenth century known as the Concert Room, is to be found a typical instance of the progress from the eighteenth-century tradition to that of the nineteenth-century music hall. In the 'thirties were already to be heard artists from the neighbouring taverns, such as Mr. Darking (of the London Concerts), Miss Anderson (from the Mogul), Mr. Sutton and Mr. Gibson (from Sadler's Wells), and Mr. Clifford (from the Yorkshire Stingo).

As early as 1775 there had occurred at Marylebone Gardens (which was a little later to present a burletta written by the poet Chatterton), an interesting example of the " one-man entertainment," a type of performance resorted to by a great many nineteenth-century music-hall artists. This was a "comic lecture" given by Baddeley the actor, and presented in three parts, with the help of " the modern magic-lantern." In this instance, Baddeley was probably imitating the methods of George Alexander Stevens, whose famous " lecture on Heads " originally given in 1690, survived him by many years, being performed in John Palmer's Royalty Theatre and by Palmer himself, in 1770, at the Royal Circus.

Such an entertainment, though bearing some relation to the diversions of the tavern, did nothing, in the eighteenth century, to lessen the gentility of the gardens, a gentility which did not even permit the performance of glees and catches until 1786, when they had by this time been given a charter of respectability through the formation of the Glee Club. Apart from these, the musical policy of Vauxhall and the rest of the gardens continued to limit itself to a reiteration of those vocal trifles which bore little or no popular significance.

A revival of interest in genuinely popular music was, however, in the air from the beginning of the century and steadily gained ground. Its origin may be traced to the work of one man, Tom d'Urfey ; whose vast collection of ballads, for the most part adapted from earlier sources and set to traditional airs, was first published in 1675 under the title of *Wit and Mirth*. An enlarged edition was issued a few years later with the better-known secondary title of *Pills to Purge Melancholy*. It is difficult to overestimate the influence of these volumes ; their appearance formed an important link with the past and provided a mine of material for the future. Baskervill[1] has pointed out that one of them, *A Dialogue*, is a survival of the Elizabethan two-character " ballad-jig " ; and d'Urfey's method of choosing the tunes for his songs from traditional airs, a method made easier for him by the publication of large numbers of old melodies for fashionable dance measures, has affected the comic and sociable song in all its subsequent history. His great influence on this method has, therefore a special interest for the student of the music hall. He is to be held directly responsible for the introduction of ballad opera. *The Beggar's Opera*, when it appeared in 1728 (the first complete ballad opera), accomplished more than the intention of its godfather Swift, who demanded a Newgate pastoral from Gay ; it is a genuine and very effective reaction from the cultural musician. D'Urfey and the " Pills " supplied the purge

[1]The Elizabethan Jig.

to the Italian aria writers, and for sixty years drew everyone back in song, to the strains of *Joan's Placket is Torn* and the rest of the native tunes. The political and social satire of *The Beggar's Opera* meant nothing to the majority of the audience. On the first night things were going none too well, until Lavinia Fenton, kneeling at her "father's" feet, burst into the pellucid Elizabethan melody of *The Children in the Wood*, to Gay's words: "O ponder well, be not severe." The irresistible force of the tune, accompanied by words of such genius, melted the house, and a triumph was assured. Here, in the strange but perhaps intuitively wise reading of Gay's work on the part of the audience, was to be found the element which was later to become the basis of music hall singing. This naïveté, which fastened on the antithesis of the author's conscious intention, expressed itself in the discovery of a common denominator—the invincible appeal of the tunes inherited by the common people.

Gay's work, which in an age of wit revealed an unusually humane quality, came perhaps too early in the eighteenth century to produce more than a superficial school of imitation. Gay himself, with all the delicacy of approach evidenced by many of his lyrics, was sufficiently of his time to fail of becoming a pioneer. The way was, indeed, somewhat congested. Appreciation in song of the comic side of life gave way to the vogue for bacchanalian lyrics.

Leveridge in his *Roast Beef of Old England* struck a note of coarse good cheer combined with a patriotic boastfulness; a note reflected in the singing clubs and in the growing number of societies which were given to convivial meetings, but what was yet lacking was the effort to obtain release from the shackles of domestic and everyday life, by laughing at them. Down to the days of Dick Swiveller, with his "Glorious Apollers," such release was only created through drinking; poor Dick could only forget his duns and the existence of all the streets he was unable to walk down because his creditors lived in them, by an appeal to the sentiment of the current "toasts" of his day, which instructed him to see that life was always crammed with "conwiviality," and that the "wings of friendship" were never allowed to "moult a feather."

In the singing assemblies of the eighteenth century, therefore, we are little better off in searching for signs of what was to come, than in the Gardens; and the records are scantier and more scattered. Unfortunately, the "night cellars," ancestors of the tavern sing-songs of the organized kind, seldom appear in recorded history. We know that one famous place, the Cider Cellars, was at least one hundred and fifty years old when Ross created his furore there in the late eighteen-forties; we know

also that many, if not all, the more important taverns already had the sing-song habit, and that they became unpopular with authority after the revolution of 1688, because of the Jacobite songs which were sung in them. One valuable record may be quoted at length. In 1763, George Alexander Stevens (*The Adventure of a Speculist*), describes a visit to a tavern concert, conducted on lines identical with those of at least seventy years later. I give a full quotation :

"We went to Comus's Court, as they called it, one Jack Speed's *White Horse, Fetter Lane*, where these very high humourists were to assemble that evening. When we had taken our seats, and I had once or twice looked round the room, and examined the many persons who were placed on each side of two long tables, I could not observe that their eyes discovered the least symptoms of jollity : on the contrary, their faces were mere blanks, and they seemed most earnestly looking about as if they wanted something they could not describe, like Curiosity in distress ; and appeared more like mourners at Mirth's funeral, than companions fit for fun and merriment.

I told this to my conductor, who whispered to me to have a little patience ; that the *Stars* did not appear soon that night, but that I should see them shine, or at least twinkle, by and by ; that the company I now saw did not meet to make one another merry, but to be made merry by others ; that these Comus' Court meetings were on the same plan as Sadler's Wells, where people might sit and smoke, and drink, and hear singing, and see all the posture-masters and tumblers, yet only pay so much for liquor, and have all these comical fancies into the bargain.

On enquiring who those Stars were that we should see by and by, he gave me their history, as follows :

"There are a set of people about this town, who, from attending to everything but what they should do, have made themselves masters of some particular tones, or oddities, which are by those who know no better, admired as supernatural qualifications.

"These people are invited from Club to Club by the landlords of public houses, to play off their fools tricks to all the guests the publican can jumble together. One plays with a rolling-pin upon a salt-box ; another grunts like a hog ; a third makes his teeth chatter like a monkey ; and thus they each have something to make the Million laugh, and put common sense out of countenance.

"But here, here they come !—take notice of their figures as they come in.

" That fellow[1] was originally a journeyman-shoemaker, and had the name of the *Singing Cobbler*, then he turned strolling-player, next publican, and is now, I believe, a publican again. He lately published a volume of songs, several very obscene ones, and at the top had the effrontery to put his name, as if they were his songs.

" The next is the *Grunting Genius*,[2] and *Broomstick Fiddler*. When he sings, I beg, as you can write shorthand, you will write down in your pocket-book, with your pencil, the words of each verse as he pronounces them.

" The next is a very fine German-flute player, a good honest fellow, who means no harm, and is friendly as far as he can be so, but has an odd whim : he fancies himself to have been a great traveller, and imagines Madame POMPADOUR and he have been *tête-à-tête* together, and that the Grand Monarch took a great liking to him, and made him great offers, provided he would embrace the Catholic religion.

" That fresh-coloured fellow who follows him is an unaccountable being.[3] He has wrote some tolerably droll songs, but spoils them by his attempting to sing them. He has belonged to both Theatres and never could make himself of consequence in either : he has too much sense for a fool, and too little to be prudent. He might be either better or worse than he is, if he would take any pains to bring it about. GEORGE, however, is either unable or unwilling to think as he should do, but lets things come or go, just as it may happen, too careless to consider of any moment but the present, and, grasshopper-like, merry one half the year, the other half miserable."[4]

Observing to my companion, that none of these STARS paid as they came in, he told me that the landlord always franked them for the tricks they played to divert his customers.

Now " silence ! silence ! " was bawled out by almost every person in the room, and every body stood up on the President's rising, who had been a very wealthy tradesman formerly, but had ruined himself by attending upon such meetings as these, merely to get the name of a CLEVER FELLOW.

After most deliberately hitting three strokes upon the table with his hammer, he began with telling the company, " that he had a toast or two to propose, after which Mr. GRUNTER should either give them the organ, the broomstick, a French-horn tune, or a song first ; but that if he might take the liberty of speaking before a set of such gentlemen of merit as he saw there, he

[1]*Bob Summers.*
[2]*Matt Skeggs.*
[3]*Dick Bowyer.*
[4]*Mr. Stevens* has here delineated his own character.

presumed that if Mr. Grunter opened with a song, it would be most agreeable".

This speechifying was applauded most vehemently, and "A song, a song, a song, from *My lord!* A song from *My lord!*" called out for.

The President once more took it upon him to inform the company, that a gentleman near him had requested Mr. Grunter to sing a song called,

"When Phoebus the tops of the hills does adorn."

This notice was applauded, and several repeated bursts of "Bravo! bravo!" were heard from different parts of the room, one after the other, occasioning irregular explosions, like the train-bands firing."

The phrase "Comus Court" appears to have been used as a definitive title for this kind of thing (one of the arcades at Vauxhall ended in a shrine dedicated to the jovial god), and in addition to its being used to describe a variety entertainment at Ranelagh in 1754, we meet with it in the cases of public houses devoted to some kind of performance. The following reference to a "Court of Comus" appears in E. T. Raymond's *Life of Robert William Elliston.* The passage may be given a rather full quotation almost as much for the sake of the manner in which the anecdote is told, as for its very interesting matter (the description applies to the latter part of the eighteenth century):

"London affords a vast variety of scenes to lads of metal, other than halls of science, or the chambers of the polite . . . scenes which being, fortunately, hidden from the world, and loving darkness rather than light, are sometimes sought under the most curious plea which was perhaps ever advanced—namely, of seeing the world! . . . There existed at this period, certain conventions, yclept clubs, which . . . had a quality of their own Here was no narrow mean exclusiveness . . . the doors, like a box. of charity, were open to the whole world, *pro hac nocte*, on the payment of sixpence. . . . One of the principal establishments of the above kind was the 'Court of Comus,' which had laid its foundations in Wych Street, whereof a certain choice spirit of the name of Desborough was rated to the poor; or in other words the landlord. This Desborough, as dull a rogue on most points as any in Christendom, was yet famous by a kind of concentration of genius, the light whereof became more vivid by the illimitable stupidity by which it was encircled. This outrageously stupid man was famous, in fact, for doing one thing well—well! Surpassing, in sooth, any effort of the 'Comus Court' itself—and

this was, singing Dibdin's song of *Fortune's Wheel.* But to return to Comus Court. Precisely at nine o'clock, by the chimes of St. Clement's Dane, the door of this sanctuary was thrown open to devotees . . . and the 'flamen' of the sanded floor, ascended the curule chair before whom a pickled herring, some strong waters, and an ounce of tobacco, were regularly placed. . . . On Cussans (the chairman in question) taking the chair, the official club cocked hat was handed to him by the Serjeant-at-arms, Sands . . . and the court was declared sitting. The first thing, as we have heard, was *Fortune's Wheel.* Then the renowned Cussans, the court improvisatore, gave a canzona, with some ability, he identified each visitor present; afterwards, in turn, every one present was separately called on to "do something." . . . 'Doing something,' implied either a song, a speech, poising a tobacco pipe or coal skuttle; an imitation of cat, dog, or fowl, posturizing, or the more classic feat of quaffing to the dregs the pewter Amystis of some potent compound. . . . On gala nights . . . Cussans descended, like Jupiter himself, into a beast—not, indeed, as a rampant bull, but as a dancing bear!"

On these foundations the tavern concert of the nineteenth century was built, whose physical features are identical with the early music hall. One easily perceives how, by a natural process, the performances moved from an amateur to a professional status, though there is, I think, a differentiation to be drawn at all times between those places which tended to organize as centres of public entertainment and those given to the meetings of "club" coteries. As we have already seen, the idea of making a charge for entertainments held in public houses is of older date than the nineteenth-century tavern concert. Stevens' reference to this custom in *The Speculist* is, however, a trifle obscure. In the paragraph in which he compares Jack Speed's to other Comus Court meetings, he seems to suggest that no actual charge is made for attendance; but in that dealing with the landlord's "franking" of the "stars" in exchange for their services, the matter is left in no doubt. The only way of reconciling the apparently conflicting statements is to assume the existence of what became to be known as "wet money," that is, a payment partly returnable in drink, which we know had been the custom from time to time at Sadler's Wells. This system, levied as a tax on the first drinks, for defraying expenses in connection with the entertainment, is probably the step by which all sing-songs of the more primitive kind adopted professionalism. It was most certainly the manner in which the music houses attached to *alfresco* resorts were organized.

We have now to note a rather curious cross-influence occurring in the early nineteenth century. One would expect that a

A Scene before the Curtain.

By courtesy of British Museum

A PENNY GAFF

By courtesy of British Museum

A "COMUS COURT"

transition from the non-paying audience would lead, by uninterrupted sequence, to the music hall, but this is not quite the case, for a major influence came from two famous places of entertainment at which no payment was exacted, except directly, from the sale of food and drink. These were the Cider Cellars and the Coal Hole. Both houses were by this time related to the " clubs " held at such places as Offley's in King Street, Covent Garden, the Wrekin in Broad Court, and other taverns in the vicinity of the theatres and the West End. These places belonged especially to the Regency " man-about-town." The note struck was therefore modish rather than popular. Renton Nicholson in his *Autobiography of a Fast Man* describes Offley's as a " resort of the Corinthians," and Bernard Blackmantle in his *Metropolitan Sketches* as a place " frequented by baby bucks, blacklegs, and half-pay officers." It is of importance that the former writer notes the house's business to have been seriously affected by the establishment of the new fashionable clubs and from this time the higher class tavern gradually ceased to be of importance in the history of entertainment.

At Offley's there was singing of excellent quality at the Wednesday evening meetings, but for the most part, provided by singers of amateur status, and entertaining such as that provided by Theodore Hook. Hook in the character of an *improvisatore* is recalled by Nicholson in his *Autobiography*, and as a mimic by Edmund Yates in his *Reminiscences*. Not only at Offley's but at all his places of call, Hook was willing to enliven the company with his performances.

Offley himself belonged to the type of tavern keeper who not only personally supervized the cooking and serving of food, but at an harmonic meeting would take the chair and contribute to the singing. We later encounter similar personalities in Evans of the Song and Supper Rooms, and his successor Paddy Green, and even in 1849 Charles Morton helped to popularize the first Canterbury Hall by giving the same personal note to his management.

But at Offley's the centre of attraction was undoubtedly the singing of such talented amateurs as Pearson Foreman—described as the " Incledon of the Tavern Concerts " : the array of chariots to be found on every Wednesday evening at the door was an evidence of the great popularity of tavern entertainment, a popularity to be far exceeded when, later, its organization became more democratic.

Let us now turn for a while to another influence in the domain of variety entertainment, august in origin and provided by the two theatres functioning under the special privileges of Charles II's patent. This was the establishment, already

mentioned, of pantomime at Drury Lane in 1717. At first only an incidental innovation, it was destined, largely by the effects of the Monopoly Act of 1737, to engender and disseminate widely characteristics which embody a very important aspect of the later music hall, for beyond the stricter boundaries of pantomime in its historical form, there lie all the forms of entertainment which on this foundation turned the theatre into something like a vast booth.

The first and most significant effect of pantomime in the theatre was, however, the fact that it occasioned the return of the English clown. As in the days of the Elizabethan Kempe, he had, to begin with many foreign attributes, for as member of the great international strolling theatre he was always giving and receiving influences. But later these were to be weeded out, for as has been seen, in this character national traits assert themselves without difficulty.

Pantomime, or as it was at first properly called, harlequinade, came to the English regular stage, by way of France, at the end of the seventeenth century. It is true that in the reign of James II a harlequin bearing those rustic characteristics which we associate with clown had appeared in a piece by John Day, but this occasion was isolated, so far as the legitimate stage was concerned, as this rustic conception of harlequin was not uppermost when, in 1687, Aphra Behn produced her " Emperor of the Moon " for a comedy of masks performed by the Parisian-Italian company of the Hotel Burgoyne.[1] The part of harlequin in this piece was played by Pinketman, the actor and showman whom we have encountered at Bartholomew Fair and elsewhere. The first English stage harlequin was therefore placed at once in the hands of a low comedian lacking the cultured attributes of Italian artists such as Riccobini. By this admixture was virtually created a new character, developed in the later English pantomime and handing down a wealth of technique to the music halls.

But it was on the additional blending-in of ballet and pure spectacle that the pantomime in England took roots and became finally acclimatized. In this is to be perceived the influence of the masque—the association of architectural ornament, music, and movement, of which the opera, under D'Avenant, made full use. The process, following on the Aphra Behn experiment, began again from such simple schemes as that of a " Dance between the various characters of the Italian Comedy," and from these dance movements John Rich elaborated the dumb-shows, in which under the name of Lun he appeared as harlequin. John Thurmond supplied him in 1717 with the introductory play

[1] *The Emperor of the Moon* is full of those tricks and transformations which became essential to pantomime production.

which was used as a means of introducing a magic transformation into the unreal world of the harlequinade—its subject being *The Necromancer, or the History of Doctor Faustus*. By this device, the acting of a play as an explanatory prologue to a dumb-show, he created English pantomime, on a plan which subsequently became rigidly traditional, consisting of the " opening " followed by the " harlequinade." The method involved a twofold innovation, the separation of the subject from the traditional characters, and the presentation of those characters in dumb-show. The idea, which was an extension of the use of these characters in ballet, is said to have commended itself to Rich because his diction rendered him unsuitable for speaking parts. He is certainly remembered as a being uncultivated, and illiterate of speech. Under Rich, harlequin retained the features of the foreign productions, that of a rascally but elegant character ; the subsidiary clown did not at once acquire a dominating position. But even without the aid of clown, the invention, followed quickly by that other innovation, ballad-opera, was sufficient to threaten the ascendancy of legitimate drma for a considerable period.

Meanwhile, the Act of 1737 was a great stimulant to the growth of pantomime. The minor theatres, as the legitimate drama was forbidden, at any rate legally, to them, were free to exploit unmolested the most popular theatrical invention of the day.[1] They were forced, however, from time to time, to observe the letter of the law, whereby it was, at least in theory, not permissible to speak any dialogue unaccompanied by music.

Here the powerful voice of vested interest was only heard when the particular minor theatre concerned had done something to alarm or exasperate its superior. The classic instance of injunction in the case of pantomime is the arrest of Delpini the clown, in consequence of his having spoken the words " roast beef " unaccompanied by music in a production at John Palmer's Royalty Theatre in Wellclose Square. Provocation for this amazing attack was, as we shall later in more detail see, here provided by the fact that Palmer was an actor of the patent theatre in revolt against their system ; he had set up an independent house under distinguished patronage by means of which he was hoping to establish the cause, so long advocated in the Press, of what came to be known as a " third theatre."[2]

[1]The enthusiasm for pantomime was even carried into normal life. As late as 1838 Spencer, the harlequin, during the proprietorship of the Garrick's Head, reproduced some of the tricks of the pantomime stage, trap-doors for bringing up table, sliding panels, into his bars.

Spencer was famous for his stage jumps, a fact which won the nickname of the Jump for the Garrick's Head.

[2]*See* Chapter V, p. 86, *et seq.*

Neither Palmer's hopes nor the attack on Delpini achieved their ends. The mention of dialogue in connection with pantomime may give the reader pause, and it will be as well to make clear an element in the development of the art in England, over which a considerable veil of confusion has been somewhat wantonly thrown by commentators.

Long before Delpini's transgression, dialogue had been introduced into pantomime by a natural process which grew out of the introduction of songs and choruses. Indeed, it was chiefly by Lun's emphasis on dumb show that a strange confusion of idea as to the nature of pantomime was perpetuated. The original misconception, however, probably slightly pre-dated Rich. A ballet, perhaps the first purely danced scenario performed on the principal stage of the country, had appeared in 1716 on the classical subject of the Loves of Mars and Venus. This ballet had been hailed as pantomime, or, at any rate, when this work was immediately followed by other ballets in which the characters of the *Comedia del arte* were introduced, the whole group of productions was classified in this way. In so doing the English producers were echoing the dictum of the Duchesse du Maine, who decreed, in 1706, that her presentation of the action of a classical play in dance form should be known as a ballet-pantomime. This has been pointed out by Willson-Disher, who has added the pertinent comment that " no savant pointed out that ' imitator of all ' (literal translation of the term) does not signify speechlessness." It may be conceded that the Duchesse had invented, or, at any rate, revived the " ballet of action," but had by no means revived the art of pantomime. This, in any case, was a lost art—the question of its complete revival could not be contemplated. What the movement actually stood for in England, and by means of which the devices and humours of the later variety stage were, by a fantastic turn of events, profoundly affected, was the adaptation of the Italian comedy of art to English buffoonery. But the French conception, with eighteenth-century neo-classical enthusiasm, had been seized upon ; and Garrick, in a prologue to a speaking ballet performed under his management, had implied a corruption of the art by this rhymed apology to the audience :

" 'Tis wrong,
The wits will say, to give the fool a tongue,
When Lunn appeared, with matchless art and whim
He gave the power of speech to every limb,
Though masked and mute, conveyed his quick intent,
And told in frolic gestures all he meant."

We have, then, to take cognizance of three important features of pantomime as it worked its way from classical misconceptions to become a living vehicle of the stage ; the character of clown, brought back as low comedian ; the stage tricks, mechanical devices and " jokes of action " which it revived ; and its comic and fantastic use of ballet. The public had to wait until Grimaldi appeared on the scene for the complete triumph of clown ; and it should be remembered his achievement was facilitated by his being a half-Italian who had learned the art from his predecessor Dubois, a Frenchman.

Grimaldi's father was a famous balletmaster and mime. He died when Joseph was still a young boy, but at an early age the latter came under the influence of the man who, to a large extent, anticipated his work ; Dubois, the creator of one of Grimaldi's most famous " serious pantomine " parts, Orson, in *Valentine and Orson.* Grimaldi, English on his mother's side, and with a thorough and complete instinct for low comedy of the English kind, was to his audiences the embodiment of the native type, and was especially held in their affection by his performances of hearty English characters such as Squire Bugle in *Mother Goose ;* though it is of interest to note that he himself regarded this part as his worst performance. For all this, he clung to many continental theatrical traditions, such as the whitening of his face in the manner of Pierrot, over the groundwork of which he painted bizarre coloured patterns. To this he added a blue headpiece, which had a certain resemblance both to a cockscomb and the plume of a French Hussar's helmet. His costume with its white shorts abandoned all trace of the rustic characteristics of the earlier clown. The baggy, cross-gartered trousers worn by certain Italian harlequins ceased with Grimaldi, and belong only to clown, while still a minor character. With the triumph of clown as chief personage of the harlequinade, " certain grosser elements " of th character passed from the former to the latter, and it should not be forgotten that these elements were based on foreign models. It is this borrowing which, from reducing harlequin to the second rank, finally denuded him of all individuality beyond that of a shadowy tinsel figure of the ballet. According to Willson Disher[1] the change-over was initiated in 1727 in a pantomime called *Harlequin's Triumph* (an ironical title in the circumstances), in which the leading character was given to harlequin's servant, Clown. Thus by becoming the servant's servant, Clown gained mastery of the stage. Simultaneously the character reverted by inheritance to the type of artist one may call " mimus," to which it properly belonged.

It is to be noted that Grimaldi's immediate predecessors and

[1] Clowns and Pantomimes.

comrades on the English state were artists of foreign extraction—Dubois, Johannot, Laurent, Decastro, Delpini. Bearing a foreign name himself, but bringing a dominantly native influence to bear on the part, his successors, Tom Mathews, Jefferini (Jefferies), Barry and Usher, were Englishmen. Thus through this strange medium of pantomime, the English comedian of sheer entertainment became one of the most influential figures on the stage, and what had at first been only an experiment, developed into a system based upon the old tricks of buffoonery, which for a time got rid of all lines of demarcation between contrasting types of theatre. And only after a century of faithfulness to the methods practised by Grimaldi was room found for another kind of expression, the music hall, which in a disintegrated form embodied the same influences.

It is impossible fully to appreciate the earlier (and for that matter, many of the later) experiments of the variety stage, without observing the complete preoccupation of the theatre during Grimaldi's career, with pantomime methods. The romantic melodramas of the time are indistinguishable, in scenic treatment, from the pantomimes. One instance of this may be quoted ; it is the concluding incident in the play of *Rugantino*, an adaptation by M. G. Lewis of his own romance *Abellino, or the Bravo of Venice*. At the conclusion of a scene of general rejoicing there are the following stage directions : " The folding doors open —the background is lighted by the moon. Neptune and Amphitrite enter with the Nereids and Tritons. Last a machine representing a rock of red coral, floating on a silver sea whose waves are in motion. On the summit of the rock is a brilliant conch shell—in which is Rosabella."

The effects of this dramatic hybrid upon actual variety programmes will be clearly seen in later stages of the book.

Into these fantastic surroundings Grimaldi brought his unexampled gifts for low comedy, dancing, acrobatic mime, and melodrama. Unexampled, because one feels that in all these divisions his work had equal distinction. Report of his fame for the most part rests upon a consensus of popular enthusiasm. Contemporary criticism hardly touches Grimaldi. Hazlitt's appreciation of him limits itself to praise of his meagre use of spoken words in the harlequinade. Though writers like Lamb are said to have been worshippers of Grimaldi, their works contain nothing but the most fugitive references to the great clown. Thomas Dibdin, who wrote so many pantomimes in which Grimaldi played, including the famous *Mother Goose*, has nothing to say of him as an artist, beyond reporting that " he was the best clown ever seen on a stage." John Decastro, who was a fellow artist of distinction, fails in his *Reminiscences* to amplify

his one mention of Grimaldi's work with anything of a critical nature ; and finally the *Memoirs of Grimaldi*, having passed through the hands of two editors, one of whom was Charles Dickens, who rearranged them in the third person, contain nothing but a collection of unreliable anecdotes. Though this silence may, in itself, be taken as implying an admission of his greatness, I think the idea of his fame rendering comment unnecessary an insufficient explanation. Nor do I find Mr. Willson Disher's interpretation of the absence of criticism as being due to the fact that pantomimes appeared as a late feature of an evening's entertainment very convincing.[1]

I think the explanation lies rather in a general attitude, shared by Grimaldi himself, to his stage personality. To the world, the artist was merged in the character he assumed. He was " Clown," and as such—completely the embodiment of this creation—he was, as it were, outside critical standards, scarcely felt to possess a separate individuality. It would appear that with him had returned that identification of the performer with his part, which caused the Italian comedians of earlier centuries to be known by the names of their stage creations rather than by their own. When, in partial glimpses, we are able to take Grimaldi by surprise, we discover something touching in his simplicity and complete lack of any realization of being more than a humble and devoted servant of the theatres in which he worked ; conscious only of his specialized task of supplying a continuous stream of jokes, songs, and contortions.

He was born to the stage and, under the rigid discipline of his father, no doubt developed an obedient habit of mind. His triumph, when it came, was amply expressed for him in the acclamations of the pit and the gallery. To the great ones he was " Clown," to his managers " Joe," to the public " Old Joe Grimaldi." Though he made large sums of money during his career, and though the theatres in which his benefit performances were given were surrounded by crowds twelve hours before the plays began, he was continually harassed by the managers for whom he worked and, at the end of his career, was even refused a farewell performance at Covent Garden by Kemble and his partners, in a manner insulting in its mixture of patronage and official coldness.

He was trained for his art as are those athletes who accomplish marvels on the high wire and the trapeze. Such artists are to be compared to Grimaldi in the absence of any expectation of personal fame from their accomplishment.

His first important success occurred in 1817 in a pantomime called the *Talking Bird*, through the medium of the song *Hot*

[1] op. cit.

Codlings, composed by John Whitaker.[1] The enormous vogue of this song, reaching till the middle of the nineteenth century, must be attributed to Grimaldi himself. It is not a particularly good example of the pantomime song—the theme is rather feeble and the humour dependent on the device of leaving out the rhyming word at the end of each stanza, yet it was included later in the production of *Mother Goose*, and was Grimaldi's most famous song in that favourite pantomime. Comic singing was perhaps Grimaldi's most popular accomplishment. Even now ephemeral songs are remembered for his sake, among them, in addition to *Hot Codlings*, *Me and My Neddy*, *Tippitiwitchet*, and *Poor Putty*.

The bare bones of Grimaldi's stage achievements do little to reveal him as an artist. He was particularly fond of external equipment: a great many of the mechanical devices used by him were of his own invention. This fact, in itself, is not inspiring. Extravagant costumes and "properties" are often resorted to by indifferent comedians. Yet sometimes they are of importance in the effects obtained by a genuine artist—W. H. Berry being an instance of this in our time. In any event, Grimaldi was making the most of a prevalent fashion.

His serious acting may unhesitatingly be put into the category of forceful melodrama, which relies on physical achievements in voice and movement rather than on subtle shades of characterization. His *forte* lay in such things as 'the Red Indian's death agonies,' and in scenes of that kind he is said to have been studied by Edmund Kean. He played occasionally in parts belonging to the classical repertory. A type of part in which he excelled, and which he transferred to pantomime, was that of the hearty English squire. In such characters he was assisted by his own physical characteristics, a round face and a rich laugh.

Before the age of fifty Grimaldi was crippled by overwork, and that mixture of anxiety with a ceaseless drain of nervous vitality which shortens life. Nothing in stage history is more touching than his struggles in his last years against loneliness and an increasing poverty, punctuated by such incidents as the begging visits of his profligate son. Most pathetic of all is the humility he showed towards the managers whom he persisted in regarding as his benefactors. Hood has left us a description of Grimaldi's visit to him to sue for the favour of a "farewell address" from his pen. Hood hardly recognized the broken elderly man, who approached him so respectfully with the request, and begged him to make the address short as "he was a bad study."

[1]Whitaker was organist at St. Clement's, Eastcheap, and in addition to the composition of light opera and humorous songs, produced oratorios and settings of the Odes of Anacreon in English translation. He was the composer of the celebrated song. *My Old Dog Tray.*

Hood was deeply impressed with the simplicity and charm of the great clown, and wrote the last words which Grimaldi spoke from a stage.[1]

[1]The MSS. of what may be Grimaldi's last letter written to an intimate friend, is in the Weidener Library at Harvard. It is dated December 5th. The year, though not given, is undoubtedly 1836. The letter is probably addressed to his fellow-artist, Ellar :

MS. Letter from Grimaldi to
Vol. 2 of Coll. Weidener Library, Boston.

Arlington Street,
Nr. Sadlers Wells.
Dec. 5th.

Dear Old friend,

I shall not be able to come—Poor Joey's laid up in lavender, this cold weather, and will never again make Christmas folk grin with his anticks, his buffooneries, and his quips and cranks.

No more concealment of sausages in his capacious trucks pockets—no more bottles stored away—no more merry songs, sayings and gibes.

O my heart grieves ! Well, there must be an end to everything mortal, and, as poor Palmer said (his last words) : " There is another and a better world." I wonder if I shall be able to " *clown* it " THERE ! Well, *adsum*.

Would I come to your son's benefit and give him the advantage of pranks and humour. But I can't go—impossible. I am hipped. Will, however, put my mite down, which will not be a " mighty " one, I tell you, for I am far from being a millionaire. O that pain—it is coming on again, and I must drop the pen that quivers in my hand. Come and see poor Joey—come, dear friend, and talk to me as of yore. The sight of your jolly, rubicind mug will mayhap ease me, drive for the nonce, " dull care away."

Yours as ever,
Joey Grimaldi
(" Grim-all-day.")

Joking till the last, as you see.

CHAPTER III

Night House to Music Hall

In the early days of the nineteenth century, two houses, sometimes rather loosely described as "night cellars," emerged from obscurity. These were the Cider Cellars in Maiden Lane (at the corner nearest to Bedford Street), and the Coal Hole in Fountain Court, Strand. Probably in these earlier days both places bore a considerable resemblance to such houses as Offley's, but in their development towards the middle of the century they acquired characteristics differing materially from the convivial haunts of the Regency period.

Both the Coal Hole and the Cider Cellars were a convenient resort for journalists and men of letters, and under their patronage they flourished and became famous. The man who attracted this world and held its interest securely was William Rhodes, an actor and chorister who, before turning publican, had performed at Covent Garden.

Less is known of his stage career than of his bent for convivial singing and song making, undoubtedly the basis of the popularity he earned for the Cider Cellars and the Coal Hole. He acquired both houses early in the 'twenties ; undertaking the management of the former, and installing his brother at the latter. In a general sense, these taverns, at first holding only amateur or semi-amateur sing-songs, may be said to have looked back to the assemblies of the eighteenth century ; but with the difference that there was lacking, in these cases, the class limitations of the earlier institutions.

For the professional tavern artists, introduced by Rhodes as the singing elements developed in importance, the Cider Cellars and the Coal Hole provided a new and important milieu. Here they were facing an audience of Bohemians and intellectuals, considerably removed from the lower middle-class patrons of the Eagle or the Yorkshire Stingo, well-known houses of the same date. The fact that actors such as Edward Knight occasionally performed at these concert rooms are no indication of their social status. A great deal of interest might be written on the equivocal position of the theatrical folk of the time. It is

sufficient to say here that an actor could frequently accept a singing engagement of this kind during the rather long periods between the seasons given by the stock companies. Contemporary references to the tavern artists such as those by Renton Nicholson in his journal *The Town* are of a disparaging kind, and emphasize the vulgarity of an entertainment which had abandoned the gentlemanly habits of the old-time harmonic club meeting.

The principal characteristic of Rhodes' management was the upholding of the atmosphere of good-fellowship. Both houses excluded women from their concerts though they did not altogether, as has been suggested, exclude women performers. Here they followed the tradition of the majority of those indoor tavern resorts (though there were many exceptions to the rule) which did not survive the development of the sing-song of the late 'forties and early 'fifties. Nicholson varied the precedent for his *Judge and Jury* shows, by allowing women to attend the " Poses Plastiques " which followed the trials. But by this time both the houses were declining, the original proprietor having died.

In these respects the Coal Hole and the Cider Cellars differed from equally early resorts such as the Doctor Johnson tavern in Bolt Court and the Mogul in Drury Lane, which later fell into line with the policy of the Surrey and the Canterbury Music Halls. The conservatism of the Coal Hole and the Cider Cellars, broken into by Nicholson, did not, on the other hand, survive as it did at Evans's and popularity waned completely under the competition of the new influences. A contributory reason for their failure to make the transition to music hall may have been that they were both hemmed-in places, in which enlargement of the stage or the auditorium was not practicable.

John Rhodes took the Coal Hole before 1825, in which year he is described by Bernard Blackmantle in his *New London Spy* as " the poet Rhodes." His venture along these lines probably pre-dates the similar evenings held at Joy's Tavern in Covent Garden which later became Evans's Song and Supper Rooms. There is little doubt that the Coal Hole's growing fame in the early 'thirties contributed to the career of the rival house, and there is therefore some reason for regarding Rhodes as a pioneer. It is in these days that artists of celebrity made their appearance at both houses ; among them, Tom Hudson, John Caulfield, Charles Sloman, Robert Glindon, and the locally famous Joe Wells ; to be joined a little later by John Labern, Tom Penniket, G. W. Ross, J. W. Sharpe, John Moody, and Sam Cowell.

Rhodes himself led the musical proceedings and affords an early example of a professional tavern concert chairman. He is described in Stuart and Park's *Variety Stage* as an " ideal chairman

and a past-master in the art of the raconteur." It probably needed someone with the strong personality and gift for management which Rhodes undoubtedly possessed, to lift this house, known as the Fountain Tavern, out of the disrepute into which, according to the *Epicure's Almanack* for 1815, it had then fallen.

Charles Sloman may be selected from among the performers at the Coal Hole and Cider Cellars, as the type of artist nurtured by the better class of tavern concert. He was born in 1808 of Jewish parents and made his first appearance at the White Conduit House pleasure gardens in Barnsbury at the age of sixteen. Immediately, it appears, he exhibited those qualities of "weaving into a song any subject proposed by his audience," which gave him a claim to be regarded as the "only English improvisatore." This art, with its ancient tradition, although his most highly appreciated gift, was probably not in Sloman's own estimation his most important one. This, he would have said, lay in his composition of songs dealing romantically with the history of the race to which he belonged. According to the *Era Almanack* for August 10, 1870, Sloman achieved a success in 1830 at Saville House, Leicester Square, and elsewhere, by his performances of the first of these ballads, *The Maid of Judah*, of which he wrote both words and music. His racial enthusiasm later produced a number of other ballads and recitations on the Semitic theme, and these appear to have provoked the typical music-hall reaction of sentimental sympathy not unmixed on occasions with affectionate banter.

Though known as a humorist, the greater number of his published songs consist of this heavy-moving stuff, and indeed, he must have been a man rather obsessed with ideals above the immediate range of his occupation, for he published (by subscription) a strange little volume of literary fragments entitled *Fitful Fancies of an Improvisatore*. This includes two unfinished tragedies, a sermon, and a moral tale dealing with the reclamation of a fallen woman.

The story of his long professional life is, after the 'forties, one of gradual decline. In the height of his fame an important attraction at Evans's and all the leading assemblies of the kind, he is rather pathetically described in his obituary notice as having "of late years chiefly displayed his talents at the smaller rooms of the Metropolis." Indeed, Sloman, after having held a unique reputation as entertainer, song writer, chairman and concert-room proprietor, and achieving a further celebrity in the pages of *Pendennis* as the original of "little Nadab," broke down completely under the loss of his wife in 1866, and died in the Strand Union Workhouse in July, 1870. He was particularly

unfortunate in not having been voted a grant from the funds of the "Dramatic, Musical and Equestrian Sick Fund" of which he was a founder, and an officer for many years. He may have been disqualified for help by the fact that he had received some small grant from the Freemasons.

He was the most respectable, the most ubiquitous and in some ways the most typical of tavern concert artists. As a performer, in spite of certain versatility, he may be regarded as negligible. True, he sang, played the piano, composed, wrote verses and extemporized them. But, though he was no doubt quick-witted and accomplished, his work had really little importance; it was rather as a personality with the gift of popularity that he succeeded in attaching himself to history. Clement Scott had a soft spot for him, and in *Drama of Yesterday and Today*, revealing the fact that his rendering of Shields' song "The Wolf" was especially in favour, though again, the psychology of the music hall audience may here be taken into account, there being some strange alchemy about this song's opening phrase, "Locks, bolts and bars," which in similar surroundings will even now still the voice of criticism. Occasionally his ballad singing is said to have tried the patience of his audiences to protesting point, his voice being an unpleasing one; and this, on an occasion, manifested itself during a performance of one of his Jewish romances.[1]

A classic example of the very serio-comic singer, he appears frankly to have bored Ewing Ritchie, author of *The Night Side of London*, to whom such unenviable experiences must frequently have occurred during his incessant visits to the tavern concerts in the interests of morality. But even Ritchie has nothing uncomplimentary to say of Sloman on the moral side, commenting as follows with more than a touch of critical discernment: "The little Hebrew, who has been at it, he tells me, for forty years, is not an improvisatore like Theodore Hook, but he does it well enough for an audience, good natured, and a little the worse for drink." (A reference to the date of the book (1857) suggests that the "little Hebrew" was pulling the leg of the censor of morals.)

On the other hand, Renton Nicholson, who may have had some genuine feeling for wit, though little appreciation of the sense of humour is evinced in his autobiography, recalls that Sloman in the days of the "Partiality Club" (about 1830 to be precise), was "one of those who were wont to keep the table in a roar."

Before leaving Sloman for the moment—and it is impossible

[1]The story is told by Clement Scott in his *Drama of Yesterday and Today*. At a charity performance in 1840 at the City of London Theatre, Sloman, on giving voice to the sentiment, "No more shall the children of Judah sing," was answered from the gallery, "I should think not, with a voice like that."

to be without him for long at this period—it may be well to make some mention of his connection with the Colosseum in Regent's Park.

The day of the overwhelming flood of "improving entertainment" was at hand—a movement which will be dealt with elsewhere—and an impressive and early instance of activity of this kind was to be found in the immense domed building which stood on ground between that part of Albany Street, which is now called Colosseum Place, and the road frontage of Regent's Park. This edifice was erected over a period of five years and opened in 1829, with the avowed purpose of gathering under its roof and in its rather limited grounds, objects and exhibitions of instruction combined with amusement. Unlike the contemporary Polytechnic Institution, it soon, after a rather disastrous effort to maintain the ideals which it was established to propagate, gave up attempting anything more than a shadowy suggestion of educational background, and in this amorphous situation came under Sloman's management in 1838.[1]

He inaugurated a full policy of variety entertainment. In the Grand Saloon the vocal and instrumental concert was to be heard, with Henry Howell, Master Hutchings in impersonations, and Miss Harrington. In addition, there was a Hall of Mirrors, an Indian Supper Room, a "magnificent theatre for the performance of Vaudevilles and Ballets," and, of course, the Dioramas. Thus we have the multiple entertainment, originating in the exhibits and "side-shows" of the public gardens collected under a roof, perhaps for the first time. Sloman's energies were at their height. He found time, while conducting the complicated affairs of the Colosseum, to take over the chairmanship of the Duke's Head Tavern in Whitechapel under Sieby's management, and it was here that Miss Fraser James, so much praised by Renton Nicholson, played the syren without compromising her virtue. Unfortunately, the Colosseum proved a disastrous venture for Sloman and the following year found him again the chair at the Mogul tavern, a post he had held previously.

The figure of W. G. Ross, though less representative than that of Sloman, is perhaps the most considerable of those connected with the Cider Cellars and the Coal Hole. He is an instance of an artist whose career hinged upon the performance of one song; the rather foul-mouthed, and universally-styled "infamous" *Sam Hall*. Ross, whose early history as an unsuccessful and untalented actor is obscure, leapt into the most astonishing

[1]Edmund Yates in his memoirs describes visits to the Colosseum as a boy. These would have occurred not long after Sloman's management of the place. He gives particulars of a Glyptoteka, an exhibition of plaster casts, and of an aged eagle languishing among stucco rocks in the grounds, which were also embellished with stalactite caves and sham ruins.

fame with this song, itself of equally obscure origin. "Sam Hall" was first sung by Ross at the Cider Cellar in the 'forties, and so greatly titillated the *habitués* of that place by its outspoken refrain of "damn your eyes," that, for a number of years, a crowded room was assured whenever Ross was announced. A version of the song is given from memory in *The Days of Dickens*, by A. L. Hayward: another version to be found in the appendix is from a scarce broadsheet. From other authorities we learn that he sang the song "in character," sitting astride a chair, the effect of his tattered clothes and bedraggled hat increased by the blackened clay pipe held between his teeth, which was removed only for purposes of expectoration, and for the greater emphasis of the oaths which bespatter the verses. It is supposed that the song is of earlier date than Ross's singing of it and bears reference to a forgotten but historically existing criminal.

There undoubtedly were extra verses in Ross's version not revealed in Hayward's quotation, verses which may well have rendered the song an unpleasant and unremitting piece of realism, and Ross's rendering was unanimously held to possess a degree of power amounting to the horrible. F. C. Burnand, A'Beckett, H. G. Hibbert, and the rest of the commentators, speak almost in awe of *Sam Hall*. It became more than a performance, it grew into a kind of rite. Burnand records that during a visit which as a boy he paid to the Cider Cellars, a waiter called at the various adjoining rooms and announced that "Mr. Ross was about to sing *Sam Hall*," whereupon everyone hurried into the concert room, though they might have heard the song fifty times before.

It is significant that *Sam Hall* never penetrated to Evans's though it was permitted at Vauxhall in 1847. Ross received the usual invitation to return to the regular stage, and under Buckstone appeared in an Irish farce. But his talents being essentially those of an entertainer, he was not successful. The drawing which accompanies Percival Leigh's description in *Punch* depicts a Ross who had been singing this song for eight years before the same audiences. At last in the 'fifties the vogue declined. Ross's career was probably maimed by its one extraordinary success, the kind which makes the discovery of suitable material to follow it so difficult a matter. While the range of his talent was probably similar to that of Robson on a lesser plane, no attempt was made either by him or by his managers to develop it along these lines. One hears vaguely of his other songs: of his use of a narrative burlesque on *Richard III*, originally written for Sam Cowell, together with performances of the well-worn Tom Hudson parody of the *Ivy Green*, called the *Lively Flea*; and of a song called *Going Home with the Milk in the Morning*, a title which reminds one of the Edwardian star, Hetty King. But such

things were obviously of supreme unimportance. After losing grip on music hall audiences Ross eventually drifted back to the stage, this time as a member of the chorus in musical comedy. He was one day pointed out to Chance Newton, who barely recognized the poor down-at-heel singer. He died while working as a super in one of Hollingshead's Gaiety companies.

The Coal Hole and the Cider Cellars under virtually the same management, had identical policies : both suffered from the same disabilities—or advantages—as to the impossibility of enlargement on theatrical lines, and both came under the same blighting influence of a term of tenancy by Renton Nicholson. Of the artists already mentioned, who made appearances at both the houses, Tom Hudson is interesting both as a representative composer of popular songs and as a link with the Regency tavern concerts. He was born in 1791 and is described in the British Museum catalogue as "Thomas Hudson, Grocer." To this avocation he added those by which his name survives, the singing and writing of songs ; and the management of his celebrated theatrical tavern, the "O.P. and P.S." in Russell Court, Covent Garden. Hudson was an industrious publisher of his own songs, the first volume of which was printed in 1818. In range and style they are representative of the comic standard achieved at the time. In them are to be found certain links with the garden songs of Dignum and Darley, there being a considerable trace of the Bacchanalian note of the eighteenth century, but added to these characteristics may be perceived the signs of change. These consist of a development towards a purely domestic source of humour—a reliance on the commonplace and intimate occurrences of everyday life. A different class angle is visible : in Hudson the lower middle-class became articulate. Parody was also a favourite device with Hudson, and for purposes of burlesque he used the popular ballad-poets of his time—notably Haynes Bayly, Tom Moore, and Dibdin. There are songs whose themes survive well into the nineteenth century such as those which make reference to animal life—*The Mouse Trap*, *The Spider and the Fly*, *The Hungry Fish*, and others whose homely parables are revealed by titles such as *Back and Belly* and *Petticoat and Breeches*. There are, moreover, topical songs which have the true music hall flavour. Many of them were sung extensively by comedians of note : *Jack Robinson*, *The Dogs' Meat Man* and *Walker the Twopenny Postman* being prominent in the repertory of Robert Glindon and Henry Howell.

Efforts were made by Hudson to secure his songs from the universal pirating of the time (with little success, as contemporary chap-books clearly indicate) and the albums continued to appear for a number of years, preserving an unabated raciness of style,

and by no means free from that vulgarity of which the authors of *The Variety Stage* are so anxious to acquit them. An example of his work is to be found in Appendix B.

The other artists already mentioned will be dealt with later. They were all vocal comedians of one kind or another, a type of artist which predominated at the Cider Cellars and the Coal Hole, although the programmes at times included other elements of variety. Conjuring and juggling found a place there, and when the nigger minstrel craze set in after Rice's visit to London, J. A. Cave led the way with his Æthiopian performances. It is difficult to ascertain at what date the " lady serio-comic " vocalist invaded these houses, the innovation probably did not occur until they had come under the management of Nicholson who, rather late in a career devoted alternately to " flash " journalism and the shadier branches of the amusement industry, broken intermittently by visits to the King's Bench Debtors' Prison, turned his attention to Mock Trials and the " Poses Plastiques," which he brought to the Cider Cellars in 1853 and to the Coal Hole in 1858.

The trials, or " Judge and Jury Shows," were probably suggested to Nicholson by those given in Dublin in the eighteenth century, with which Alexander Stevens was connected. As its name suggests, the setting of the entertainment was a burlesque court of law, over which Nicholson himself presided in the character of the " Lord Chief Baron." Counsel and witnesses were impersonated by professional entertainers, the jury was usually made up of enthusiastic amateurs. The former included Richard Hart, " the celebrated debater," Alfred Hoffner, the comic song writer, H. J. Brooks, an actor who supplied a variety of character studies in the witness-box and is credited with much originality, and Edward Thompson, a comedian. The first of these shows was probably given by Nicholson at the Garrick's Head Tavern in Bow Street in 1841, where he was leading a forlorn hope, the house having recently failed under two successive managements. They proved to be an immediate success and remained a feature of London life for about twenty years. John Hart, by this time the proprietor of the Cider Cellars (Rhodes' widow being in management at the Coal Hole) actually enlarged the premises to accommodate Nicholson's performances, but they did not flourish there for long. Hart, at some of the trials, was in the habit of impersonating a prostitute, and in connection with this characterization, stage business of unquestionable lewdness was introduced. Indeed, this practice was on one occasion the cause of proceedings in a real court of law.

The " Poses Plastiques," a variant of those living exhibitions of classical statuary which had been shown at an earlier date at

the saloon theatres and elsewhere, served as a means of introducing women to the audience at the Cider Cellars, their presence being invited for this part of the entertainment though not for the Judge and Jury Shows. An unequivocal female element, having also been brought on to the stage for these exhibitions, the Cider Cellars and Coal Hole lost for ever the characteristics which had made them famous and lingered only a few years as public places of resort.

Towards the end of the 'sixties Evans's, the last stronghold of the male sing-song, also capitulated to the lady serio-comic, and such artists as Mrs. Caulfield were heard there for the first time. The early association of this singer with those places which had previously excluded woman performers, probably accounts for the fact that she was claimed by H. G. Hibbert to have been the first of the female serio-comic singers. The statement as it related to the concert rooms as a whole is completely inaccurate, the humorous song, performed "in character," being one of those features which the music houses and garden saloons had borrowed from the theatre.

Nevertheless, an evolution in humorous songs sung by women was in process, and Mrs. Caulfield's early appearance at the newly opened Canterbury Hall where, for a time, she was the only female soloist, marks the beginning of a new epoch. The only respect in which Mrs. Caulfield's repertory deviated from tradition and anticipated the work of the later comediennes, was her introduction of "ladies' versions" of the popular comic songs of the day. The fashion for such versions increased as time went on and gave an emphasis to songs sung by women in male costume, a practice already in vogue in the theatre. Vesta Tilley is credited with being the first music hall artist who wore realistic male attire.

For the rest, Mrs. Caulfield's singing was sufficiently conservative in character. A favourite with her public was the arch and old-fashioned *The Captain and his Whiskers*, which dates from the 'thirties and is set to the tune of *The Wearin' of the Green*. She also had much success with a nigger minstrel song brought to England by Mrs. W. J. Florence, called *Keemo Kimo*.

On the whole, Mrs. Caulfield, so far from being an innovator, leaves one with the impression of being a typical member of the theatrical profession who had strayed to the concert rooms, and with her husband, John Caulfield (late of the Haymarket Theatre)—whose son played the harmonium at the Canterbury—of belonging to the older tradition, rather than to the newly born music hall.

The Cider Cellars and the Coal Hole disappeared in the rebuilding of their sites: the latter being converted by an Australian actor called Charles Wilmot into a well-known

theatrical resort known as the Occidental Tavern. Later, in its place, he built a theatre in which to house the celebrated comedian Edward Terry, to whom eventually he sold the property.

Though they contributed so materially to the growth of the song and supper movement, these two famous houses stop short, for the reasons which have been indicated, of making the true transition to music hall. Where neither traditional nor architectural barriers obtained, the movement towards theatrical presentation and the presence of mixed audiences were paving the way for the triumph of the new régime at the Canterbury and rendering the old-fashioned sing-song an anachronism. The single exception to this tendency was Evans's Song and Supper Rooms, which, while retaining the conservative non-theatrical policy and the male audience, succeeded in capturing the central position in the entertainment world of the following decade. Evans's, however, was so far outside the line of the logical development of the time as to suggest a separate treatment in a later chapter.

The Cider Cellars and the Coal Hole were by no means the only other important tavern concerts which for one reason or another failed to effect a transition. Of such was Hudson's O.P. & P.S. in Russell Court, a resort of members of the theatrical profession and of men about town. Its performances were enlivened by John Hart, late of the Cider Cellars ; by Nicholson's friend, Morton Box ; by Joe Wells, the old pro. of the Coal Hole ; and by a number of those convivial men who sought to carry on the glories of the Regency nights.

An interesting assembly, true to eighteenth-century tradition, where the young sparks, members of the flash community of both sexes and of the respectable working class, happily rubbed shoulders, was the Hare and Hounds, a public house in the vicinity of St. Giles, the proprietor of which was known as "Stunning Joe Banks." Well into the century it held place as a popular resort though, and even perhaps because, it was in the midst of a notorious and somewhat dangerous neighbourhood. The scheme of entertainment at the Hare and Hounds has been described by John Richardson in his *Reminiscences of the Last Fifty Years*. He informs us that the proceedings always opened with the performance of an anthem—a relic, this, of eighteenth-century practice—and that a lady "presided over the revels and at intervals amused the company with specimens of her talent."

Nicholson, in his autobiography, gives more details of this female chairman : "The fair dame, elevated in the background," he writes, "is the queen for the night of the orgies which take place, as we have said, once a week at the *hotel* called the Hare and Hounds in the Rookery. Her duties are to keep order, collect subscriptions in the plate, to sing songs, and to regulate the

amusement of the evening, inasmuch as dancing, as well as singing, forms a very prominent feature therein. The queen is selected from the flowers of loveliness amongst the fair cadgers."

The locality of Buckridge Street, St. Giles, in which the Hare and Hounds stood, is described in detail as follows: "Coming from the City, our inquiring friend must pass St. Giles' church and keep on the right-hand side of the way: He will then shortly arrive at a turning, the entrance to which is obstructed by sundry intricate posts and, passing between them, twenty yards walking in a straight line, brings him into the Rookery and to the renowned lush crib maintained by the Stunning Joe Banks."

These and more respectable instances of the smaller tavern concert gave impetus to music hall development, and helped to preserve certain traditions, such as the office of chairman. But no possibility of a music hall emerging directly from them could be looked for; the essence of this development is in the introduction of theatrical conditions; although the title of "music hall" has no theatrical significance. It is a little difficult to say how this name grew sufficiently into favour to be chosen as a definite term for houses presenting miscellaneous entertainment. Strangely enough, there are few traces of the phrase in connection with the performance of serious music, perhaps the single exception is that of the Surrey Music Hall, which, though a concert hall, was the cause of the neighbouring house, which bore the same name, changing its title to the Winchester. In connection with concert performances, the term Room or Great Room is the more general one which precedes the use of the word "Hall" without any prefix. In connection with miscellaneous entertainments, the phrase music hall was probably first used as a kind of euphemism. The New Surrey Music Hall, *c.* 1840, the new music hall, Yorkshire Stingo, 1835, the music hall, Store Street, *c.* 1840, the music hall, Hungerford Market, and the Regency Music Hall are probably all early instances of a desire to give to their respective houses a well-sounding title. The phrase theatre of varieties also appeared as early as 1829, the instance being that of the Regency Theatre of Varieties, Tottenham Street: the first Lyceum, under the management of the pantomimist Laurent, was known for a time as the Theatre of Mirth.

No doubt the term music hall has some connection with the earlier phrase music house, and this connection, although I think neither a conscious nor consecutive one, is emphasized by the fact that the latter was almost always the outgrowth of a tavern, though usually not adjoining the parent house.

Whatever the exact origin of the title, its application in almost every instance was, from the first, to those tavern concerts which

strove to present theatrical features in emulation of the saloon theatres and the minor theatres which included varieties in the programmes. Architecturally, the enlarged concert rooms were taking on theatrical attributes. With the proscenium there came the addition of a balcony, or in some cases a raised platform separated from the body of the hall by a railing, behind which was the saloon bar with its somewhat more elaborate seating arrangements which justified the higher prices charged for this part of the house. On the floor, the guests still sat as of old, either at long tables placed at right angles to the stage, or at small square tables scattered over the auditorium in the manner of the Continental café. In either event the chairman was placed at a table parallel with the stage, from which he faced the audience ; and places at or near the chairman's table were occupied by those *habitues* who enjoyed that autocrat's favours, in return for which they were granted the privilege of supplying him with drinks and cigars during the course of the evening.

Thus the transition to a theatrical auditorium was effected by adding this " upper hall " or " saloon," this later giving place to a low-priced balcony ; tables gradually being supplanted by ledges at the backs of the seats for the refreshments. By these means the aspects of the tavern concert and of the old all-masculine sing-song were forgotten and those of the modern " theatre of variety " by and by emerged. From that time onward the clear outline of the music hall in its essential character as tavern concert became blurred and a junction was effected with the cheaper-priced theatre, ranging from minor theatre to penny gaff and with the hybrid saloon theatre whose short-lived career was the outcome partly of the alfresco habit and more particularly of the legal anomalies preceding the Act of 1843. The Britannia Saloon was perhaps the most notable instance of this junction, becoming as it did, after the theatricalization of the tavern, indistinguishable from all those music halls (as they were now universally called), which strove to retain as many dramatic features as was compatible with their more narrowly defined status under the Act.

This effort to retain a semi-dramatic programme was later to develop into a struggle as bitter as that which had previously been carried on between the minor theatres and the patentees. For the time, however, they made hay while the sun shone and the competition which their very low prices created was a cause of complaint among the old-style gaff theatres whose portable shows, insecurely lodged in stables or sheds, were now subject to a keen competition.

The prices of the tavern shows, even after the introduction of theatrical display, certainly left little margin to the gaffs, ranging

as they did from 2d. to 1s., with special rates for women and children. The Yorkshire Stingo was as high-priced as any, charging for the upper saloon (to which no person was admitted without tickets to be had " on application at the bar ") a 1s. for " gents " and 6d. for ladies and children. A really helpful announcement tells us that " a new orchestra embellished with illuminated crystal columns " has been installed, together with " a saloon communicating with a new balcony overlooking the grand concert room." Here is clearly shown the association of saloon and balcony—the latter being an adjunct of the former. The Yorkshire Stingo partly, but not extensively, depended on its outdoor attractions. It was in origin one of the quiet tea garden taverns standing back from the main road in Marylebone which led out of the town on its western side. The name is retained by the public house which stands on the site but the Marylebone public baths occupy the garden space from which Green made some of his celebrated balloon ascents. Its arbours were a favourite haunt of those miserably paid journalists, numbering among them E. L. Blanchard, who for the price of a pint of ale could borrow pen and ink and write their " copy " in undisturbed seclusion.

The Yorkshire Stingo, under the energetic management of George Hodson, an actor, vocalist and composer, with a considerable talent of showmanship, entered in 1835 on a career which rendered it something of a West London replica of the Eagle Tavern in the City Road. An early stroke of good management was the prominence he gave to the singing of Robert Glindon. The latter, with his wife, was closely associated with the Yorkshire Stingo throughout its concert-room career, giving to the performances exactly that steadying respectability needed for the type of audience to which appeal was made. Glindon's two best-known songs, *The Literary Dustman* and *Biddy the Basket Woman*, the first of which he wrote himself, are character studies entirely lacking in that raciness which gave the songs of his contemporary, Tom Hudson, some relation to real life. Not even the mildest of Rabelaisian qualities disturbed the dullness of Glindon's domestic humour, yet he came to great celebrity as a concert-room artist, and towards the end of his career was heard in company with the leading singers of a newer school, at Vauxhall and Cremorne. Until he transferred his energies to the Bower Saloon in Stangate, Hodson maintained the prestige of the Yorkshire Stingo at a high level ; and the house, but for the existence of its garden, might be adjudged one of the most important of the earlier music halls.

This disqualification does not attach to the Rotunda in the Blackfriars Road, at its junction with Albion Street, one of the earliest houses to use the term " music hall " (it was known by

that designation in 1838) when it came under the management of John Blewitt, the composer. The place was built in 1790 by a man called Parkinson, who had won by lottery the collection of curiosities made by Sir Ashton Lever and publicly exhibited in Leicester House, under the name of " Holuphusikon." In its new home the exhibition, called by Parkinson " The Museum Leveriarum," was never a prosperous venture and failed in 1806. From this time onwards the career of the Rotunda became extremely chequered. In turn, melodramas, waxworks, exhibitions of mechanical devices and panoramas were offered as attractions. Charles Sloman appeared there in 1829. In 1833 it was giving drama and variety performances under conditions of a penny gaff. In 1838 came Blewitt's management, when it assumed the features of a music hall, and for many years carried on an intermittent existence, gathering a kind of fame in the locality, and often harbouring artists of note ; one of the last being the infant Dan Leno. The licence lapsed in the late 'eighties, and for a time the building was used as a chapel. It must not be confused, as it so often is, with the " Ring," a boxing centre a few doors away from the site.

Of far more importance to music hall development was the " Grapes " Inn in Southwark Bridge Road, whose enlargement into a music hall was a clear-cut and satisfactory instance of the tavern outgrowth. The Grapes, under its various titles of Surrey and Winchester music hall, did not survive into the period of the modern variety theatre ; it ceased to exist when the type, of which it was a leading example, was beginning to become out-moded. Following on the period during which a sing-song had been held in the tavern long room, the hall was built in the 'forties, the new house neatly adjoining its parent tavern. It had a single balcony and seated about a thousand people. A cosy affair, essentially part of the neighbourhood from which it drew its audiences, it was an admirable and representative example of the music hall movement in true perspective. Its reconstruction was effected by Richard Preece, who retitled the hall the Surrey. Though possessing a fully equipped stage, theatrical elements made no special appeal to Preece, whose programmes retained the flavour of a professional sing-song. A family atmosphere pervaded the house, for William Warde, who acted as chairman and manager, had a son and daughter both of whom took part in the performances. With the Dauban family the Wardes later made a considerable reputation in ballet, and the two families became fused by marriage.

The house was run upon pleasantly respectable lines and the separation of the public bars from the auditorium helped to render it an early example of a *rendezvous* for a bourgeois

audience of both sexes. A high standard was set by the orchestra, which from the first was in the hands of an accomplished musician. In every respect the Surrey anticipated the claims made later by Morton for the Canterbury, though Preece lacked the ambitious and acquisitive intelligence of that manager. Indeed, the early success of Morton at the Canterbury was not a little due to his seizing of the possibilities implicit in the new standard set by the Winchester and going one better. The move to checkmate took the form of vastly more elaborate and roomy premises and of the famous picture gallery—that "Royal Academy over the water" which *Punch*, by this encomium, almost raised to the dignity of a national institution. It is amusing to note the retaliation made by Preece, who also became a picture fancier in rivalry to Morton, two examples of whose collection may still be seen in what is now a private room in the present Winchester Tavern. During the 'sixties, ballet and pantomime were introduced at the Surrey, a policy which was probably dictated also by the rivalry of the Canterbury. It was then that the famous Vokes family appeared at the house before they made their West End début in pantomime at the Lyceum in 1868.

It was in 1856, early in its history, that it became necessary to change the title of the hall attached to the Grapes, to the Winchester; owing to the erection of the gigantic building in the Surrey Zoological Gardens, to which was given the name of the Surrey Music Hall, and which was built for the purpose of housing the fashionable concerts of Jullien, the waltz composer, then fresh from the triumphs achieved by his promenade concerts at Drury Lane Theatre. Both houses were doomed, however. The latter was burned to the ground in 1861, only a few of its pillars remaining to provide the artist of the *Illustrated London News* with material for a drawing suggestive of some relic of Imperial Rome. The former got left behind in the competitive struggle set up by the music hall boom of the 'seventies. Its respectability, its intimacy, and its local fame being no longer qualifications for success, it petered out and was demolished in or about 1878. In the Winchester, the public house music hall reached its peak, and with it this institution in its most characteristic form may be said to have come to an end.[1]

The era which closed with the closing of the Winchester should, logically, have brought to an end the use of the term music hall. For the change wrought by the formation of big

[1]I was shown round the present "Winchester" by the kind proprietress of the establishment who, among other interesting things, showed me a door at the back of an adjacent shop still bearing the inscription "Gallery" on its glass pane. She also showed me a window upon which Preece had scratched his name with a diamond ring.

syndicates was inevitably to bring the movement into the zone of purely theatrical speculation. Thus that form of miscellaneous entertainment which had been nurtured as a branch of licensed victualling was finally superseded. In a sense, of course, this orientation of the art is as old as any other, but the organized period during which it achieved the definitive name of music hall was a brief one, and its collapse involved what was virtually a return to the older and smudgier methods of the minor theatre, though the great variety palaces were at the time hailed as a sign of innovation and reform.

The title name of music hall died hard, though an immense gulf of time is marked between the first use of the phrase theatre of variety in 1814 and its more general adoption. The early choice of this name fell on a little theatre in Tottenham Street, Fitzroy Square, which, originally built as a concert hall in the end of the eighteenth century by Paschali, housed for a time the Concerts of Antient Musick. The house, or rather its site, has, after innumerable vicissitudes, become the Scala Theatre. The vagaries of the Tottenham Street theatre began early in its career. On the removal of the Concerts of Antient Musick to the Hanover Square Rooms, it was the scene of the inauguration of Colonel Fulke Greville's "Pic-nic" Society. Quickly deserted by Greville, various efforts were made to adapt the house to forms of miscellaneous entertainment, such as Mr. Hyde's performances on the cornet or the feats of Saunders, the equestrian. One or two ventures were made in regular theatrical production and it was leased for six years and successfully conducted under the name of the Regency Theatre of Varieties by the actor and circuit manager, Beverley, who not only had the honour of receiving the unknown Edmund Kean into his company, but of championing him under the derision of his fellow actors. The interest of Beverley's management is confined to his choice of name, as his policy did not in any way deviate from that of the normal minor theatre of the time. It is a little odd that this term used by Beverley at the beginning of the nineteenth century should have remained almost completely dormant until its revival at the end of it as a descriptive title for the new type of hall introduced by invading syndicates from the Midlands.

The Bower Saloon in Stangate provides an instance of a music hall with a history differing from the usual line of development. Built, it is true, in connection with a tavern which boasted a small garden and which had housed a "free-and-easy," it nevertheless jumped fully grown from the brain of its founder, Philips, who was a scenic artist and painter of Dioramas connected with the Surrey Theatre. It was from the first supplied with a

fully equipped stage and orchestra. Philips' scheme was the presentation of an elaborated form of Diorama at the Bower, and he inaugurated his management by exhibiting pictures of his own to the accompaniment of a musical programme, under the direction of John Blewitt. This policy failed, and in 1841 the property was acquired by George Hodson of the Yorkshire Stingo. Under Hodson the Bower Saloon for a time enjoyed a moderate success. He conducted the house on the lines of the Apollo Saloon in Marylebone,[1] that is, by the production of songs, vaudevilles, and melodramatic spectacles. The two Miss Hodsons appeared there in a *Buy a Broom* duet, one of the prolific stream of songs which had reference to the Bavarian girl pedlars who, in the previous decade, were to be seen everywhere in the streets of London. An important singer who, early in his career, appeared at the Bower was J. B. Howe. Howe was a successful and varied singer and song writer famous for his performance of one of the burlesque narrative songs founded on the dramatized legend of Alonzo the Brave, the lyric of which was written for him by Blanchard. Another song writer equally prolific but more obscure, connected with the Bower, was G. E. Palmer, who took a benefit there in 1845. Hodson himself continued his activities in his new house, as a purveyor of sentimental songs. In this capacity he earns a recollection as the composer of *Tell Me Mary how to Woo Thee*, which at least enjoyed a considerable popularity. He also set Haynes Bayly's lyric *He knew she never blamed him.* In the very heart of the Bayly tradition was a further song of Hodson's entitled *He never said he loved*, the poem for which, by a happy coincidence, was the work of F. W. N. Bayley. The art of plagiarism was not unknown to Hodson, as is attested by a note in the British Museum Catalogue to the effect that the vocal line of his setting of *Oh Give me back My Arab Steed* reproduces the finale to the opera of *The Barber of Seville.* Hodson's undoubted versatility is instanced by his assumption of the musical conductorship of Renton Nicholson's Poses Plastiques and Musical Illustrated Lecture in 1846. His ability as a chorus master was also recognized by Nicholson, who entrusted him—the idea originating with Hodson himself—with the organization of his troupe of "Female Æthiopian Serenaders," which appeared at the St. James's Rooms in the 'forties and subsequently toured in the provinces.

The years immediately preceding and following the opening of the Canterbury in 1849 were those during which the process of germination in the music hall was approaching completion. When the Oxford opened in 1861 the full flood of activity was

[1]The name of the Hall at the Yorkshire Stingo : *see* page 57 *et. seq.*

at its height. The list of halls nearing maturity during the 'fifties is a long one, especially if to it are added the many which died by the way. The East End of London was perhaps the most prolific quarter. Such Halls as Gilbert's in Whitechapel, the Rodney, the Lord Nelson, the Eastern, the Apollo in Bethnal Green, Macdonalds near the Britannia Theatre, the Cambridge in Commercial Street, Shoreditch, Wiltons in Wellclose Square, the Foresters (earlier the Artichoke) in the Cambridge Road, and many others, had all during the 'fifties laid the foundations of the considerable popularity which they enjoyed in the following decade. Notably in this quarter of London the Eagle Tavern and Gardens in the Mile End Road which from the early 'thirties had been devoted to the blend of entertainment given by its namesake in the City Road, had under William Lusby been rebuilt as a hall of major importance. Under Crowder and Payne (a partnership which had first brought the Britannia Saloon into prominence) the hall after having suffered a fire was further refashioned in 1878, and became still more widely known as the Paragon. In its final and recent phase the house has been known as the Mile End Empire.

In the West End, at least in the more fashionable part of it, there was understandably less music hall activity. Though in very much earlier times the ancient Boar and Castle in Oxford Street, the site of the Oxford Music Hall, had with its Long Room been numbered among the musical taverns, no trace of this remained when it was demolished to make room for Morton's venture. The Black Horse, by Piccadilly Circus, in whose yard the London Pavilion was erected, boasted only a sing-song of the older type ; and the Tivoli, where, later, a beer garden gave the hall its title, was not to come into existence for many years. Among the number of smaller public house concerts the Swallow Street Hall was emerging, and had by the 'sixties taken its place among the music halls. Though the smallest of the West End houses, it received most of the well-known singers during a career which ended about the same time, or a little later, than the Winchester.

Somewhere between 1850 and 1860 Leicester Square developed one of its cosmopolitan resorts in the Parisian Hall (later the Eldorado), whose character, reflecting that of the immediate neighbourhood, possibly influenced the policy of the succeeding Empire.

Nearer the centre, the Mogul in Drury Lane had under J. L. Graydon established a music hall reputation before the opening of the Oxford, on the basis of a well-known tavern concert of many years' standing. Edward Weston's operations in transforming the National School adjoining the Seven

Tankards and Punchbowl Inn, Holborn, into a music hall synchronized with Morton's founding of the Canterbury.

In the city the Doctor Johnson Tavern was already a fully developed music hall in the 'fifties ; in north London, Deacon's is of the same period, in the south-eastern quarter the Surrey had a neighbour in the Salmon, which was later known as the Raglan and the Borough. South-west London was developing halls from the garden taverns of the Sun and the Trevor in Knightsbridge. The latter site was adjacent to the existing public house of that name at the corner of Charles Street.

In Pimlico the Standard had, under May been organized on music hall lines in the 'forties ; W. G. Ross appearing there and also Charles Sloman in an entertainment entitled *Myorama.* In Marylebone no house of importance had as yet taken the place of the Yorkshire Stingo : the sing-song at the White Lion in Edgware Road and that of the Rose of Normandy in High Street not having yet been transformed into the Metropolitan and Marylebone Music Halls. The Cosmetheka in Bell Street belongs to the 'sixties : the other house in Church Streeet (the Marylebone Theatre) was of the minor theatre type which included sporadic varieties.

In addition to many houses of the latter type existing in the 'fifties—such as the Effingham in the Whitechapel Road—all of which were making their contribution to miscellaneous entertainment, there are to be taken into account houses which, though they did not precisely belong to the spate of " improving " entertainments (being organized on a frankly commercial basis), yet provided varieties inspired to some extent by this movement.[1]

They were, of course, not licensed premises. Among these the music hall in Store Street is of interest on account of its transitional use of the term. The house stood near the corner of Bedford Square and together with the Polygraphic Rooms and the Adelaide Galleries, presented a type of non-theatrical " varieties." In 1837 this establishment was announcing entertainments designed to demonstrate the effect of the Patent Aeolophon on the pianoforte technique of Mr. Philips' pupils. The one-man entertainment was also represented there in the person of Orlando Parry, who at this house gave performances of his *Notes Vocal and Instrumental.* In this category may also be included the Egyptian Hall in Piccadilly, some of whose varied programmes will be mentioned elsewhere. It may be stated here, however, that Philip Astley had anticipated many features of the later music hall in a room on the site of the Egyptian Hall. The room was hired by Astley for the purpose of a very astute form of advertisement for his Amphitheatre in Lambeth. The entertain-

[1]*See* Chapter VIII.

ments consisted of performances by Signor Rossignol, who in addition to giving imitation of bird-songs, achieved the feat of performing a violin concerto " without strings " ; a " foreign gentleman " who played five instruments at one time, together with a contribution to the programme by Astley himself, which was no less a matter than " to exhibit and discover tricks of legerdemain." Between these rooms and his headquarters Astley was in the habit of forming those street processions which since became a familiar feature of the arrival of a circus in a country town. At these " parades," as they are technically known, a chariot was to be seen which contained " a clown and a learned pony, which distributed handbills."

Apparently Astley experienced a change of heart at a later date, for he afterwards announced that he had " abandoned these disgusting exhibitions for ever."[1]

[1] *See* Chapter VI, p. 105, *et. seq.*

CHAPTER IV

Pleasure Gardens

We have seen in the last chapter how, early in the nineteenth century, those of the concert rooms attached to taverns which were able to add a proscenium and a tableau curtain tried their hand at pantomime and ballet ; and thus laid the foundations to the theatrical and spectacular elements of the later music hall.

The larger pleasure gardens were caught up in the same movement. By the early 'twenties Vauxhall had for theatrical purposes altered its Rotunda (the large umbrella-like building which had been used till then for concerts and assemblies) ; ballets and " vaudevilles " by Haynes Bayly and others, together with the " first act " (thus it is expressed in the advertisements) of the vocal and instrumental concert were performed there, the second part of the concert being still given in the open-air orchestra.

This is sufficient evidence that a new note was being struck in this industry. The tea garden ideal was passing away : some of the most famous eighteenth-century haunts had, indeed, not survived beyond the century in which they were established ; those which had, persisted by means of their theatrical and concert saloon developments. Marylebone and Ranelagh suffered the decay of fashion before the nineteenth century opened, Islington Spa held on until 1840, Bagnigge Wells until 1843, White Conduit House until 1849, the Albert Tavern and Gardens, by taking up a theatre licence, until 1857 ; and a remarkably long run, comparable to that of Vauxhall, was achieved by the St. Helena Gardens, Rotherhithe—1770 till 1881. Bermondsey Spa, though it eked out an existence with concert entertainments and fireworks, died in 1804 after a pitiable struggle, graphically described by J. T. Smith in *The Book for a Rainy Day*.[1]

[1]Smith's visit was in 1795 : " that once-famed place of recreation was most rapidly on the decline. I entered under a semi-circular awning next to the proprietor's house, which I well remember was a large, wooden-fronted building, consisting of long square divisions, in imitation of scantlings of stone. My surprise was great, for no one appeared, but three idle waiters, and they were clumped for the want of a call. . . . As soon as we had reached the orchestra, the singer curtsied to us, for we were the only persons in the gardens. ' This is sad work,' said he [Keyse, the proprietor,

The two triumphant survivals, Vauxhall and St. Helena Gardens, whose careers overlapped by many years the later creations of Cremorne and the Surrey Gardens, went about things in the same way. That is to say, all pretence of fashionable glories was abandoned, their appeal being frankly to the new class of patron, who demanded cheap fun. Vauxhall, after a struggle in 1833, reduced its price of admission from half-a-crown to a shilling and gave itself up to the whims of the moment. By the 'thirties the tin cascade had been replaced by a diorama : the converted rotunda was embellished with " optical effects and laughable mirrors." Steamboats, by 1837, were carrying visitors to the river-gate in place of Tyers' State Barge,[1] Ducrow, Astley's distinguished successor, was giving an equestrian entertainment, described as the *Curriculum*, in the grounds and, most revolutionary of all, the genuine tavern concert singer invaded the orchestra—and even before this innovation occurred his influence had been felt, for ln 1829 the concert had been advertised as " consisting entirely of comic and other duets." (It is perhaps only just to add that in the same year something of the old grandiloquent note was struck by the installation of a " Hydropyric Temple.")[2]

It is in 1831 that we first hear of a variety concert in the rotunda, the performers including Paul Bedford, Miss Horton, Van Joel, and a man called Cornie, who sang the humorous song called *Nothing*.[3] These artists were also to be heard out of doors. Joel,i as a kind of resident buffoon, was as popular at Vauxhall in the 'thirties as he later became at Evans's. He gave strange exhibitions involving ventriloquism and the imitation of birds, and was allowed to wander in the grounds that he might jump out on visitors in unexpected places.[4] He is not to be confused

who had joined the solitary Smith] ' but the woman must sing according to contract. . . . As the lady retired . . . ' this is too bad,' again observed Keyse ; ' and I am sure that you cannot expect fireworks ! ' However, he politely asked me to partake of a bottle of Lisbon, which, upon my refusing, he pressed me to accept of a catalogue of his pictures."

[1]The extended steamboat service introduced in this year led to the establishment of the Rosherville Pleasure Gardens, on the banks of the Thames, in the west suburbs of Gravesend; a familiar reference to which occurs, many years later, in T. S. Lonsdale's song, *Tommy, Make Room for your Uucle*.

[2]Continuing a long line of such eighteenth century toys. In the *Gentleman's Magazine* for June, 1822, reference is made to the installation of a Heptaplasiesoptron : " an illuminated area, with several pillars, around which are entwined sepents, shaded under the foliage of palm trees. The centre is occupied by a cooling fountain, and looking glasses, skilfully placed in the background, reflect both the ornamental objects and the spectators, with something approaching to magnificence of effect."

[3]The Rotunda auditorium is described as containing " Boxes, Pit, and Gallery, in the circular part ; and on one side a Stage. . . . Also an arena for horsemanship."

[4]A Vauxhall playbill in the Francis Edwards Collection (Brit. Mus.) reveals the Christian name of Van Joel as Julian. He is announced as " the celebrated siffleur from Altona " (Hamburg's Fair-ground suburb). The wording further states : " Herr Joel will amuse the Company with his imitations of birds, etc., etc., etc." (dated 1842).

with Joel il diavolo, an acrobat, who at this same period figures in a bill as " sliding on a rope from a Tower above to a *bosquet* beneath." The place, moreover, abandoned its old atmosphere of mystery, by opening in the daytime, for Vauxhall architecture was designed for nocturnal effect. Dickens, writing in 1837 in *Sketches by Boz*, found the disillusionment hard to bear. To his disgust, he discovered the famous rococo decorations of the gardens to be " Nothing but a combination of roughly painted boards." " *That* the Moorish tower," he cries, " that wooden shed with a door in the centre, and daubs of crimson and yellow all round, like a gigantic watch-case! *That* the place where night after night we had beheld the undaunted Mr. Blackmore make his terrific ascent, surrounded by flames of fire and peals of artillery. . . . *That* the——." Then a bell rings, summoning Boz to the concert in the orchestra. Here a " small gentleman in a dress coat leads on a particularly tall lady in a blue sarcenet pelisse and bonnet " and they perform " a plaintive duet." Significantly, the comic singer is the " especial favourite." His distinguishing characteristics are a wig approaching to the flaxen, and an aged countenance. He bears the name of one of the English counties, if we remember aright." (By this, we are able to identify the artist as Paul Bedford.) He sings " a very good song about the Seven Ages, the first half-hour of which affords the assembly the purest delight; of the rest we can make no report, as we didn't stay to hear any more."

Mingled with the comic singing at Vauxhall were the rotunda vaudevilles, whose composers included John Blewitt, Charles Horn, Haynes Bayly, and T. Cooke, a musical director for the gardens, who as a frequent actor in his own works must not be confused with T. P. Cooke, the creator of William in *Black-eyed Susan.*[1] The great Sir Henry Bishop occupied the conductor's chair from 1830 until 1833, and under him *The Bloom is on the Rye,* Fitzball's famous song to Bishop's music, was sung by Robinson of the tavern concerts. By 1847 the "comics," a somewhat later appearance of whom a contemporary newspaper describes as an invasion of " the fast school," that is, the authentic music hall artists, arrived at the Gardens—Cowell, Sharpe, John Moody, Mackney, W. G. Ross, J. A. Cave, and Robert Glindon.

Meanwhile, the Gardens were not without some features to remind visitors of other days. After his death in 1835 an

[1]Thomas Cooke was a Dublin man. As a boy he played in its theatre orchestra and became leader. His first composition was performed in 1803, when his finale to *Love Laughs at Locksmiths*, improvised on the non-arrival of the manuscript, was pronounced superior to that written by the composer of the work, Michael Kelly. Both as a violinist and a performer of comic operatic parts, Cooke was equally proficient. His singing in Storace's opera, *The Siege of Belgrade*, in 1812 procured him an engagement in London under Arnold at the Lyceum.

By courtesy of British Museum

PAUL PRY.

The Inquisitive, Quizzical, Satirical, and Whimsical Epitome of Life as it is.

No. 8. PUBLISHED WEEKLY. Price One Penny

THE LORD NELSON TAVERN.

Puff is the order of the day. From the highest to the low... puff is the salve with which that great fool—the public— ...anointed. People have no faith except in chicanery, and ... dence to charge sixpence for admission to an entertainment—only distinguished for its utter want of talent—is no great wonder to us, but that such an exhibition should be patronized ... the talent which should adorn such a musical hall in London. The room is too great for the company, and the singers by far too impudent for the room. They take liberties with the au-

Miss Enid Brett's collection

illuminated effigy of Simpson, the famous master of the ceremonies, which by a clockwork device continually raised its hat in salute, was placed near the entrance to the grounds, and in 1840 an entirely new set of Gothic Ruins was erected. Tableaux-vivants, described as " groups of sculpture by male and female artists," appeared on the scene in 1837, comic ballets were performed by the Ravel family, and humorous glees specially written for the Gardens by Alexander Lee. Displays of fireworks (it will be remembered that they were not introduced by the reluctant management until 1798) now took an important place among the entertainments. In 1827 the Battle of Waterloo was represented and an open-air concert was announced to " commence as soon as possible after the battle." In 1833, in addition to the fireworks, the list of alfresco entertainments included comic songs and glees, tight-rope dancing by a lady, double juggling, slack-wire dancing, the Italian balance master, and Chinese postures.[1] And so on, into the 'fifties, when E. L. Blanchard so much admired the performances of the Bedouin Arabs. Thus Vauxhall kept pace with the increasingly complicated development of variety.

In the 'thirties the Britannia Saloon, "Hoxton Old Town, Old Street Road, near Shoreditch Church," is numbered by John Hollingshead as among the garden taverns. The place was then beginning to rear its head under the management of Crowder, at a later date important promoters of the music hall movement. Most of the ground surrounding the saloon was absorbed when Samuel Lane built the large theatre in 1841. Lane at once instituted a minor theatre policy and spectacles introducing the talented " Infant Taglioni " were produced with the additional attraction of real armour. Before the passing of the Theatre Act of 1843, when Lane at once availed himself of its provisions, the element of variety was preserved. A programme for 1842 includes a Pas Chinois, and several songs. In the same year the price for admission was raised from 2d. to 6d. inclusive of refreshment, upper stalls being sold at 1s. Lane's ambitions, shared by other saloon managers, were entirely theatrical. Hollingshead, whose narrative is for the most part lucid and unbiassed, is nevertheless among those who place too much importance upon the coercive effect of the 1843 Act, which in his judgment forced the precursors of the music hall to become theatres. In the majority of cases, the alternative was accepted with alacrity. As

[1]A description of the open-air stage erected for acrobatic displays is given in the *Vauxhall Observer*, a publication inspired by the management, dated May 1823. In 1841 the open-air stage was replaced by " a large building presenting in front the appearance of the proscenium and stage of a theatre."

will be seen, it ensured legal stability, in many cases, for the pursuance of the already adopted theatre policy, and the Britannia Saloon provides an example of this. Its programmes immediately following the announcement that the house is " licensed pursuant to Act of Parliament by the Lord Chamberlain," are identical in their intermingling of drama and the type of spectacle-ballet which includes singing and dancing. In other saloons the same position evidenced itself, so great were the freedoms taken with the law with or without the help of the burletta licence in the years immediately preceding the passing of the Act. Thus it was that the buildings put up in the grounds of taverns became gradually more ambitious and were given the general title of saloon theatre. Of this type of house the most prominent example was the Eagle tavern with its Grecian Saloon, in the City Road, by the corner of Shepherdess Walk.

Thomas Rouse took over the Eagle Tavern in 1831, and began developing its already existing Harmonic Meetings. These were held in the usual manner, in the Long Room on the first floor of the building, but under Rouse they took on a semi-professional character. There was convenient ground adjacent to the tavern on the east side, which had been known as the Adam and Eve Tea Gardens ; here Rouse began laying out walks and putting up ornamental buildings ; he also purchased the decorations to the Abbey entrance and robing rooms used at the coronation of William IV and erected them as an entrance to his gardens, advertising them not only as the identical fittings but as re-erected by the identical mechanics.

Probably the first building erected was that known, until it was later converted into a theatre, as the Moorish Saloon. But very soon after, perhaps at the same time, Rouse put up a solid and rather handsome building containing a semi-circular room, or " Rotunda " as it is called by Dickens, at the southern end of the grounds, with its façade towards them. This was expressly designed for the performance of varieties and vaudevilles and is the house shown in the handbill belonging to the year 1836, and which about the same time, " Miss Ivins " and her party are described in the *Sketches by Boz* as having visited. The document issued by Rouse in this year also gives particulars of the organ built for this saloon : the cosmoramas in the garden, the self-acting piano and the gas chandelier are also mentioned. We have to trust to Dickens' description of the physical features of the interior of the first " Grecian." The word rotunda is applied to it, presumably because the word was in fashion, although it was an irregular semicircle in shape. The stage—Dickens describes it as an " orchestra "—was most probably of a transitional type, without tableaux curtain. Curtainless stages were

in use at Evans's in the 'fifties and as late as 1852 at the second Canterbury Hall. It was in the nature of the saloons to have raised portions on which was placed a refreshment bar at the end opposite the stage, but in the Grecian of this period the arrangement was probably of a different kind and the words " the audience were seated on elevated benches round the room, and crowded into every part of it," suggest an arrangement of tiers.

In describing the grounds, two bands which performed alternately are referred to, reminding one of the methods of the modern " palais de danse." Singing in the grounds in the manner of Vauxhall was a habit at the Grecian, as also the rather peculiar practice of holding a " miscellaneous concert " late in the evening, on the conclusion of the performance in the rotunda.

The manager was an energetic man and was affectionately known to his patrons as " Bravo " Rouse from his habit of sitting in the stage box of his saloon and leading the applause. He was a builder by profession and soon reconstructed his rotunda, adding ornamental features to the exterior and re-conditioning the stage for the purpose of presenting a full burletta programme. The Grecian then entered on the most famous period of its history. The best-known concert room vocalists and comic singers were engaged. Robert Glindon settled down there as a permanent favourite, acting in burlettas with his wife and interspersing them with his own songs. Henry Howell and Kitty Tunstall, the latter also a great favourite at the Yorkshire Stingo, were to be seen there as well, together with other artists from the London theatres.

Early in the 'forties the celebrated Frederick Robson joined the company, his first character being that of John Lamp in the burletta of *The Wags of Windsor*. He is also said to have appeared at the Grecian in his famous character of Jem Baggs in Mayhew's comedietta, *The Wandering Minstrel*, for which E. L. Blanchard wrote his narrative song *Villikins and his Dinah*.[1] The history of the song is a little obscure. Mayhew's comedietta had been revived for amateur theatricals organized by Blanchard in 1836, but it is not certain that *Villikins* was written at this time. Indeed, there is a passage in his diary which suggests that the song was written especially for Robson when he appeared in 1853 in the same play at the Olympic Theatre, though this entry may refer to Blanchard's writing of an extended version. Still, *Villikins* and the Grecians have always been associated with one another by commentators, and it is true that Blanchard had already attracted Rouse's attention with a mock pastoral called *Arcadia*, which was performed there with an excellent cast in 1836. If it is true that *Villikins* was sung at the Grecian, it could

[1]Clement Scott : *The Diaries of E. L. Blanchard.*

have created no special attention as no indication of the song's great vogue occur until 1853. It has often been claimed for *Villikins* that it is a song of great antiquity, by George Augustus Sala for one.[1] There is, however, no familiar ballad on the theme though, of course, it is not impossibly an echo of some earlier dramatic ballad.[2] Robson had other songs of this kind, notably Sloman and Westrop's *As I was a-walking beside the sea-shore*, which, together with *Villikins*, later became popular in Sam Cowell's repertory—indeed, Cowell's choice of doggerel narrative as his principal song medium was probably an inheritance from Robson. Whatever the origin of *Villikins*, Sala's light-hearted claim of a remote antiquity may be confidently set aside. The passage, in his sketch of Robson in which he refers to *Villikins*, however, is of some interest. "The story told in the ballad, of a father's cruelty, a daughter's anguish, a sweetheart's despair, and the ultimate suicide of both the lovers, is, albeit couched in uncouth and grotesque language, as pathetic as the tragedy of *Romeo and Juliet*, Robson gave every stanza a nonsensical refrain of Right tooral lol looral, right tooral lol lay." At times, when the audience was convulsed with merriment he would come to a halt and gravely observe, "This is not a comic song." But London was soon unanimous that such exquisite comicality had not been heard for many a long year.- *Villikin and his Dinah* created a *furore*.[3]

Robson achieved nothing but local popularity at the Grecian, which he left in 1850 for a visit to Ireland. In 1853 he joined Farren at the Olympic, and here, after a rather lukewarm start, he leapt into fame with his performance in Talfourd's burlesque of *Macbeth*. This was followed eventually by *The Wandering*

[1]" The words and the air of 'Villikins' were, if not literally as old as the hills, considerably older than the age of Queen Elizabeth."—(G. A. Sala, *Robson ; a Sketch*, 1864.)

[2]Indeed, I have discovered a Broadsheet in the British Museum of *William and his Dinah* which has essentially the same narrative, and possibly pre-dates Robson's song.

[3]An anonymous writer quoted by Sala in his memoir of Robson states that, at the conclusion of the burletta performance, Robson was in the habit of singing his songs in a large saloon attached to the grounds. Other commentators have it that these songs were sung in the open air (possibly in the orchestra). The probability is that the saloon referred to was that which afterwards became the theatre and was used for these concerts only in wet weather.

Sala exhibits a rather unexpected note of snobbery not untinged with ignorance, in his references to Robson's work at the Grecian in the following passage : "He had come timidly to London and accepted at a low salary the post of buffoon at a half-theatre half-saloon in the City Road, called indifferently 'The Grecian' and 'The Eagle,' where he had danced and tumbled, and sung comic songs and delivered the dismal waggeries set down for him without any marked success, and almost without notice."

The fact was that he was seen there in Shakespeare and in a number of characters of the classical English repertory.

Minstrel, which contained *Villikins*. From this time, his career belongs rather to the history of the legitimate theatre. Other burlesques were written for him by Talfourd, though his most famous characterization was probably the title part in *The Yellow Dwarf* by Planché, in which he carried to a great height his genius for blending the comic with the macabre. He is remembered at this period of his career by Henry James, who as a child was taken to see him act at the Olympic. James in *A Small Boy and Others* writes: "At a remarkable height . . . moved the strange and vivid little genius of Robson, a master of fantastic intensity, unforgettable for us, we felt, that night in Planché's extravaganza of *The Discontented Princess*. . . . I see still Robson slide across the stage in one sidelong wriggle as the small black sinister Prince Richcraft. . . . Everything he did at once very dreadful and very droll . . . the greatest point of it all, its parody of Charles Kean and *The Corsican Brothers*."

From the first, Rouse's policy at the Grecian was in the direction of pure theatre; and by the early 'forties a full operatic repertory was established. The following advertisement bearing the date 1843 has the following list of operas cited as "but a few of those presented at this popular place of public resort:"—Auber's *Massaniello*, *Fra Diavolo*, Bellini's *Sonnambula*, Barnett's *Mountain Sylph*, *The Marriage of Figaro*, Rossini's *Barber of Seville*, and Boiledieu's *John of Paris*.

The place under Rouse, who retired in 1851, carries with it considerable suggestion of charm—this little cockney arcadia in the City Road, its walks and illuminated buildings at the edge of a crowded thoroughfare; bands playing or crowds dancing on a small platform, a burletta in performance in the rotunda, and the great Robson, singing for the amusement of a crowd of shop-assistants, unaware that they were listening to one of the greatest actors who ever lived. By 1844 the scene had changed somewhat: Rouse had built the larger theatre on the site of the old Moorish pavilion and the rotunda was now reserved for suppers and dancing. The theatre had taken up a full dramatic licence and was becoming famous on its own account.

When, in 1851, the Grecian passed to Benjamin Oliver Conquest, it was reopened with a performance of *A Midsummer Night's Dream*, preceded by a rhymed prologue by E. L. Blanchard. Neat reference was made to the fact that its new status as a theatre forbade the sale of intoxicating liquor in the auditorium.

"The talents of all nations shall be shown;
Especially the talents of our own;
All that is British you shall here find handy.
Excepting one thing British—that is Brandy."

Conquest introduced a monster dancing platform in the grounds, and thus sowed the seeds which twenty years after brought a harvest of official displeasure, when the place was earmarked as an undesirable resort. An atmosphere of immorality was discovered there by the late Lord Balfour, who deplored the presence of supper boxes, dark walks and prostitutes. It is to be feared that Conquest had made matters worse by the introduction of fancy dress dances, a move which, in England, appears to be fatal to the good name of any public resort. Finally, but not before a new Grecian theatre had been erected in 1879, the place having sunk financially as well as morally, General Booth made a dramatic bid for the premises in 1882, and the theatre and grounds became a Salvation Army citadel. The public were now admitted to religious services in the grounds, and the monster platform became the evangelist's rostrum. It is not without a trace of satisfaction that one learns that by the terms of his purchase the General was obliged to keep the Eagle Tavern open for the sale of intoxicants.

The Grecian is the last important instance of the fusion of three elements of entertainment, the pleasure garden, the theatre, and the variety saloon; and survived into a time when such a fusion had become an anachronism, for it was a survival of the tavern garden and tavern club habit of an early time.

The arrival of free trade in the theatre gradually put an end to such pleasant places, in which the sublime and the ridiculous jostled one another, and in which the comic vocalist might also be seen acting in Shakespeare.

Those contemporaries of the Grecian whose attractions were divided equally between the saloon and its surrounding gardens existed in considerable numbers; they housed to a greater or lesser degree elements of variety to be found in the tavern concerts. Nearly opposite the Grecian was the Green Gate tavern, one of the last in the neighbourhood to relinquish its garden, which established a stage with auditorium composed of lower and upper saloon. All over the town the same process was taking place. The Tivoli Gardens and the Eagle Tavern, in the Mile End Road, for instance, established well-known saloons; these in both cases survived as music halls. By 1838 the Yorkshire Stingo had a number of activities, including fireworks, balloon ascents, and a variety theatre which made it one of the most popular pleasure centres in the district.

Hollingshead's list of the leading saloon theatres of the 'thirties is as follows: The New Bower Saloon in Stangate, the Yorkshire Stingo, the Globe Gardens at Mile End, the Effingham Saloon in Whitechapel, the Albert in Shepherdess Walk, the Britannia Saloon, and the Grecian, the Albion, and the White

Conduit House. Apart from those already dealt with, the Globe Gardens, the Albert, and White Conduit House, in Pentonville, concern us in this chapter. The last-named had been a place of entertainment from a date shortly after the erection of the small stone conduit house which stood in an adjacent field.[1] The large concert room attached to the tavern in the grounds, flourished exceedingly in the 'thirties, and although known facetiously as the *Vite Condick* (affectionately so called in the stage cockney of the time) and a resort not unmentioned in flash literature, yet it was the resort of the worthy and even of the distinguished also. Well-known artists graced its boards ; Sloman appeared there early in his career, and J. W. Sharpe is said to have made his first appearances there.

The big concert room was a later feature of White Conduit House, a bandstand and a small open-air stage did duty in 1829, when Chabert, the fire and poison resister, appeared there. Chabert, who created a great stir, but was afterwards found to have resorted to fraudulent methods, also appeared at the Argyle Rooms, used for entertainment purposes after the break-up of Colonel Greville's Pic-Nic Society, and not to be confused with the later Casino in Windmill Street, Piccadilly. Chabert's exploits are described in John Timb's *Curiosities of London* and a contemporary pamphlet.

. . . " M. Chabert returned, clad in a coarse woollen coat, to enter the heated oven. Before he entered it, a physician ascertained that his pulse was beating 98 times in a minute. The company were horrified when they saw him enter the oven. . . . In this fiery furnace he remained five minutes, in which time he cooked two dishes of fine beef-steak and a dish of potatoes also, for his dinner. . . . At length the oven door was opened—he came forth without injury. The thermometer stood at 600 degrees within the oven, and the Fire King's pulse was found to be at 168 vibrations in a minute."

The little monograph exhibits on the cover a picture of this intrepid Frenchman standing in the midst of what appears to be an ingenious arrangement of gas jets—fiercely directed on to his fully clothed figure—the clothes apparently sharing the fire-resisting qualities of their wearer. Leffler, a famous ballad singer, Miss Smith of the Strand Theatre, Howell, Joseph Plumpton, who wrote *The Periwinkle Man*, and was later retained as resident singer at the Britannia Theatre, were also favourite performers at White Conduit. Another artist well known there was William Pearce, known as " Storm " Pearce in allusion to his admired rendering of the song of that name composed by J. T. Hullah.

[1]But styling itself in 1826 as the Vauxhall of Pentonville.

The large concert room was the scene of a number of mass political meetings, and became a vortex of the excitement provoked by the Reform Bill. The place succumbed in 1849 when the site was built over ; the present Warren Street, named after one of the proprietors, marks the position of the gardens.[1]

Bagnigge Wells, having led suburban fashion in the eighteenth century, fell into line with the prevalent demands of the nineteenth and by 1831 a concert room had been installed in which the usual type of programme was offered. The price charged for admission was 3d. Braham, the famous tenor who built the St. James's Theatre, and whose early history was largely concerned with variety, is said to have sung at Bagnigge Wells as a boy. Though the place ceased to function as a centre of entertainment in 1840, when the house in which Nell Gwynne lived was pulled down, the licence did not lapse, and a public house bearing the same name still stands upon the site in the King's Cross Road opposite Riceyman Steps.[2] The list of other and more obscure garden saloons of the period is a long one. We may often trace appearances of well-known artists in obscure corners ; Henry Howell and his wife, for instance, being mentioned in advertisements of the tiny City Vaudeville in Snow Hill, and Harry Sidney in those of the Colosseum Saloon in Albion Street, but their presence need not lead us to attach historical importance to these places. The method of seasonal engagement at the theatres left artists free to undertake many unimportant engagements by which they could swell their annual earnings without prejudicing their theatrical status. Apart from the *cachet* which appearances at Drury Lane or Covent Garden undoubtedly gave to an artist, the theatrical community was still largely democratic. (Mr. Jennings Rodolph's bitter complaint in *Sketches by Boz* that, though such a favourite at White Conduit House, his talents had not been recognized by the patent theatres, will be remembered by Dickensians.)

The Royal Albert Saloon and Standard Tavern and Tea Gardens in Shepherdess Walk, separated by only a few yards

[1]The following is a bill for the entertainments at White Conduit House in 1843 : *White Conduit House Tavern.* Extraordinary success of the American Wonder, or Creole Screamer. Proprietor, Mr. R. Rouse, who invites the public to view the Gardens and witness the surprising Performance of the American Phenomenon. . . . The entertainment consists of a Great Instrumental and Vocal Concert. Gymnastic and astonishing evolutions by the Arab Bros. Laughable Burlettas, Comic Ballets, character singing and dancing. Mr. Henry's novel Panoramic Cosmorama, etc. The electro-magnetic apparatus is in operation every evening. Admission to the garden 6d. Chaste and elegant interpretation of the Grecian statues. Laughable Burletta, " Our Uncle Tweedle." Uncle Tweedle, Mr. Saker. Under the management of Mr. Saker.

[2]Arnold Bennett's name for them.

from the Grecian, was an instance of a house which in presenting the typical medley of entertainment disguised its true ambition : the achievement of full theatrical status. This was acquired under the terms of the Act of 1843, when the Albert developed less notably along the lines of its more celebrated neighbour. An outgrowth of the original tavern and garden, its theatre backed on the roadway, and was of sufficiently flimsy structure to allow the children of the neighbourhood to bore holes in the back wall of the stage and so to penetrate to its mysteries.[1] In the year after its memorable revival at the Grecian, the Albert Saloon was giving performances of the *Wandering Minstrel* with Howell in Robson's part of Jem Baggs. Appearances in 1840 may be mentioned of the famous de Castro on the " flying rope " and the performing elephant of the celebrated circus proprietor, Van Ambergh.

As at most of the saloons, the Albert was let on occasions for performances given for the benefit of some group or society, and in the same year, 1840, a really elaborate function was held in aid of the Zinc Trade's Society. At the " well-selected concert in the gardens," Howell sang the song called *Commonsense*, and Miss Tunstall sang *Banners of Blue*. There were also *Feats Gymnasium* (*sic*) by the Incredible Brothers, a comic ballet with Paul Herring, in a character bearing the traditional name of Simpkin ; the programme rounded off with two historical dramas—*Robert the Bruce*, and *Gilderoy*. The admission fee for this entertainment, including a reserved seat for the plays, was 1s. The fact that tickets were to be had only at various private addresses given may perhaps have had its origin in enthusiastic canvassing for the affair, but it is just possible that the promoters may have felt that the non-theatrical licence held by the Albert was being a trifle strained by the performance of two full-length plays.

Paul Herring, a clown and pantomimist of some distinction, was closely connected with the Albert Saloon. Born with the simpler name of William Smith, he gained a reputation in the larger houses, but spent much of his time as major attraction of the cheaper saloons such as the Albion in Shoreditch, and a number of penny " gaffs," of which some particulars will be given later. He qualified for his profession with " Muster " Richardson of the Fairs, and as an eminent recruit from the canvas world his name is spoken of with reverence by one of the showmen whom Mayhew interviewed in the early 'fifties. Smith was christened Herring, perhaps with some thought for the ancient clown name of Pickleherring, by Hector Simpson, the

[1]Hollingshead : *My Life*.

proprietor of the Albion.[1] He was an eminent performer in the minor houses of the name part of *Bluebeard*, the phenomenally successful pantomime founded on Colman's romantic drama, and was the creator of the part of "Drolinsko" in Astley's production of *Mazeppa*, in 1831. The Albert Saloon was remarkable for the unusual arrangement of its two stages, which were contiguous, one facing the saloon and the other the gardens. In more than one reference to these stages they are described being at right angles to one another. This is a slightly bewildering statement, as to ensure economy from the use of such a plan (and Chance Newton mentions that he had often suggested the plan to managers for this reason) the stages should surely have been placed back to back.[2] Nelson Lee, another well-known pantomime artist and a later proprietor of Richardson's Show, was manager of the Albert in the 'forties[3], and in his time balloon ascents were made from the gardens by the famous Green, who died triumphantly in bed, after having achieved much popular idolatry. In 1857 the place was closed, and was shortly afterwards rebuilt as the Standard Theatre, finishing its career as a music hall.

The Albert was, on the whole, an interesting receptacle of the medley of entertainment arising from the complex nature of the theatrical situation: if it did not achieve the status of its neighbour the Grecian, it contributed to the enlivening of its neighbourhood in no unworthy manner. An impression of the place may be summarized by the contents of two bills, immediately preceding and following the passing of the Theatre Act. The former announces the appearance of the Morocco Arabians from the Victoria Theatre, "the admired Drama of the *Pirate's Vow*, a concert, a ballet, and a finale by the whole company"; and the latter, when the house had come under the control of Henry Brading, a production of *Black-eyed Susan* with Henry Howell in the part of Jacob Twigg, and (astonishing period) the tragedy of *Venice Preserved*.

[1]Hector Simpson has stood in danger of confusion with T. B. Simpson owing to the fact that the latter had been head waiter, previous to his career as Manager of Cremorne Gardens, of the Albion Tavern in Russell Street, Covent Garden.

[2]This arrangement was made use of by Fred Karno when he rebuilt the Tea House on Taggs Island—a sliding shutter separating the two stage areas.

[3]A biography of Nelson Lee appeared in the *Era Almanack* for 1868. He was born in 1806, and was destined to a naval career; it is reported that he was attracted to the stage by the performance of Ramo Samee in front of the looking-glass curtain at the Coburg Theatre. So delighted was he with this artist's tricks that he acquired proficiency in them, and, joining the troop of Gyngell, the conjurer, performed all the balancing and juggling feats of the Indian. He became a lessee of the Standard Theatre and of the Marylebone Theatre. His most successful management was, however, that of the City of London Theatre in Norton Folgate, where he remained until his death in 1865. At one time he was a proprietor of Richardson's Show. His celebrity as a clown and low comedian was considerable.

Two of the more extensive type of pleasure gardens overlapped and outlived the vogue of Vauxhall ; the first was Cremorne in Chelsea, whose name, possibly by virtue of literary and artistic associations, still stands for the popular imagination as a symbol for the Victorian pleasure garden.

Cremorne, the centre of which is now marked by the four chimneys of the Chelsea Power Station, was founded in 1832 by one of the self-created Barons who appear from time to time in nineteenth century social history, born with the name of Charles Random de Berenger, but trading under that of the Baron de Beaufain. He took the pleasant manor house which stood in spacious grounds and opened it in 1832 as an athletic club and equestrian training school, which lingered on till 1843.

In 1837 he took out a music and dancing licence. In this year and in 1839 John Hampton's balloon ascents and parachute experiments were made at Cremorne. In 1838 an ascent of Mrs. Graham's balloon, together with a *fêté-champêtre*, was advertised for June 16, and, five days later, was announced "A *fête-champêtre* to the Foreign Ambassadors."

In 1843, the Baron having failed in this and other ventures, another "Baron" equally devoted to speculation in the entertainment world, none other than the celebrated Renton Nicholson, arrived on the scene. Under him Cremorne began to assume the aspect it retained until the 'seventies. He reopened the place with a "Thousand Guineas' Fête," which, records Wroth,[1] "during three days (July 31, August 1 and 2), at one shilling admission, provided among other diversions, a mock tournament, a pony-race, a performance by Tom Matthews, the clown, and a *pas de deux* by T. Ireland and Fanny Matthews."[2]

A programme of varieties at Cremorne in its earlier period, though probably of a date later than Nicholson's short tenancy, is a typical example of the method by which the diversions of the place were organized. Proceedings opened with a performance by Bean's Band, on the lawn. There then followed :

at 4 p.m. The Cremorne Punch and Judy, a pyramidal and tumbling performance and The Wonders of St. Petersburg.
at 5.30. The Cremorne Punch and Judy.
" 6.30. New Grand Amazon Ballet.
" 7.30. The Great Natator Frog.
(Novel entertainment under water.)
" 8.0 Boorn's Russian Circus.
" 9.0 Burletta, "Low life above stairs."
" 10.0. Fireworks. Dancing Continuous.

[1] "Cremorne, and the later London Pleasure Gardens."
[2] In 1845 Matthews, at Cremorne, is said to have sung Grimaldi's *Hot Codlins* before making a balloon ascent.

In the same decade the Bosjemonds, a minstrel troupe mentioned in Maddison Morton's farce of *Box and Cox*, appeared at Cremorne.

The theatre at Cremorne, in which the burlettas were performed, was a long room with a stage at one end, open to the gardens down one of its sides. It was alternatively used as a banqueting hall. Dancing took place on the circular platform in the grounds, which at night were illuminated with coloured gas-lamps.[1] In many respects, this resort had features in common with the Grecian. As at Vauxhall, the music hall note was struck in the year 1847 by the inclusion in its concerts of the fashionable Sam Cowell and the worthy Glindon ; Whistling Van Joel appeared there in 1848.

Cremorne has handed down the tradition of the saloon theatre and pleasure grounds to a number of places which are still in existence. The spas and health resorts such as Harrogate, derive their parks and winter gardens from it. But changes in the regulations of local bodies, affecting the supply of refreshments in the auditorium, have modified the Victorian quality of their entertainments. For an exact parallel one has to go back forty years or so. Devonshire Park at Eastbourne was an instance, at that time, of a minor and very respectable Cremorne. Under the management of Mr. Standon Triggs it had a pleasantly mid-Victorian flavour. In its glass-roofed " Floral Hall " was a small and elegant stage devoted to the performance of varieties, and the auditorium comprised a number of roped-in stalls, flanked by small tables at which refreshments were served. On fine evenings an instrumental and vocal concert was held in an illuminated bandstand, set very prettily under the trees in a secluded part of the gardens. On Saturday nights, the programme concluded with a display of fireworks, followed by a military tattoo ; and at midnight the strains of bagpipes penetrated the inmost recesses of the surrounding boarding-houses. Devonshire Park was also most delightfully given to " athletic gymkhanas," the progress of which was interrupted by the antics of circus clowns.

I do not propose to enlarge further on the catalogue of garden resorts and saloon theatres of the earlier nineteenth century, period of transition. For the smaller houses, the vanishing point of differentiation between the alfresco and the purely indoor saloons is reached by the 'forties. Then, building encroachments, gradual changes in social habits (so small a change as the ousting, perhaps from lack of ground space, of the bowling ground by the billiard saloon is not to be overlooked as an influence) and

[1]In 1846 the orchestra for the dancing was conducted by De Laurent, who founded the Argyll Rooms.

municipal interference, together contributed with the effect of the Theatre Act, to a new orientation. Thence forward the movement of large-scale undertakings created by the attraction of capital to the entertainment world leads directly to the modern music hall.

Some important schemes for alfresco pleasure haunts were yet to come; the Surrey Zoo had already developed in the 'thirties from the menagerie in Exeter 'Change. But its later development, which embraces the vast and ill-fated concert hall called the Surrey Music Hall—the home of Jullien and his waltzes—although reproducing some of the features of Vauxhall does not, by reason of the new specialization, concern itself with the main development of variety relevant to this book;[1] the same may be said of the North Woolwich Garden, the creation of William Holland. Highbury Barn, originally a typical eighteenth-century product, and in the mid-Victorian period a kind of suburban Argyll Rooms, is exceptional in that it finally developed an important music hall of the modern type, but particulars of this belong to a later chapter.

The position up to the years which immediately precede the founding of the Canterbury Music Hall is as follows. The music hall, though anticipated in its most complete form at the Surrey, had not as yet come under the spell of its greater progenitors. Charles Morton was still dreaming of vaster sing-songs and lengthier betting slips behind his bar in the Belgrave Road, and Sir Edward Moss and Sir Oswald Stoll were as yet unborn. But all the elements which were to be a stimulus to the music hall idea were already present and have been fully exploited in their various combinations. Apparently divergent to an almost irreconcilable degree—they are yet in all cases the late flowering branches of an ancient and deeply rooted growth. In most cases they have now been to some extent outlined, but attention must still be paid to the part played by the legitimate theatre itself, together with the complementary art of the circus with which the theatre made a temporary alliance under Dibdin and Hughes, and Philip Astley.

[1]Varieties were attempted there, however, in the 'forties, and an anonymous article on the Gardens deplores the "fatal element of variety" which was introduced by the appearances of Ramo Samee. But the morale of the place was reinstated by the building of the Surrey Music Hall, which did not long survive. The choice of this term is of interest as emphasizing the fact that it was originally applied to houses giving variety entertainments, as a euphemism. The Surrey Zoo had some pleasant garden features; a lake in the centre of the grounds rendered effective various panoramas exhibited there. There was a permanent exhibit of Wigwams, and there were rustic cottages in the manner of the "village" at the Petit Trianon. In 1844, General Tom Thumb appeared in the gardens; also Blackmore, the wire-walker. Another attraction was the Heptaplaspcoptron, an arrangement of objects which were reflected seven times.

The gulf which divided the tavern concerts from other forms of entertainment was a social one, only to be bridged in the music hall by the vastness of the scale on which eventually it was organized. The lower middle-class character is mirrored in the excessively low prices charged for admittance to them, often depending only on a minimum guarantee of liquor consumption, a method directly arising from their origin—the club coteries formed from haphazard local assemblage. Until the 'fifties the entertainment centres arising from this source had not yet come sufficiently into prominence to be held to warrant any reference in the columns of any periodical publications but those of a rather questionable character, and even in these are awarded only cursory and somewhat belittling mention. Although often attracting talent of the highest order, they were yet in almost all cases completing a lengthy period of transition from amateur to professional status.

The saloon theatre was on a somewhat higher plane, though even here the same reluctance to give them any critical attention is manifest in the journals of the day. The prices charged were somewhat higher than in the public house concerts, the average charge being 1s., though as much as 2s. was frequently made for the upper saloon or the balcony; the price rising to 4s. for boxes, when any existed.

A fairly accurate analogy may be drawn between the tavern concerts and the concerts of the social and working-class clubs of the present day. Here the entertainment is still described as a variety concert, and a chairman still presides. The main difference is the absence of performers of standing or, at any rate, any of those who have achieved a position on the theatre or music hall stage; for there is no relic now of the conditions which accounted then for the presence of performers such as Knight or Caulfield, willing to sing their songs for a few shillings and a hot supper. It is therefore highly unlikely that in these clubs of to-day the entertainment will be found, as in the tedious array of "obliging talent" of the older sing-songs, to be punctuated by the performances of genius such as those of Robson or Sharpe. This is not to say that even now such artists are not to be discovered at these humble functions at an early stage of their careers; just as in the days of music hall supremacy Marie Lloyd flashed on to the scene. In the garden saloons the same incalculable quality had prevailed. There were, of course, great discrepancies. The Dog and Duck, in St. George's Fields, might well have exhibited those characteristics which are ascribed to it in the attack on the Hedger family which appeared in *Paul Pry*.[1] But it is a far cry

[1]In which an atmosphere of villainy, rapacity and disreputability is painted in very heavy daubs.

from such a place to the Grecian. In many of the gardens, such as the Montpelier in Newington Butts, the erection of a flimsy outdoor stage sufficed for the entertainments, and in such circumstances one may deduce an atmosphere which was no less vulgarly boring than that pervading a pierrot show in some public-house garden at Barnes, Richmond, or Winchmore Hill. But even so, and allowing for a dangerous but almost unavoidable tendency to idealize the past, some quality was undoubtedly present which now is irrecoverable ; for the existence of these places arose from a desire, or the rebirth of a desire, to create a form of experience which should communicate an illusion to actual life, by the association of sunlight and trees with fantastic and non-utilitarian architecture, with dancing, song and posturing. Irrecoverable also is that strange intermingling of value which associated " Rossini and refreshment tickets, Auber and alcohol, Bellini and bottled beer," and, we may add, comic singing and *Venice Preserved.* It may be said that such a scheme of things leads directly away from the theatre and the music hall, and certainly the music hall has little to do with the elements of quietude and leisure in which an individual reaction takes the place of the mass reaction; engendered by the sense of a delightfully enclosed world, set in the midst of every-day life, but apart from it. Yet with all the differences, psychological and physical, there is a fundamental link ; for both gardens and music halls have been in their day the vehicle by which the masses have effected a momentary escape from reality. In the music hall there was added something unknown to the garden theatre period, a revealing cynicism which, by bringing into comic relief the unpleasant facts of daily life, removed the sting from them.

CHAPTER V

Legal Intelligence

In the year 1737, by the passing of the Licensing Bill, the curtain was rung up on the second act of the strange history of theatrical privilege in England. The effect of this Act, indicated by events already described, was to give some reality to the monopoly conferred by the patents for the erection of theatres in London granted by Charles II to Killigrew and D'Avenant. This monarch's intervention in the dramatic field immediately followed the proscription of all forms of theatrical activity by the Act of 1647, and was the arbitrary action of a man to whom the peculiar situation had given the opportunity to pursue a purely personal policy. The patents in each case were granted for sentimental reasons : to D'Avenant, because a similar grant had been previously made him by Charles' father in 1639, and to Killigrew as a reward for his active service in support of the Restoration.

The general political situation had placed the stage in a position of the greatest stress : plays had been performed behind locked doors, or in dismantled playhouses, by means of a dangerous resort to bribery. The licence to erect playhouses was therefore a gesture of absolute monarchy, unaccompanied by any formal repealing of the legislation which had placed the theatre outside the law ; it was this choice of method which, somewhat paradoxically, eighty years after gave to the theory of monopoly a measure of legal sanction. It is important to bear these facts in mind, for when, upon the rapid growth of population, the field of theatrical activity demanded extension, Charles II's solution of the problem stood revealed as an an achronism, and became productive over a period of nearly two centuries of a most complicated and mischievous conflict of vested interests.

The excuse made by the King in his preamble to the grant was that " he had heard that in London and the suburbs, certain persons were assembling for the purpose of acting plays and interludes for rewards " ; that these plays contained " matters of profanation and scurrility . . . though if well managed . . . such kinds of entertainments . . . might serve as morall instruc-

tions in humane life." Here, at the outset, we have the altruistic motive brought forward as a cloak to motives altogether of another kind; for a single reference to the actual dramatic output of the Restoration period will show how completely (and mercifully) the sentiments of this preamble were disregarded.

For a time the patent grants worked smoothly enough, though there was a certain friction arising from the partitioning of the plays and actors between the two houses. Actors, other than those protected by their engagement at one or other of the patent theatres, were still under Act of Parliament, rogues and vagabonds, but were tolerated while their activities were still of so insignificant a nature as to cause no embarrassment.

The first signs of trouble came from within the patent theatres themselves. Although the granting of the licences to D'Avenant and Killigrew nominally brought these managers directly under the patronage of the Crown, that patronage did not carry anything in the nature of a subsidy. So far as guarantees of material safety were concerned, the royal ownership was a myth. The theatres did not pay their way, and were soon deserted by their audiences for the music houses and the fair booths. This was an unlooked-for development ; although no infringement on the privileges of the patents could be alleged, the most vitiating effects resulted.

In this quandary the patentees attempted an unfortunate remedy. In an effort to economize, they dismissed a number of their most experienced actors, and undermined the position of those whom they retained by engaging novices. This led to a revolt, headed by the great actor Betterton, and after a somewhat prolonged struggle, the situation took on a new aspect in the reign of William the Third, when as Sovereign he decided that it was in his power to extend the licence to build theatres, and so granted to Betterton the right to erect a new independent theatre in Lincoln's Inn Fields. This occurred in 1694, and was in effect a death-blow to the unchallenged superiority of Drury Lane and Covent Garden. For this departure gave occasion for more theatre building, sometimes with a pretext of legality and sometimes without. The Opera House designed by Vanbrugh was erected in the Haymarket in 1705, and by purchase of the original patents in 1691 came into the possession of Christopher Rich, father of the celebrated harlequin. A further oppression of the actors by Rich involved him also in a dispute with the reigning Sovereign, Queen Anne, who adopted the very spirited plan, made possible by means of a revival of the Lord Chamberlain's powers, of ejecting him from Covent Garden. Rich retired to the Lincoln's Inn Theatre, which he was about to open on the exceedingly simple expedient of transferring his patent to that

house, when he died. His plan, however, was carried into action by his son, the Queen also having in the meantime conveniently died. The theory of the patent had, in a measure, survived these occurrences, but the position was weakening, and the Lord Chamberlain was now acting in the old shadowy way, controlling the destinies of managements and of plays, as the political situation and the royal will dictated. Theatres began to multiply; strange new permits to perform in the summer months, during the vacations of Covent Garden and Drury Lane, were instituted. An enterprising builder called Potter, acting entirely on his own initiative, opened the Little Theatre in the Haymarket in December, 1723, which under the management of Henry Fielding, who took the house a year or so later, rapidly became a storm centre.

Meanwhile a theatre had been erected in Goodmans Fields, on the site of the present Baptist Chapel in Great Alie Street. This house was outside the direct jurisdiction of the Lord Chamberlain, whose power was restricted to the precincts of the Court and the City of Westminster. The house had not been built without encountering local opposition: a number of tradespeople, alleging danger of business arising from congestions of traffic caused by the assembling of audiences, but probably actuated far more by the old Puritan distrust, applied to the justices hoping for intercession on the score of public nuisance; they strengthened their plea by an appeal to an Act passed in Queen Anne's reign which restricted the limitation of the actor's licence to the permit held directly from the Crown, and made illegal the transference from one company to another. The appeal to the local magistrates being fruitless, and the movement gathering momentum from the actual erection of the theatre, a petition signed by the Lord Mayor and Aldermen was presented to the King.

The situation was by this time becoming almost an exact repetition of that which had occurred in Elizabeth's day, when the Privy Council was continually disregarding the opposition of the City authorities to the erection of public theatres by the royal and baronial companies. A difference in the situation existed, however, for the licensed companies were no longer supported from the Exchequer, and the rights of the barons to form companies of their own had been abrogated. But, as in the earlier century, higher authority was not seriously hostile to the multiplication of theatrical companies, provided it had no reason to suspect political subversiveness. In other words, Government was only concerned with its own particular form of vested interest, and was willing to allow that of the patentee to take care of itself; and it is important to note that the premise of the

1737 act, though theoretically limiting to vanishing point the existence of all theatres except Drury Lane and Covent Garden, was far more concerned with the endorsement of the Lord Chamberlain's powers of veto on plays and entertainments, than with regulating the number or constitution of the places in which such entertainments occurred. This is the explanation of the ease with which, in spite of the repeated intervention of the patent theatres, the precedent of monopoly was so successfully overridden, and of the consistent lukewarmness of the justices in all cases when they were appealed to by the patentees for the upholding of their privilege.

In the case of Odell, the promoter of the Goodmans Fields theatre, however, the Crown behaved with some perfidy. After having given him a form of permission for his venture, it listened, or appeared to listen, to the Lord Mayor and Aldermen, and officially reversed the position. Odell retired from the fight. But Giffard, who had been associated with him in the venture, reopened the theatre after a suitable interval had elapsed, without hindrance of any kind. The play chosen for this occasion was *George Barnwell*, and the seasons continued uninterruptedly till 1733. On the face of it, this is a strange sequel, but it is typical of the theatrical situation throughout the whole period of durance. The position of the patentees was indeed a rather baffling one; without any real support from the Crown, and in a legal position which finally rested on royal privilege, the only line of attack left was an appeal to the Queen Anne Vagrancy Act, which subsequently proved a completely ineffectual weapon. Indeed, events would have taken a much stranger turn had the promise given to the Lord Mayor in reference to Goodmans Fields been sincerely made, for this would have meant the raising of a dam against a virtually national tendency. The taste for theatrical performance had definitely taken root, with the additional urgency of an immensely increased population. Moreover, a release from the tedium created by the continual performance of the conservative stock plays had been provided by the invention of pantomime. The fairs had rapidly developed along the same lines, had definitely set up in the business of theatrical production, and even the public streets were honeycombed with booths in which performances similar to those given in the theatre were to be seen. It was abundantly clear from this attitude of toleration that tacitly the recognition of theatrical free trade was, in all cases where no subversive behaviour was attempted, an accomplished fact.

The realization of this attitude must have been sufficiently alarming to the patentees; the first direct effort to retrieve the lost ground was made in October 1733, when the Vagrancy Act

was invoked in a second attempt to dislodge the occupants of Goodmans Fields. Charges of acting without licence were preferred by the patentees against members both of Giffard's company and of the company at the Haymarket. In both cases the magistrates' decision was given in favour of the defendants. The patentees' next effort was to secure the arrest of an actor in the Haymarket company on a direct charge of vagrancy. The actor in question was acquitted of the offence. Again, it is a little difficult to follow the legal line of argument by which the acquittal was obtained. It is probable that, as stated by Colley Cibber, prominence was given to the contention that, as the defendant in question (Harper, formerly of Drury Lane) was a householder, he could not, in any circumstances, be adjudged to be a vagrant. But the pith of the matter lay in the fact that the Vagrancy Act had not been called into existence to meet the type of situation in which it was being invoked. It had been introduced only as a disciplinary measure in relation to places of irregular entertainment such as the Sadler's Wells Music House and had been intended to make the patent-house actors conscious of their Royal Licence. We may surmise that the justices before whom Harper appeared had sensed the inappropriateness of applying the Act to his case, a proceeding which would have been in the same category as an attempt to enforce their legal prerogative of whipping all practising members of the theatrical craft, and imposing a fine of five shillings on every person witnessing their performances.

The position of the minor theatres was, by this acquittal, retrieved for the moment, and the management at Goodmans Fields survived to sponsor the first London appearance of David Garrick. But trouble was soon brewing in another quarter. In 1734 the Little Theatre in the Haymarket, which had from its early days given sanctuary to a company headed by Colley Cibber's son Theophilus, and which was in revolt against the Covent Garden management, fell into the hands of the great Henry Fielding. Here he organized his "company of the Great Mogul," and began operations, harmlessly enough, with a satirical play called *Don Quixote in England.* In 1736, however, he entered on a bold campaign, the production of an exceedingly provocative series of political burlesques, the first of which was called *Pasquin*, written in the manner of Buckingham's *Rehearsal.* This was followed by others in which political and social satire was intermingled with jokes directed against the Drury Lane management. Finally, a farce called the *Golden Rump*, containing the most pointed and personal satire on Walpole and the practices of the Government, brought him into conflict with the hitherto neutrally disposed authorities. Walpole took a copy of the play

to the King, with the result that the Theatre Licensing Act of 1737 was framed. That Act, when it appeared, was found to contain a clause of fundamental significance. This was the definite establishment of the Lord Chamberlain as the licenser of all plays produced in the area of his control, and it provided that all plays earmarked for production were to be sent to him, or his representatives, at least fourteen days before their contemplated production. This clause was the real crux of the Act. Its affirmation of the monopoly of the patent houses was secondary in that it amounted to no more than a restatement of the terms of the Queen Anne Vagrancy Act, by which all performances other than those given under royal licence were deemed illegal. It will thus be seen that Fielding's temerity, though it had produced but little change in the position of the minor houses, had provoked a serious curtailment of the freedom of all dramatic output. Power had now been completely invested in the governmentally inspired control of the Chamberlain, and it was clear that the operation of the so-called monopoly was to be overwhelmed by this weapon. And so it proved. The balance of freedom enjoyed by the minor theatres shifted with the varying attitudes of succeeding Chamberlains.

The one certain result of the act was the effective muzzling of free speech. The Chamberlain's powers were deemed to be retrospective, affecting the production of old plays as well as new ones. And there were Chamberlains who did not hesitate to exercise this power when political motives appeared to justify its use. Later in the century, performances of *King Lear* were prohibited, as reflecting on the mental condition of George III, and within memory, these powers not having been subsequently repealed, *The Mikado* was similarly banned, because it was feared that it might offend the susceptibilities of royal visitors from Japan.

Outwardly, the restatement of the position of the minor theatres naturally led to greater severity but, as before, they were by no means daunted, for immediately there began the series of elaborate evasions which give such a bewildering quality to the playbills of the time. An enthusiasm for giving "concerts of music" which included "recitations" of the plays of Shakespeare and others rapidly developed. The simple device of charging an audience money for witnessing a miscellaneous entertainment and then following it, entirely gratis, with the performance of a play, was also adopted. Macklin opened a "Dramatic Academy" at the Haymarket, and the public were allowed to pay to be present at his rehearsals of *Othello*. Samuel Foote, the wittiest and most intellectually nimble actor of his time, appeared on the scene at the Haymarket Theatre, with a

form of one-man entertainment called *The Diversion of a Morning*. As it contained a burlesque on one of the patent holders, it was promptly suppressed. He thereupon resorted to his celebrated device of inviting the public to drink a cup of chocolate with him, and while the chocolate was preparing, " begged leave to proceed with his instruction of certain pupils he was educating in the art of acting." In 1760 the Richmond Theatre was calling itself the " Histrionic Academy "—and while it held this name Charles Dibdin sang there with Shuter and Miss Pope. All performances of Shakespeare's plays, a monopoly in which the patentees looked upon as their most cherished privilege, were disguised in some way, and among the rest, Garrick's first appearance as Richard III became an item in a semi-musical programme.

The moment had clearly arrived for testing the sincerity of the Government's restatement of the " monopoly," and a very significant occurrence soon gave a clear hint on this matter. Though a momentary success had been effected by the interdiction of Foote's *Diversions of a Morning*, it was very short lived ; for, as a final result, instead of committing Foote for his further misdemeanours, a permanent licence was granted to the Haymarket Theatre, the licence being valid during the months in which Covent Garden and Drury Lane were in the habit of closing.

But a further effort to break down the ascendancy of the patentees' theatre by establishing a theatre with an avowedly dramatic repertoire was unsuccessful. This attempt was made by John Palmer in connection with the building erected by him in Wellclose Square, to which he gave the name of the Royalty Theatre. The facts briefly are these. Assuming the existence of powers by local magistrates to give dramatic licences outside the domain of the Lord Chamberlain—powers which certainly had no existence whatever in fact—Palmer got as far as the completion of a handsome house for which the money had been raised by subscription, when the axe fell heavily on him. The patentees' action in this instance was successful, and the house had, perforce, to join the swelling number of minor theatres forced to present miscellaneous programmes.

The patentees upheld a specially vindictive attitude in the case of Palmer, who, as a particularly valuable actor and eminent member of their company, naturally earned their bitter enmity by thus endeavouring to cut the ground from under their feet. It is indeed difficult to understand how he could have hoped for any success from his plan. Apparently he had misread the terms of a twenty-years-old Act passed in 1766, by which the magistrates governing areas outside a twenty-five mile radius from London were empowered within certain limitations to license seasons of

plays in their respective districts. But, principally, Palmer was relying on the support of public sentiment which was being vigorously roused in the Press; notably in his publication *The Prompter*, by Aaron Hill, who as early as 1730 had complained that "trade in amusements was developing into theatrical madness." Hill and those who supported his contentions, which were based on a passionate advocacy of the literary theatre, had indeed been successful in inflaming public opinion against the privileges of the patentees to a considerable degree, and the movement for an independent or "third" theatre had already found expression in several parliamentary attempts to amend the situation. This unwavering dramatic purist had even gone so far as to recommend a reversal of the *status quo* by which the minor theatres, so far from being given the option of performing legitimate drama, should be compelled to do so.

But general efforts were not successful in securing any modification of the law, and were powerless against the vigilance and malignity of the patentees. Even after Palmer had, at the eleventh hour, cancelled his original plans and was at work on pantomime and varieties, they watched for their opportunity to trip him up, and found it in a fantastically minute instance which has become historic, that of Delpini the clown speaking the words "Roast Beef" without any musical background. The decision of the local magistrates in this instance favoured the plaintiffs, but the ridiculous charge no doubt had a salutary effect for the advocates of free trade, as almost immediately after there followed an act of concession by the Lord Chamberlain which, in the process of time, amounted to a virtually complete enfranchisement of the minor theatres. This was the introduction, not, it is true, universally granted, of the "burletta licence." The word "burletta," borrowed from Italy, had been introduced as a description for a type of trivial dramatic entertainment, whose musical counterpart had been allotted the name of "vaudeville," a term first introduced in this connection, I believe, at Marylebone Gardens. Once the word burletta had been admitted as a formula, and a licence been made available under this description, the battle was virtually won, for it is obvious that the minors would lose no time in driving the wedge further home. Many battles were still to be fought and won, and quite a number to be lost; but the formula remained, and on the whole served all reasonable purposes except in the matter of Shakespearean production. The patentees themselves further unwittingly eased the situation by reviving, under the title of burletta, Fielding's burlesque play of *Tom Thumb* (it is true, with additional songs introduced by Kane O'Hara), in September 1780; an incredibly injudicious proceeding.

One of the first managers to establish his claim to the new form of permit was Philip Astley, to whose career attention will be given later. By 1787, the useful word was snugly embedded in his licence, admitting every form of equestrian and spectacular melodrama for which his amphitheatre became famous. At this date the younger Colman was Examiner of Plays, having qualified for the post in a manner repeated on later occasions, by producing a work of a somewhat amoral character, entitled *Broad Grins.* When appealed to for a definition of the ambiguous term, he gave the following : " A burletta is a drama in rhyme, which is entirely musical ; a short comic piece consisting of recitation and singing, wholly accompanied, more or less [*sic*] by the orchestra." This is, at least, a guarded statement on the subject, befitting the novelty of the permission entailed. But by 1833, expounders of this remarkably elastic form had confidently come to the conclusion that practice had settled its meaning as " a drama with amusing plot, sprightly dialogue, and light sketchy characters, without the addition of music."

This really completes the story. It spelt a triumph for the minors with the single troublesome exception of Shakespeare, in the matter of whose plays the patentees remained adamant. Not that, as has been indicated, the ingenuity of the minor theatres was baffled by the restrictions, for many ludicrously evasive productions were attempted, culminating in 1809 in the supremely ridiculous achievement of Elliston's presentation at the Surrey Theatre of *Macbeth* in rhymed couplets with a musical background, which, described as a " ballet of action," contained the unforgettable lines :

> " Is this a dagger which I see before me ?
> My brains are scattered in a whirlwind stormy."

At this apex of folly we may leave the subject for the moment, always remembering that though many and valiant as the efforts were towards a universal extension of the legitimate drama under the thin disguise of such absurdities, there had yet been engendered a taste and a practice for miscellaneous performances in a definitely theatrical milieu, so firmly established as to render in a large measure nugatory any differentiation between the various types of entertainment.

In the period intervening between the Act of 1737 and the granting of the first burletta licence, there had been passed another Act of Parliament, " to amend and explain " the Vagrancy Act of Queen Anne's reign and aiming at the disciplining of such irregular places of entertainment coming under the heading, in the wording of the statute, of " public dancing, music, or other public entertainment of the like kind " ; in other

words, all such minor theatres or saloons, which could not hope, by nature of their humble and undefined origin, for any of those capricious privileges such as Foote's summer licence at the Haymarket. This was the act which survived as the only source of authority over the music halls until it was superseded by the added force which the " General Powers " Act gave in the Metropolitan area to the already considerable authority enjoyed by the London County Council. The Vagrancy Act, as had been said, was directed against the freedom of the tavern sing-songs and music houses, at which it was observed songs of a Jacobite character were being sung ; and of all these places, Sadler's Wells was most conspicuously in the mind of the authorities. A further Act of 1751 was aimed quite specifically at Sadler's Wells and followed on the lodging of the uncomplimentary report of its transactions, made in 1744. This Act applied to an area within twenty miles of London and was made perpetual in 1745 ; it referred in its preamble to " the multitude of places of entertainment for the lower sort of people " as a " great cause of thefts and robberies," and proposed, in order to eliminate the possibility of these occurrences, that " any house, room, garden, or other place, kept for public dancing, music or other public entertainment, of the like kind, in the City of London or Westminster, without a licence had for that purpose from the last preceding Michaelmas Quarter Sessions of the Peace . . . shall be deemed a disorderly house or place, and every person keeping such house, room, etc., without such licence as aforesaid, shall forfeit the sum of £100 and be punishable as the law directs in the case of disorderly houses." This law, which the infuriated " practical John Hollingshead " used to refer to as the Moll Flanders Act, has never been repealed. As we shall see, by contemptuously placing all places of non-dramatic entertainment outside the careful control of the Lord Chamberlain, it left such places with that collateral freedom enjoyed by vagabonds and others to whom the responsibilities of citizenship are not accorded.

The irregular houses also numbered among their privileges the exemption from closing their doors in Lent. In this instance, the protection of the Lord Chamberlain was a serious embarrassment to the patentees. The matter, as it stood in the 'thirties, is best explained by requoting the passage, selected by Watson Nicholson in " The Struggle for a Free Stage," from an article in *The London Times*. The passage, which refers to the position of the patent theatres, reads : " The term monopoly has come to imply their not being able to do what the other theatres do. . . . At the Adelphi a series of entertainments, of which comic humour is the leading feature, are given without interruption (i.e., during Lent) ; while at Covent Garden a sacred drama on the story of Jephtha,

conveying solemn impressions, with some of Handel's finest music, is prohibited as a profanation of this period of fasting and mortification."

In this matter, the patentees were indeed hoist with their own petard, and handed on this legacy to all the minor theatres when they came under the Lord Chamberlain's jurisdiction in 1843.

By 1875 the regulation by which the regular theatres were closed throughout Lent had been relaxed, to the extent of permitting opening except on Good Friday and Ash Wednesday. John Hollingshead carried on a vigorous campaign against the continued Ash Wednesday embargo ; preparing a protest, signed by a great many leading theatrical personages, referring to the fact that while " three millions of people, more or less, in London " were at liberty " to work on that mysterious day," the right was denied to the members of a particular branch of the theatrical profession only. He also threatened to present a special bill at the Gaiety Theatre on Ash Wednesday, consisting of " A Wooden-headed Farce, A Dog Pantomime, and A Ventriloquial Comedy." The battle was, however, won in 1885, when Lord Lathom, the Lord Chamberlain, removed the ban.

Not the least of the privileges retained after the Act of 1843 by houses not in possession of a dramatic licence was that of drinking and smoking in the auditorium, which the theatres lost on the passing of the Bill. Such collateral privileges have in part disappeared, for the London County Council, rejoicing in the wide extension of the powers previously held by the local magistrates, has proved a far more motherly influence than any previous authority. Still, but for the vexed question of the dramatic aspirations of the music halls, the system governing them offered at first, perhaps, fewer restrictive disadvantages than that under which the theatres laboured, at all events, until well into the 'seventies, when the increase of vigilance on the part of the magistrates rather belatedly began to reflect the work of the various societies for promoting temperance and public morality.

Then there began a campaign for restricting the number of licences granted, followed by a slow but steady increase of interference with the conduct of management, and the behaviour, material and costume of the artists. Over the entire earlier period (between 1737 and 1843) no legal differentiation had been made between the non-patent theatres and the tavern concerts and gardens. Excluded from all theatrical status by the reaffirmations of the Act of 1737, all types of houses, however dissimilar in character, were in the same position of outlawry, but those most nearly approaching the status and social prestige of the patent

theatres were the most narrowly watched and suffered most from their disabilities.[1]

At that time the position was, on the whole, less precarious for those outside the West End area ; a thin trickle of music justified such theatres as the Britannia in the production of almost every kind of play, and, with a few exceptions only, their life was not seriously impinged on. But such houses as the Strand Theatre (reconstituted from Rayner's Panorama) were liable to experience checks on their proceedings similar to those inflicted on Palmer at the Royalty, and the old subterfuges continued to be practised. Both at the Strand and the Victoria, the attempt was made to raise the embargo on legitimate drama by a method of rendering the performances technically private. As the test of a public performance seemed chiefly to rest on the taking of admission money at the doors, the Strand hit upon the brilliant scheme of selling, through a window, an ounce of rose lozenges for four shillings, with a free admission to the house. The attempt at the Victoria was less complicated, consisting merely of the old device of buying tickets at an address in the Strand, and then exchanging these for a free ticket of admission at the door of the theatre. Needless to say, the authorities did not allow themselves to be frustrated by these ingenuities.

As time wore on, the insistent growth of theatres, the vagueness which surrounded the burletta licence, and the demands of the public and the Press, all converged to undermine by fatigue the dying pretensions of the monopolists, and the matter was adjusted by a simple act, automatically licensing as theatres all houses in possession of the " burletta " permission. This Act, nevertheless, had in it a clause involving an important change, that dealing with permissions as to refreshments in the auditorium, to which attention has already been given. This, of course, was effected by a new angle being taken on the question of theatrical management only, and by leaving all other places of entertainment under the provisions of the Act of George III. These were by inference still to remain in the category of the haphazard and undefined meeting places liable on any misdemeanour being proved against them to be penalized as disorderly houses. As in the case of the Act of 1737, the outward effects of the new Act were, at first, negligible. Houses, such as the Britannia, which were glad to avail themselves of the theatrical status, were nevertheless forced by usage to retain considerable elements of variety. The real cleavage was a slow one, resulting from the economic rise of the

[1]This and the succeeding paragraph may appear to the reader to embody some contradiction of the earlier references to the Burletta Licence as a solvent of the minor theatres' difficulties. The fact is that these conflicts came in waves, and after a comparative lull (broken, it is true, by the exploits of Elliston at the Surrey Theatre), they tended to become fiercer and more frequent again in the 'thirties.

non-theatrical house, rather than from these legal changes. With the achievement of this economic weapon a new line of conflict between the music halls and the houses elevated to the rank of theatre, arose ; inaugurated by Morton and Strange's attempts to stage ballet and extravaganza at the Canterbury and elsewhere. But the story of this later war, which developed again in the first years of the twentieth century as the "sketch war," will be treated in later chapters of this book.

The main conclusions to be drawn from the quarrels arising from the partitioning of privilege in theatrical life by Act of Parliament is that the law's yeas and nays are not the fundamental driving force behind the situations which they appear to create. That driving force is reflected by these legal adjustments of power, distorting temporarily the natural curve of events ; but social institutions are themselves inherently charged with that principle of change and growth which is stronger and more insistent than external laws of governance. Such laws only provide certain stimuli or barriers to the inevitable evolutionary process, and give occasion for a vexatious conflict of vested interests. Briefly, the theatre, though freed from its shackles, remained much as it was, until causes, germinating beneath the surface, found expression in new forms; and a genuinely spontaneous dramatic revival replaced, by a natural process, the era of pantomime, vaudeville, burletta and the like.

On the other hand, the music hall eventually discovered its moments of highest vitality, primarily by a reliance on the methods, surviving in the song and supper room, of the old form of tavern concert adapted to larger and more highly organized houses, rather than by attempting to outwit the veto placed upon it, in relation to theatrical forms of production.

CHAPTER VI

" *Minor* " *Variety*

A CLOSER inspection of the life of the minor theatres at the beginning of the nineteenth century further reveals the very complex ingredients from which modern variety has been supplied. It is impossible, in spirit, to draw any line between one form and another in the extraordinary turmoil of entertainment which succeeded the classical managements of Garrick and his contemporaries. The rise of the minor theatres to comparative freedom, won by means of the convenient fiction of the " burletta " licence, had, as has been already pointed out, completely overwhelmed the pretensions of the literary drama to its claim on the possession of a sanctuary. The minor theatres proclaimed an almost insolent freedom to continue those strangely distorted presentments of the national dramatic literature, at first evolved under the stress of legal disabilities but now pursued as a commercial policy which penetrated to the stages of Drury Lane and Covent Garden. Even while the great Garrick was still in control of affairs, the repertory of the patent theatres had come under the compulsion of a competitive policy brought about by their own obtuseness, so that Goldsmith, in his *Vicar of Wakefield*, speaking by the mouth of a strolling player, had remarked, " it is not the composition of the piece, but the number of starts and attitudes that may be introduced into it, that elicits applause." So little, indeed, were the patent theatres relying, before the end of the century, upon the presentation of an unadulterated drama, that Philip Astley is reported to have remarked with bitterness, in reference to the borrowed vogue for " equestrian " productions, " Why do they steal my horses? I never try to engage Mrs. Siddons."

In the early nineteenth century the leading variety theatres in the West End of London were the Adelphi, called, until the building of Adelphi Terrace by the Adam brothers, the Sans Pareil; and the Lyceum, known at its inception in 1765 as the Lyceum Great Room. These houses led the way in miscellaneous entertainment. The former was erected to the designs of a certain John Scott, an oil and colour merchant whose business was

conducted on an adjacent site. At the first small house which dated from 1802, the lack of a " burletta " licence was responsible for the very modest nature of the musical entertainments inaugurated by Mr. Scott's daughter—" the whole being written and composed by the performer."[1] The piano used in this entertainment was placed over a trap-door in order to make room for the " mechanical and optical exhibitions " with which the entertainment was embellished.

In 1806 a larger theatre was built and named the Sans Pareil. A burletta licence was then obtained and Miss Scott was able to turn her talents in the direction of the lighter types of dramatic production. For a number of years the performances were devoted to the typical miscellany. A bill for 1812 makes mention of " a flight by Mr. Pack, the celebrated agilist," a burletta, and " songs in character " (the phrase is thus found to be used in a definitely theatrical milieu). These songs included the well-known " Visit to Bagnigge Wells," sung by Mr. Huckle. About the same time Charles Dibdin gave a number of his entertainments there, and in 1819 the theatre was let to Rodwell and Jones, which resulted in the production in 1821 of Moncrieff's celebrated *Tom and Jerry*, adapted from Pierce Egan's *Life in London*.

Writing in 1826, Brayley, in his *London Theatres*, remarks in a notice of this theatre, that " more recently Messrs. Reeve and Wilkinson performed their inimitable imitations, etc., and Mr. Alexander executed his wonderful power of ventriloquism on this stage." I am able to add that, in the Lent of 1825, Mr. Henry exhibited his *Phantasmagoria*.

At this time Rodwell died and the management passed to Terry and Yates. In 1828, Charles Mathews the elder, the celebrated comedian, replaced Terry, and with Yates gave an entertainment consisting of songs, sketches, and character studies. Later, in 1829, a work written round the personality of a performing elephant called Djeck provided an attraction which drew the town for a period of three months.

Some time after the death of Mathews, Yates took over the sole management and presented, though not for the first time in England, the renowned T. D. Rice, known universally as " Jim Crow," in honour of his impersonation of the negro of that name, whose performances were indirectly responsible for the strange Victorian craze for minstrel troupes.

Meanwhile the Great Lyceum Room, built by James Payne, contributed some interesting experiments in variety. The house

[1]George Frederick Cooke, the celebrated actor, who spent the last four years of his life in America, visited the Sans Pareil in 1806 and commented, with tremendous force of implication, upon Miss Scott's talents, in his private diary. He wrote as follows : " Miss Scott provided the first part of the entertainment at the Sans Pareil. The second and third parts of the entertainment are very pleasing."

was originally intended for the exhibition of pictures and was used on several occasions by the Incorporated Society of Artists, a body extinguished by the foundation of the Royal Academy in 1768. Its demise was the opportunity of a Mr. Lingham, a breeches-maker in the Strand, who developed a number of varying entertainments in the rooms. The plural is used advisedly as one may gather from contemporary allusions that the place consisted of a large saloon with a number of smaller rooms adjoining.

In 1794, Dr. Arnold, the composer, rebuilt the "back part of the premises" which he converted into a small theatre; this constituted the first Lyceum. Arnold's purpose was to develop native opera, but as no licence could be obtained from the authorities, he was forced to surrender his lease to Lingham, with its additional advantages. Fully equipped as it now was, the place was available for the most diverse entertainments. In 1789, Dibdin gave there his "Entertainment Sans Souci"; both Astley (his amphitheatre having been burned down in 1794) and a rival equestrian of the name of Handy, exhibited feats of horsemanship in the theatre, and Cartwright gave his performance on the musical glasses, that fashionable accomplishment which, together with the works of Shakespeare, was the favourite diversion of the Hon. Amelia Skeggs.[1] An illusionist called Philostal also hired the place for the presentation of his *Phantasmagoria*. Not so profitable, apparently, as the foregoing attractions, was "Lonsdale's chaste and classic display, called the 'Ægyptiana,' which consisted of "a series of well-painted representations by Porter, Mulready, Pugh, Cristall and others in illustration of the scenery, buildings, manners, etc., of Egypt, accompanied by explanatory readings and other instructive divertissements." The latter, by way of leavening variety, consisted of recitations from Milton's *L'Allegro* and the *Legend of Sir Boris of Southampton*, with scenic illustrations on the stage behind the reader, "corresponding with the progression" of the subjects involved.

Five balloons were exhibited in the Great Room just before the erection of the theatre, one of which is alleged to have been entirely overlaid with gold. Waxworks and Flockton's puppets, together with sleight-of-hand tricks, were early listed among the attractions. Further variety entertainments, quoted by Brayley, as occurring between 1790 and 1809, included such well-known entertainments as that of Robert Palmer (the son of the famous actor who has already been mentioned) entitled *Portraits of the Living and Dead*, Collins in his *Evening Brush*, a one-man show in five parts, and Charles Incledon, the great singer, who described, with musical interpolations, his *Voyage to India*, an entertainment

[1] "The Vicar of Wakefield."

by the Clown Bologna, called *Phantascopia*, and an " Astronomica Exhibition."[1]

In the smaller rooms of the building the ancient lust for gazing at freaks was gratified by the engagement of those " extraordinary sports of nature," The White Negro Girl, the Panther Mare and Colt, and the Porcupine Man.

In the year 1809 the lucky accident of the Drury Lane company being without a home, brought theatrical importance to the Lyceum Theatre. It obtained for the first time the burletta licence, and three seasons were given by the Drury Lane Company.

In 1815 the house was entirely rebuilt internally to the designs of Beazely, the architect of the St. James's Theatre, and its career as the English Opera House began under the management of the younger Arnold. It was stated by the terms of the licence (granted by the Lord Chamberlain as a patent), that the house was to be used as an experimental ground for the operatic artists engaged at Drury Lane and Covent Garden. Arnold's own grandiose scheme was for the establishment of a permanent English Opera House. How far this scheme achieved reality is revealed by the presence in 1818 of the elder Mathews with his " silver tongued " entertainment of *The Mail Coach Adventures*. Lent, a close period for the higher drama, was set aside for a continuation of the Astronomical Lectures, and these were touched up by the addition of scenic display and " a large orrery." Masquerades, which had been forbidden from time to time as an offence against public morality, were held and given the title of carnivals.

One would like to know more of the *Soirées Amusantes* held during the English Opera House period of the Lyceum ; it may be concluded, however, that they were an anchorage for a complete programme of varieties.

The Surrey Theatre, the largest of the houses on the south bank, had an origin in equestrian entertainment, and its existence was due to the influence in this sphere of Philip Astley. In 1771 Charles Hughes, Astley's notable rival, had constructed a " ride " close to Stangate Street in Lambeth. To this he gave the name of " The British Horse Academy." Two years later Hughes became involved in a dispute with the authorities which resulted in a temporary embargo upon both his and Astley's establishments, but about the same time, Charles Dibdin's restless and versatile mind became attracted to the idea of an equestrian form of entertainment, principally that the prevalent craze for the mediæval might be exploited by a combined stage and circus presentation of historic pageantry. To Dibdin, therefore, we

[1]The principal saloon of the first Lyceum Theatre was called the Shrubbery in allusion to the fact that in the centre and angles of the room were arranged a variety of trees and plants.

MUSICAL BOUQUET
LUCY NEAL (SOLO & CHORUS); & LUCY LONG.
SUNG BY THE ETHIOPIAN SERENADERS.

By courtesy of British Museum

SURREY MUSIC HALL,

GRAPES TAVERN,

SOUTHWARK-BRIDGE-ROAD.

W. WARDE'S BENEFIT,

AND NOVEL BILL OF FARE.

W. WARDE (Stage Manager), respectfully invites his Friends and the Public at large, to his Benefit Spread, which will take place on

WEDNESDAY, JANUARY 11, 1854.

The REPAST will vie with any of his former efforts, consisting of the *choicest delicacies of the season.* W. W. trusts from his long experience in catering for the Public Taste, the following *Bill of Fare* will meet with general approval, believing the chief art in making GOOD SOUPS depends on the judicious blending of the *different flavours*, so that nothing shall predominate to take the *fat off other dishes.* The judgment of the Cook will be taxed to render the whole Entertainment *palatable*, and as little *puff paste* as possible will be used to curry favour; each *sauce* will have its peculiar smack, and form an agreeable contrast to the preceding one.

FIRST COURSE.

Odd FISH, and Singing Birds, by Messrs. McGOWAN, F. SHORT, TEMPLETON, J. BARKER, KERRIDGE, FULCHER, &c,

ORNAMENTAL DISHES by Mrs. TEMPLETON, Misses HYDE, and KERRIDGE, &c., &c.

SECOND COURSE.

The POULTRY and GAME will be dressed by Mr. de BRENNER, from whose unrivalled Farm Yard, Fowls, Ducks, and Pigs, will be supplied, the ingredients will be varied according to the Viands by skilful Artistes.

Hasty Pudding and Comic Removes by E. TAYLOR.

The Sideboard will be garnished by numerous extra dishes; Spice Nuts and Short Cakes by the inimitable FRANK. The Rich and Rare Turnovers, variegated with innumerable Bon Bons (Sugared and Silvered) by Mons. FILLIS and SON.

Savoury Pat-ties and Mottoes by the New Irish Comic Vocalist, Mr. McGOWAN.

EXTERIOR OF SURREY MUSIC HALL.

INTERIOR OF SURREY MUSIC HALL.

The Confectionery, Sweetmeats, Carry-away Comforts Christmas Trees, and Trifles, by Miss KERRIDGE, Master TAYLOR, Master WARDE, and Young GODDEN.

A dainty dish of "BLACK-BIRD PIE," from the Queen's Larder, by the Niggers from the South.

THE DESSERT,

By W. WARDE.

(Don't desert him), in several New Dishes made for the occasion. 1st. Good Luck to Everybody; 2nd. Learning and Leather; 3rd. Fresh Invented Relishes in shapes of Comic Duets with his Son, the Fruits of his labours in the Vineyard of "the Grapes."

Extra Removes, Real Lancashire Capers, i.e., Stewed (H)eels, Broiled Soles, and Hot Trotters, by the

CELEBRATED JOHN BOOTH,

Who has kindly consented to favour with his Company.

The Audience, it is hoped, will make and bring their own JAMS and JELLIES, by attending in great crowds,

Wines and Liquers, &c., as usual at the Bar, and in the Picture Gallery.

The Tea and Coffee served up at the Refreshment Rooms next door to the Hall.

The Cloth will be laid at half-past Six, and the Band will play during Dinner.

Under-Stewards, Messrs. MONTGOMERY & BECKHAM.

Mr. CECIL HICKS will preside and attend upon the Ladies.

Lower Hall, 6d. Upper Hall, 1s.

POLICE REGULATIONS.—Cabmen charging more than their fare to set down at the Queen's Bench, and pass off to the Police Station.

By order of

W. WARDE,

Head Cook and Bottle-Washer.

Miss Enid Brett's collection

probably owe the creation of this strange hybrid theatre of which the latest London example was the Hippodrome, built in 1900. Astley had, it is true, introduced novelties with some theatrical flavour into his circus, such as the famous " Billy Button's Ride to Brentford," and was, by 1775, devoting evening performances to the *Ombres Chinoises*, but his first stage was not built until 1784. Dibdin's idea was realized, in partnership with Charles Hughes, two years earlier than this, by the erection of the Royal Circus in St. George's Fields. Difficulties were discovered in the furthering of their plan. A burletta licence could not be obtained: it had apparently not been clear to the promoters of the scheme that the Lord Chamberlain had no power to grant such a licence outside the precincts of the Court and of the City of Westminster. But the disability could not have been an insuperable one, for such a licence was granted to Astley in the immediate neighbourhood in or about 1787.

The Royal Circus, however, opened with no licence of any kind, and an attempt to disarm authority was made by devising a form of theatrical entertainment performed by children, the management benevolently arranging for the instruction of their juvenile artists between performances, in " religious, moral and useful learning." The first programme announced was duly carried out and consisted of an " Entrée " of horses, a ballet on the subject of Admetus and Alceste, a display of horsemanship and a pantomime. The season did not prosper, however, and an engineered disturbance led to the reading of the Riot Act in the house, which was summarily closed after it had been open barely a month. Early in 1783 the theatre was reopened under a music and dancing licence, but it immediately began to suffer from the effects of internal conflict; for Dibdin, always a storm centre, became embroiled with his partner Hughes, a man who, even by his apologist, John Decastro, was admitted to have possessed an irascible nature. The theatre found itself in a state of " inextricable embarrassment," and Dibdin was forced out of the partnership on a charge of neglect, a neglect which was probably the unavoidable result of his consignment to the King's Bench Prison for debt. Hughes thereupon quarrelled violently with the other sharers in the property, and, rather surprisingly, we discover Dibdin again joining forces with his antagonist in a successful *coup de main*, by which the theatre came once more under their joint control.[1]

[1]The following is from a bill dated 1784, during Dibden's absence: " *The Lover's Device* in which M. Johannot will introduce a new song to the favourite air of *Fal de ral Tit*. The favourite dance of the Coopers, by Messrs. Laborie, Flin, the Misess Simonets and others. Horsemanship by Mr. Hughes and Pupils. A Burletta called *The Jovial Cobbler*. Imitations, vocal and rhetorical, by Mr. Decastro. The Comic Song of *Four and Twenty Fiddlers* by Mr. Johannot. The vicissitudes of Harlequin. Signor Rossi's Firework."

For the moment there appeared to be some likelihood of prosperity. The magistrates granted a liquor licence, and popularity was achieved by a revival of the ancient practice of presenting blood-sport as entertainment, by the production of an actual fox-hunt in the ring, this being followed by an equally realistic presentation of a stag hunt. Such a partnership as that of Dibdin and Hughes could, of course, have only a brief existence. Dibdin soon found occasion to complain of Hughes' "unjust and violent behaviour," and proceeded, in his own words, "to shake the sawdust of the Royal Amphitheatre from his feet." The surviving partners then made an interesting experiment. They engaged John Palmer to perform three times a week, among other monologues, the famous Alexander Stevens' *Lecture on Heads*. The move was the prelude to an attempt to give rein to theatrical activities under Palmer's direction. A more provocative choice could hardly have been made. Palmer's record in connection with his attempts to establish a third theatre had made him the particular target of the patentees. Twice, while at the Royal Circus, he was arrested, at their instigation, on a charge of vagabondage, the principal charge centring round his assumption of the character of Henry Dubois in a spectacle dealing with the storming of the Bastille. The sequel was Palmer's return to Drury Lane.

The Royal Circus then engaged in various efforts at pantomime and equestrian melodrama, in which Palmer's son appeared, under the stage-management of Delpini the clown, but the theatre fell into bankruptcy during Hughes' remarkable visit to the Empress Catherine of Russia.[1] On his return to England in 1795 Hughes rented the house, which had meanwhile reverted to the ground landlord, and for a few months a junction was made with the company which had been performing at the Lyceum. In 1799 Hughes died, according to De Castro, of a broken heart resulting from the transfer of the terms of his licence to his partner Jones. After that event we hear of pony races at the Circus—a policy which in desperate straits was adopted more than once at Sadler's Wells—of the production of a successful pantomime on the subject of *Bluebeard*, and of a visit by Davis, Astley's lieutenant at the rival amphitheatre, with his performing horse, which, in a tournament scene, was able to "rear up, seize hold of, and tear down a streaming banner from the rampart walls."

Still holding nothing but the magistrates' licence for singing

[1]During Charles Hughes' visit to Russia he executed a commission for Count Orloff, favourite of the Empress Catherine, who entrusted him with the task of securing blood horses for the Imperial stables. It is said that he was only allowed to return to England upon condition that he left his grooms and performing horses behind him for the Queen's amusement.

and dancing, the theatre produced, between 1795 and 1806, a number of historical and romantic melodramas, many of them written by Cross, one of the sharers in the management. Productions with titles such as *Louisa of Lombardy, or the Secret Avenger, The Fire King or Albert and Rosalia*, and *The Cloud King or the Magic Rose*, were often written as vehicles for performers of " specialities " such as Ireland, " the celebrated Yorkshire Flying Phenomenon."

On the heels of a second bankruptcy the theatre was let for a period of five years to the enterprising actor-manager, William Elliston, who, entering on his tenancy in 1809, renamed the house the Surrey Theatre. The most spirited campaign was carried on by this manager against the authority of the patentees, only to be interrupted in 1814, when, becoming as manager of Drury Lane a patent holder himself, he immediately reversed his attitude and became one of the bitterest persecutors of the minor theatres. While at the Surrey, however, Elliston earned the highest eulogia as a liberator and to him was largely attributed that freedom which, " combined with the awakened spirit of the public, relieved the theatre from the arbitrary restraints of recitative and inexorable dumb-show." Although Elliston's career at the Surrey was thus hailed as an impressive struggle for theatrical free trade, it must not be supposed that he achieved anything important in legitimate drama at this house. An early bill in his management, in addition to advertising the comedietta of *John Bull in France* and the melodrama of *Timour the Tartar*, announces the appearance of Sieur Sanches in his feat of " walking against the ceiling," a performance repeated by Hervio Nano, the " Gnome Fly," at Covent Garden, and by others. His direction of the theatre mainly exhibits Elliston as an astute purveyor of the familiar mixture of dramatic spectacle and variety.

Until the passing of the 1843 Act, and, indeed, for a considerable period beyond, the Surrey continued in this course. A bill of 1831 illustrates admirably the methods by which it was found necessary to assist the presentation of a work of Shakespeare by the allurements of variety.

The performance, for the benefit of Osbaldstone the dramatist, was announced as follows :—

King Lear and a variety of singing and dancing.
" My Desire." Sailor's Hornpipe.
The Old Maid (in character). Miss Vincent.
Military Brigand Dance. Mdme. Rossier.
The Bay of Biscay (in character). Mr. Edwin.
The Wolf (Shield). Mr. Ransford.
Tippitiwitchet (in character). Mr. T. Hill.

Evolution of the Demon Fire King. Mr. Nelson Lee.
Mr. Wild's "Song of the Country Fair."
Mr. Hubert (by permission of J. Rouse). "I want Money."

In the same year theatrical history was made at the Surrey by the first production of Douglas Jerrold's *Black-eyed Susan* (a play founded on Gay's inimitable ballad, *All in the Downs*), in which T. P. Cooke became famous in the character of the hero.

Five years later, in 1836, an event of the greatest importance in music hall history occurred at the Surrey; the first appearance in England of "Jim Crow" Rice, whose great vogue subsequently at the Adelphi has already been mentioned. Rice, while still an actor performing in his native country under conditions of comparative obscurity, conceived one of those brilliant yet haphazard ideas which sometimes make men's fortunes. This was, to reproduce upon the stage the antics of a negro street performer whom he encountered in Cincinatti.[1] The story, quoted by Harry Reynolds in his *Minstrel Memories* from an article in the *Atlantic Monthly*, published in 1867, is to the effect that Rice, while walking down the main street of Cincinatti, heard and saw a strange being singing a doggerel, the burden of which was embodied in the couplet,

"Turn about and wheel about an' do jes' so,
An' ebery time I turn about I jump, Jim Crow."

Though one hesitates to indulge in the dangerous practice of tracing definitive origins, it is perhaps true to say that this ditty, heard thus by chance, actually brought about a vogue of so deep and lasting a character, that its influence cannot be said to have entirely departed at the moment of writing. Behind this accident there has probably been functioning some hidden depth of affinity or attraction, which, from setting whole nations humming the crazy words of this fantastic song, has found an echo even in the hearts of monarchs and prime ministers. Something of the impulse towards negro melody and behaviour is, of course, to be attributed to the agitation for slave liberation in the 'twenties. Meanwhile, that awakening of conscience had been quickened into a general rather morbid humanitarianism, which, in this particular direction, reached its full development in the later demonstrations connected with the appearance of *Uncle Tom's Cabin* in 1852. Like goes to like; and slave sentiment became firmly linked with the child-worship, already carried to fatuous lengths in face of the cruel exploitation of child labour with which the industrial revolution is involved, which pervaded a vast field of drama and literature. Through the medium of the power-

[1]The actual place of this encounter has been debated.

ful appeal of the nigger melodies a junction was eagerly made among these diverse subjects, to which was added an advocacy of temperance for the working classes. The total result was the fully-developed nigger minstrel entertainment, whose echo of such moral problems as had become fashionable rendered it a kind of annexe to Exeter Hall.

For a period Rice's success in 1836 resulted only in creating some individual imitations of the type of performance he had imported. The furore was apparently the result of a single song, the original "Jim Crow," which in varying versions he introduced into the burlettas written for him—the first being probably that by Leman Rede, in the performance of which, at the Adelphi in 1838, he was supported by Frederick Yates, John Reeve and Buckstone—and his audiences were carried away by the exact representation of his prototype's peculiar manner of delivery, the fantastic veracity of the costume and by the characteristic dance movements. That Rice invested his creation with a careful realism is born out by the story, probably a true one in essentials, as to his first appearance in this character at Pittsburg in the autumn of 1830. It is recorded that he persuaded a negro porter at his hotel to exchange clothes with him at the theatre. His appearance in the picturesque rags was a sensational success from the outset, but the crowning point of his scheme was reached when the porter himself, having become uneasy about the long absence of Rice from the dressing-room, and desiring to return to his work clothed in the garb which Rice had borrowed from him, found his way on to the stage and, poking his nose round the corner of the proscenium, demanded the immediate return of his personal property. On slighter accidents than this men have been wafted into fame, and one can picture the delight and approbation of an audience already raised to a pitch of enthusiasm at this climax, which it imagined to be a carefully rehearsed effect.[1]

No such happy accident was necessary to secure Rice's fame in England. Within a few months his song had become a universal by-word. His appearances were apparently confined to the theatres, and his stay in England was a short one. After a second visit to the Surrey Theatre, when he appeared in an extravaganza called *The Court Jester*, Rice returned to America, having sown the seeds which were to be harvested by Pell and his Ethiopian Serenaders. His second and last visit to England was made in 1842.

[1]An attempt was made to supply the public with the origins of Jim Crow in an apochryphal biography of this hero. Tribute is paid to the popularity of Jim Crow in the following words : "In the fashionable colonnade, in the filthiest street, in the naked, damp cellar, and the luxuriously carpetted [*sic*] drawing-room, the words and tune of Jim Crow are constantly to be heard."

The neighbouring Coburg Theatre, famous as the Old Vic, though with no such important innovation to its credit, introduced one contribution to variety. Built by two members of the Royal Circus syndicate and designed by the machinist of that house, it was stocked with scenery and effects secured from the Surrey and opened in 1819 as a minor theatre, with the performance of a spectacle, and a pantomime called *Harlequin and Comus.* In the following year the managers were faced with a prosecution, for a performance of *Richard III,* with Junius Booth in the name part.

Then, in 1822, the famous looking-glass curtain was constructed, which was composed of sixty-three divisions of cut glass enclosed in a carved gilt frame. In the following year appeared at the house, for the first time before a London public, Ramo Samee, the magician, whose fame was so great that all street performers, as late as the 'fifties, adopted his name as a descriptive turn for this type of entertainment.[1]

His vogue was indeed extensive: at Vauxhall he was especially a favourite. Hardly less celebrated were the performances at the Coburg in 1833 of Abdul Maza, the illusionist.

An American minstrel troupe appeared at this theatre (by now called the Victoria) in 1844, and in the same year Mr. T. Thompson exhibited himself in the guise of various Greek statues—an early instance of a performance on the lines of the "poses plastiques." The minstrel troupe included Woolcot, playing the Longo Banjo; Robins, Tuckahoe Violin; Packer, Bone Castanets; Rong, Cohea Tamburine. Their repertoire included Dan Emmet's famous *De Boatmen's Dance.*

To follow the fortunes of Sadler's Wells from the eighteenth century onwards is to meet with a great many elements of theatrical variety. Its early period as a music house ended with the brush with the authorities of 1744, which did much to bring into being the Act of 28 Geo. II. In 1746, the place having experienced its most evil days, it was acquired by John Rosoman, who quickly raised its status to that of an important entertainment centre. His vigorous management amounted at first to the establishment and ordering of a recognized theatre of varieties for the Metropolis. He appealed to the authorities successfully for horse patrols by which his audiences were safely conducted through the dangers of the northern suburbs, and he engaged the able Giuseppe Grimaldi, father (though sometimes described as grandfather) of the more celebrated Joseph, as pantomime and ballet master; and also the famous wire dancer, Maddox. Maddox's tricks as advertised on contemporary bills, included the feat of balancing a coach wheel on the wire, and a straw upon his

[1]Mayhew: "London Life and London Poor."

face and shoulders. This was followed by his balancing it upon his head, the wire being in "full swing."

Another celebrated equilibrist appeared at Sadler's Wells in 1755, whose performances were said to have fascinated even those who "heretofore could not look upon feats of this kind with any degree of patience."

Rosoman, who for a quarter of a century does not appear to have abolished the system of admission by the purchase of wine, further increased the patronage of the house by instituting convivial assemblies at the neighbouring "Sir Hugh Myddelton's Head."

Like Rouse at the later Grecian, he was a speculative builder. Having built the neighbouring Rosoman's Row, he completed the erection of the first Sadler's Wells Theatre in the place of the original music house at a cost, according to Brayley, of £4,000. This, with a stage and boxes, was able to command prices ranging from one to three shillings. From this period the introduction of the burletta, under a rather precarious sanction, gave the house the character of a minor theatre, though variety elements were introduced, such as the feats of strength of Belzoni, "the Patagonian Sampson"—famous also as an Egyptian archæologist.

An innovation in 1804 was responsible for a feature later to be adopted in the construction of the London Hippodrome. For, "in humble imitation of the Naumachia of the Ancients," aquatic spectacles were in this year for the first time given at Sadler's Wells. Here this theatre had an advantage over all rivals—the tank used for these productions being easily supplied with water from the adjacent New River head.[1] In the first of these entertainments, *The Siege of Gibraltar*, attacks were made and guns fired by accurate models of battleships, and it was followed by a succession of other pieces on the same plan. Pantomime, with its medley of buffoonery and mechanical display, was a form of entertainment which one would naturally expect to find in a house of this type, and it is hardly an exaggeration to claim that the theatre holds the most important record for pantomime in the world ; since it was here that Joseph Grimaldi first appeared on April 16, 1781, in the character, as the *Dictionary of National Biography* tells us of "an infant dancer"—a testimony to that great actor's precociousness, as on this date he was exactly twenty-seven months old.

In itself the early connection would have little interest ; but not only his early triumphs, but Grimaldi's whole life history is

[1]The tank, on one occasion, acted as a life-saving apparatus to the "Patagonian Samson." The climax of his performance was a balancing feat in which he supported a "pyramidal framework" on which were perched eleven men. At one of the performances the stage collapsed under the weight and Samson and his eleven assistants were plunged into the waters of the tank beneath.

bound up in the place. His father, as we have noted, also was connected with Sadler's Wells, first as a ballet master and mime, then as a sharer in the management. Grimaldi, moreover, married Maria Hughes, daughter of the sometime proprietor of the theatre (not to be confused with the equestrian of the Royal Circus).

Grimaldi's most famous pantomime, *Mother Goose*, the "book" of which was by Thomas Dibdin (the son of Charles Dibdin, and for some period resident manager of the theatre) was first produced at Covent Garden in 1806, having, according to its author, been five times refused by Harris, the manager of that theatre. It was several times revived at Sadler's Wells. Sadler's Wells also, according to Michael Williams, claims the first performance of Grimaldi's most famous song, "Hot Codlings."

Two other famous clowns appeared at the "Wells" during Grimaldi's career; Paulo in 1816,[1] and George Wieland, aged five, in the following year. The strong highlight of the Grimaldi period at Sadler's Wells leaves the rest of its record in miscellaneous entertainment in rather profound shadow. From Rosoman onwards the house made increasingly frequent trials of a dramatic repertoire. Under the Honners, husband and wife, melodrama was in vogue, all the principal characters being sustained by Mrs. Honner. Howard Payne, "formerly the American Roscius,"[2] played there in 1821, but in 1825 Mr. Daniel Egerton again lowered the tone of the house by introducing "pony racing and the Russian Mountains." Later in the same year, under Thomas Dibdin, William Reeve, the composer, and Andrews, the scene-painter, pantomime, as might be expected, came again into its own, and the reputation for this form of entertainment, triumphantly sustained under this management, never quite deserted the theatre until the end of its first span of life, in 1900.

It is important now to turn for a moment to a house whose policy profoundly affected the minor theatres and whose influence was a far-reaching one in the history of variety, Astley's Royal Amphitheatre. The great Philip Astley, who synthesized all the various forms constitute the English circus, was a man whose range of endeavour, audacity in the execution of ideas, and force of personality, amounted to genius. He is, by his enrichment of variety entertainment, to be placed among the creative figures of the music hall. He was, moreover, devoid of all trace of the vulgarity apt to mar the work of other pioneers in that sphere.

[1]Paulo was the son of Redigé, a famous French acrobat known as "le Petit Diable," who, in addition to being the favourite performer in Astley's in London, was the original Billy Waters in Moncrieff's adaptation of *Tom and Jerry*. The son was held in sufficiently high estimation for the Duke of Kent, at Paulo's death, in 1835, to become patron of a fund raised to purchase an annuity for his wife and child.

[2]The author of *Home, Sweet Home*.

A soldier of the romantic type, possessed of a marvellous understanding and sympathy for the animals he trained, there was about him a kind of instinctive " quality " which governed all his show-making, the problems of which he approached with a simplicity which came straight out of his imagination. Mention has already been made of Astley's performances in a hall at Piccadilly by means of which he advertised his performances near Westminster Bridge. These belonged to his early middle period. His activities as an entertainer began in the early 1770's, when, having received his discharge from the Army, he began to give riding exhibitions upon a charger which was the gift of his commanding officer, General Elliot. He chose as a site for these performances a piece of waste ground in Lambeth near Halfpenny Hatch, the position of which is now covered by Waterloo Station. Astley was not first in the field with this type of show, for in the neighbourhood of Islington, similar equestrian displays were being given by three men, known respectively as Price, Johnson and " Old Sampson." With an almost sublime disregard of legal rights, he enclosed the ground and made a charge to the public, without resorting to the formality of obtaining a licence from the magistrates. According to an anonymous writer on the amusements of South London, the policy of a set charge for his performances was immediately adopted ; according to Decastro, who worked intermittently with him over a period of thirty years, the gallant sergeant for some time merely passed round the hat. Probably the latter was the case, but the method must soon have been abandoned, as, by 1770, having built a kind of pent-house on the edge of his circle for the shelter of a proportion of his audience, he was announcing upon printed handbills his " activities on horseback, doors to be open at four and he will mount at five " ; and making the charge of a shilling for seats in the enclosure and sixpence for standing places round the ring. By 1775 the charge was two shillings for gallery seats and a shilling for ringside places.

Meanwhile, Astley had bought a second horse in Smithfield and was engaged in training his son and another assistant, while at the same time he was attracting attention by advertising riding lessons to the " nobility and gentry." His pupils happily included two daughters of the Lord Chancellor, and this circumstance stood him in good stead when, through the bad offices of Barrett, the proprietor of Vauxhall Gardens, Charles Hughes, who was conducting a similar riding establishment near the " Dog and Duck," incurred an injunction, which spread to Astley at his pitch in the Halfpenny Hatch. Moreover, he was later, through the influence of the same official, successful in obtaining a magistrates' licence, under the George II Act, for his amphitheatre.

By 1778 Astley had built an elaborately-roofed grandstand, or " riding house," the lower floor of which served as stabling, and, with his two assistants, began to develop the show along theatrical lines. His next important move, and in this instance we may perhaps credit our hero with a less innocent form of astuteness, was the acquisition of a piece of ground with a valuable frontage on the south side of Westminster Bridge Road. This became Astley's as the result of a mortgage for £200 granted to the owner, who subsequently defaulted and surrendered the site. About the same time, the lucky Astley picked up a diamond ring, and on the proceeds of its sale erected the new establishment. His meeting with George III, recorded by Decastro as occurring in the year 1801, is by another authority assigned to the period immediately after his removal to the new site. Probably the story of his saving the King from being thrown by his horse when crossing Westminster Bridge is apocryphal, but it is characteristic of Astley that he should don his regimental uniform, mount his charger, " richly caparisoned for the occasion," and await the arrival of the monarch. The King, with the Duke of York beside him, upon his arrival at the spot at which Astley was stationed, observed him, and according to Decastro's delightful account, turned to his royal kinsman and remarked, " Who is that, Frederick ? " " Mr. Astley, sir," was the prompt reply ; " one of our good friends, a veteran ; one that fought in the German War." Upon this, we are told, the King turned to him and made a courteous salutation.

A moment of real inspiration came to Astley when he decided to fuse the entertainment at Piccadilly with the equestrian performances at Westminster, the first of these performances being given by candlelight, under a canvas awning. Bills of the period show the methods by which the transition to the later type of programme was effected. In 1791, " Equestrian Feats " are advertised for morning performances. In the evenings these are intermingled with " Sleight of Hand, Comic Dancing, Rossignol, imitation of Birds, the Dancing Dogs, the Polander's Tricks on Chairs, and a grand display of Fireworks."

By 1780 the medley of variety entertainment was firmly established. A break was made with the " *haute école*," by the production of an equestrian sketch called " Billy Button's Ride to Brentford," and the show gathered momentum from the varied nature of the performances, which were to make it a model for an entirely new type of entertainment throughout Europe.

The son was highly gifted, both naturally and by accomplishment. During one of Astley's many season in Paris (the amazing man completely captured the attention of the Parisians and built an amphitheatre there which survived as the Cirque Fran-

coni) both father and son appeared by command at the Court of Versailles. Marie Antoinette was so impressed with the beauty of the younger horseman that, varying the title by which the great dancer Vestris was known, she called him "the English Rose."

Astley's ingenuity and prowess were inexhaustible. Feats of strength and endurance made a special appeal to him. He was a remarkable athlete, and courted publicity on one occasion by floating between Blackfriars and where Tower Bridge now stands, holding a flag upright in each hand. He delighted in the feats of Belzoni and of Ducrow, "the Flemish Hercules," the father of the celebrated Andrew Ducrow, who was second in succession in managing the amphitheatre.

Licensed in 1783 by the Surrey magistrates, Astley was ready in the following year for his major undertaking of a fully-developed amphitheatre with the addition of a stage, an addition which he was impelled to make in competition with Hughes and Dibdin. The building came into being in a manner fully worthy of his original mind. For building material he went to Covent Garden, where hustings had recently been erected for an election. Offering rewards to the porters and loiterers of the neighbourhood, he removed the timber to Westminster and, relying on his own architectural conception, Astley's Royal Grove (the title arising from the idea of giving the auditorium the appearance of a glade in a wood), soon rose in place of the original riding-house. Here, in 1787, perhaps in memory of Marie Antoinette, young Astley taught his horse to dance Vestris' Minuet. A season in Paris about this time gave rise to one of Astley's most magnificent gestures. He had introduced a number of tumbling acts into his performance, and in these the Prefect of Police sensed an infringement of the law which permitted no duplication of entertainments in the Parisian theatres. He was warned that this part of his show was therefore illegal. He refused to be intimidated, and mounted the acrobats by means of a large platform, on horseback, and so the performance remained equestrian.

It was in the year 1787 also that Astley associated himself with the Sadler's Wells' management in a plea for a form of burletta licence which should regularize the dramatic elements of their entertainments. A similar demand was also made by the Royal Circus proprietors. The request from Sadler's Wells met with a refusal from the Lord Chamberlain, accompanied by the rather biting comment, "Is it because they are the oldest offenders that I am to grant this permission?"

However, in the following year, we may imagine, largely through Astley's influence, the permission was obtained for the three houses, which included pantomimes as permitted entertainments.

An immense variety of artists continued to pass through Astley's hands ; his clowns included Johannot, who seceded from the Royal Circus, the elder Grimaldi, Dubois, the elder Laurent and Wallack, father of the celebrated actor who built Wallack's Theatre in New York. He made considerable sums of money and invested his profits in the promotion of amphitheatres in the provinces. In 1794 a disastrous fire at the Royal Saloon, as his house in Westminster was known at the time, recalled him to England, for he was at the moment serving as a volunteer with his old friend the Duke of York. On his return he at once rebuilt the theatre : it was ready by Easter 1795 and opened under the title of Astley's Amphitheatre of Arts. The new house, De Castro assures us, cost an immense sum of money, " it was the astonishment of everyone who knew of it, how he could have realized such a sum . . . but it showed that he was that kind of man, that he was ever determined to surmount all obstacles, however hard they might appear to be effected." It was during the interregnum occasioned by this fire that Astley took his horses to Arnold's Lyceum Theatre.

On the return of the troops from the war in 1802 he made the gesture of setting aside a number of free seats every evening for the use of demobilized soldiers, an act which made for considerable popularity. While on the campaign Astley had taken part in the siege of Valenciennes, and on his return made this event the subject of a spectacle.

In 1803 Astley returned to France to parley with Napoleon Buonaparte for compensation in respect of the building attached to his amphitheatre in Paris which had been commandeered during the Revolution. The property was returned to him and a rental allowed for the period during which it had been held by the Government. While making these arrangements he heard of a second fire at his house in London. Being naturally anxious to return home he discovered that he was unable to obtain a passport : an order had just been made detaining English subjects, a measure of reprisal for the seizing by the English of French ships. By a romantic ruse Astley made good his escape. He feigned illness and obtained leave to drink the waters at Montpelier. On horseback from this place he got to the coast, with a brace of pistols " threatening the postillion with immediate dissolution " if he did not make all possible haste.

The new amphitheatre, built after the fire of 1803, outlived Astley. It was the house described in *Sketches by Boz*. Dickens' first visits probably took place in the early 'twenties which would account for his remarking that " it was not a Royal Amphitheatre in those days." The form of the house was that of an " elongated lyre," with the very unusual distance of fifty feet from the stage

to the back of the pit. The decorations were in white, lemon and gold, and the hangings of crimson. The "ride" had a border about four feet high which was painted in imitation of stonework. The ceiling was supported by trellis-work pilasters and contained a circular opening, through which a cut-glass chandelier was let down by machinery over the ring. It was this device which Dickens refers to as a "hoop composed of jets of gas." The forty-feet proscenium opening displayed a "radiant head of Apollo," and a remarkable feature of the proscenium was that it could be widened or heightened at will : one can think of no modern parallel of this device except the expanding screen which has been used in certain films. What would now be regarded as a piece of typical modernist stage technique was to be found in the various "levels" of Astley's stage ; these were formed by enormous rostrums, removable in sections by machinery, along which, hidden by painted ground rows, moved in procession the horses and other animals used in the spectacles.

At this point in his career Astley made his first serious mistake in policy. On the site of a house belonging to the Duke of Craven in Wych Street he made an attack on the West End of London with another amphitheatre. This time he called the building a pavilion, and he collected material for it in his most characteristic manner. Lying in the Thames was an old and disused barge called the *Ville de Paris*. He bought the hulk, and from its timbers he constructed the frame of his pavilion, the design of which, actually bearing some resemblance to a tent, he himself supervised. Under the management of a syndicate which included his son, the place was a complete failure, and he was glad to sell it to William Elliston. The latter opened it under the name of "Little Drury Lane," thereby offending the proprietors of the patent theatre. In spite of this very bad beginning, however, the house survived as the Olympic and became famous first by the management of Mathews and Madame Vestris, and later, under Farren and Alfred Wigan, by Frederick Robson.

The end of Astley's great career was in sight. His management, split now among a number of sharers, was deputed largely to his son. His later years, in which the idiosyncrasies of his character became more marked, were full of delightful incidents. He was incapable of humdrum activity, there is to be found a note of individuality at all the turning points in his life ; as when, pressed for money after the second fire which attacked his theatre, he met his obligations from a secret store of guinea pieces which he had hoarded over a period of many years. The vice of most great impressarii is the occasional abuse of autocracy. In Astley's case this took the form of excessive interference in the literary and musical elements in his entertainments, of which he was without

expert knowledge. His extensive blue pencilling of the burlettas submitted to him evoked the retaliation of a certain Mr. Oakman, who, after a somewhat embittered interview with the manager, chalked on his office door the words, " Mangling done here." In the same category is the well-known story of his threat to dismiss the trombone player in his orchestra for laziness, because he played his instrument so sparingly. He was, indeed, rather unlucky in his relations with musicians, if the stories of two misunderstandings are true. The first is of an occasion when a large stage flat was being sawn by a carpenter during a rehearsal in which the stringed instruments figured prominently. " Don't saw so loud ! " shouted Astley, disturbed by the intrusive sound. At the end of the rehearsal the principal violin gave in his resignation.

On another occasion a special piece of music had been composed for a stage fight. This was being tried over, and Astley being dissatisfied with the weapons of the combatants, said emphatically, " We must have Shields." He was much surprised when the composer of the music sent a message to the effect that if he desired to engage William Shields to compose for him he was at liberty to do so.

Astley died in Paris in 1814. His son did not long survive him and until 1824 the Amphitheatre in London came under the management of Davies, his assistant. During his régime the less happy plagiarism from the Royal Circus of a fox-hunt was presented in the arena. Then Alexander Ducrow, perhaps the greatest equestrian in history, took the Amphitheatre and revived its glories. He was no stranger to the house, having ridden for Astley in 1808. The year before he had been performing at the Royal Circus. Under his management, which lasted for about sixteen years, the celebrated equestrian drama called *Mazeppa, or the Wild Horse of Tartary*, was produced.[1]

In 1844 the theatre was rebuilt by William Batty, whose career, passing through all the stages of showmanship, had been earlier linked with that of " Old Wilde," the itinerant booth manager whose history will be briefly dealt with later.

The tradition of Astley's was now a major influence in European entertainment : the subsequent history of the house need not detain us. As the century advanced, its individual importance waned : in 1873 its original methods were revived by Sanger. Dion Boucicault was also in management there and conducted it as a drama house.

To Astley, more than to any other individual, the stage owed

[1]The play was an adaptation of Byron's poem made by M. G. Lewis. The celebrated Ada Isaacs Mencken appeared in a version of the same drama, also at Astley's, in the 'sixties.

the existence of that strange medley of horse-display, dancing, clowning, drama and fireworks, which for many years constituted a normal output of the minor theatres. In creating this junction between many diverse elements, he created the conditions from which the later music hall inherited its cosmopolitan characteristics. There were, of course, other sources from which this diversity was spread: the major theatres, through John Rich, had contributed pantomime, and this form had naturally reacted to the innovations of Astley, adding in the process of time further complications.

When the public-houses, the nursery of convivial singing, became involved in the general fever for theatrical presentation, they borrowed freely from the medley around them and stood revealed after the Act of 1843 as the true exploiting ground of all that which the regular theatre was now ripe to abandon.

The example set in high places had penetrated into every nook and cranny where a performance was physically possible. Even the streets teemed with imitations of the minor theatre in many of its aspects, and were particularly vulnerable to the vogue for "Æthiopian Serenaders."

Wherever a shed or a disused stable could be secured, it was put to the purpose of an entertainment which professed to reproduce the glories of the Adelphi, Astley's, or Vauxhall. Even the patent theatres' proprietary rights were invaded. Since the booths had no legal status of any kind they were, on the whole, less liable to interference, but there are not wanting cases in which, for the offence of playing scenes from Shakespeare to a juvenile audience at a penny and twopence a head, whole companies were brought before the majesty of the law. Such an instance was afforded by the arrest, in 1831, of the entire *dramatis personæ* of a penny gaff in St. Giles', "together with the band, money-takers, candle-snuffers, etc., sixteen in number," who were brought before Mr. Hall, the magistrate, on a charge of being rogues and vagabonds. In this case, however, judgment was entered for the defendants; the superintendent of police had entered the house without information or warrant, and the prisoners were discharged, "to the great joy of these poorest of the children of Thespis."

In the seedy improvised performances of the street corner such well-known creations as Sam Cowell's "Billy Barlow" were exemplified by name among the itinerant clowns and tumblers, and even "Punch and Judy" shows kept themselves up to date to the extent of including a "Jim Crow," who, as "Black Sambo," is still to be found among the caste of the few remaining examples of to-day. But the movement indoors was becoming universal. Showmen were complaining that the "Concerts" had now become so cheap (more accurately stated, so numerous at a cheap

rate of admission), that most of the performers were leaving the streets for indoor employment. With typical conservatism these concerts were held to be low-down affairs, far less respectable than the street singing.

From the earliest days of the nineteenth century the example set in high places had been followed by the booth and tent theatres. The same medley with which Astley and the Royal Circus influenced the London theatres was reproduced in miniature round the country. To the art of Vincent Crummles with his ballets, songs and fireworks was added the equestrian drama in its simpler forms as exemplified by " Billy Button's Ride to Brentford." The travelling circus visited by Alfred Rosling Bennett in the 'fifties disappointed him. The performance he describes occurred at Greenwich, and he was attracted to it by the advertisements which, with pictorial embellishments, announced " Dick Turpin's Ride to York, and the Affecting Death of Black Bess, Represented by the Leading Equestrians of the Day." It may be that a prophetic instinct for stage realism dimmed his appreciation of the exciting chase of Turpin round and round the ring, accompanied by the exchange of shots between the highwayman and the Bow Street runners in pursuit ; the climax being superbly reached when Black Bess, at a given cue, lay down and her master made a hurried exit with his face hidden in the sleeves of his highwayman's coat.

The most impressive figure among the booth proprietors of whom detailed records are available is that of Samuel Wilde, whose recollections were published in the 'eighties. He belonged to the class of showman whose characteristics were equally compounded of childlike simplicity and adventurous audacity. As the friend and instructor of some of the great men of his craft, he earned a place in theatrical history, for if he did not, as Richardson did, harbour so great an actor as Edmund Kean, he was at various times the employer or partner of William Batty and Anderson, the " Wizard of the North"[1]; Wallet, who rather

[1]As an addition to this reference and others in the book to James Henry Anderson, the following biographical details may be appended. They are taken from a work entitled *The New Universal Conjuror ; explaining all the magic tricks of the most celebrated Wizards, Magicians, and Conjurors . . . with the lives and adventures of Professor Anderson, Wizard of the North ; and Senior Bosco, Wizard of the World.*

Born in Kincardine, O'Neil, Aberdeenshire. First public appearance on his own account as a conjuror in Edinburgh ; where his success was so great that Sir Walter Scott . . . requested that he would perform at Abbotsford, on the occasion of the son of the great novelist attaining his majority.

Scott is said to have remarked to him : " They call me the Wizard of the North, but it is you not I who deserve that title." Anderson thereupon adopted the phrase. After achieving a considerable success in Scotland and the Northern and Midland counties, he erected, on Glasgow Green, the largest theatre in Scotland. After three months it was destroyed by fire, during a rehearsal of *Der Freischutz*.

Later he toured in Sweden, Denmark, and the Baltic towns. He appeared at St. Petersburg before the Emperor of Russia. He toured in Russia and erected his

gratuitously went by the name of " The Queen's Jester," and David Prince Miller, who himself from the humblest type of strolling conjuror, survived as an important theatre proprietor to present the farewell appearances of Macready and of Madame Vestris.

Wilde's management reproduced during his career every variety of minor theatre, from circus, by way of the amphitheatre, to pure theatre. His first independent venture, after a youthful term as an orchestral clarionet player, was as proprietor of a small travelling circus, which must have constituted one of the first of its kind, for it was the influence of Astley alone which was responsible for the existence in England of this type of entertainment. His numerous children and his wife all took part in the highly technical crafts of tight-rope and slack-rope dancing, in the training of performing animals, in acting the melodramatic interludes with their combats and " rides," and in the feats of magic and legerdemain, of which Wilde himself was especially an expert.

Through many incredible vicissitudes the family gradually achieved prosperity. A scheme by which they attracted their humble public, but which was frowned upon by the authorities and landed them in difficulty, was the institution of a lottery to take the place of admission fees. The prizes offered were extremely varied and remind one of Mrs. Lane's gifts at the Britannia Theatre, consisting of such articles of homely usage as sacks of flour or small coal, or sometimes, ornamentally, of tea-trays or snuff-boxes. To this list was at other times added pigs, or even horses, but of the latter it is stated that they were usually won by persons with whom the management was " on speaking terms."

It was in 1820 that the Wildes definitely amalgamated the theatrical and circus elements of their entertainment, and scenery was requisitioned from an artist at Halifax who provided the proprietor with a street scene, a " room or parlour," and a " wood or shady grove."

When the itinerant showman, " Pep Dawson," later famous as Anderson, the Wizard of the North, came into the partnership, the company was enlarged. Punch and Judy and the " Ombres Chinoises " were introduced, and a singing acrobat, of the name of Lightwood, engaged. Then came an equilibrist who balanced on his person a twenty-foot plank and a live donkey (presumably the redoubtable Billy, the learned animal who at first comprised the entire menagerie).

It is a memorable instance of the romantic vicissitudes of the

magic temple in most of the chief towns of that extensive empire. After visiting America, he appeared with great success in London at the Strand, Adelphi, Lyceum, Covent Garden, and St. James's theatres. At Covent Garden he appeared as an actor in the character of Rob Roy, and it was at the conclusion of this season, after a ball masqué, that the house was completely destroyed by fire.

showman's life, that at this period the family became friendly with William Batty, then an animal trainer of the humblest type and afterwards the proprietor of Astley's Amphitheatre and helped him when his luck was completely out, and his tent damaged by a storm.

At Rotherham, in which the Wildes gave frequent dramatic seasons in the Theatre Royal (actually a disused chapel), commands reached them from Wentworth House, the home of the Earl Fitzwilliam ; and how delightful it is to learn that these appearances were, in fact, bespoken by the men and maidservants of the establishment, " to cheer them up " ! One's heart goes out to the butler who entertained them in return for their services. " He was a good old soul," one reads, " and returned cheer for cheer."

Then Wallett, the self-styled " Queen's Jester," who had, with many of his kind, an unquenchable reverence for the Royal Family, appeared in the scene. The warmest of friendships sprung up between him and Wilde—" we were inseparable friends and bedfellows," writes the old man—and the spectacle of *The Bottle Imp* was added to the repertoire, for which the many-talented Wallett painted the scenery, which included a vision of Venice by sunset, an " illuminated saloon," and " The Dungeon of the Inquisition on Fire." The programme for these performances was completed by Mr. Hunter on the tight-rope, a duet, " Polly Hopkins and Tommy Tomkins," and a farce.

With the arrival of Powell, an equestrian who, as capital, brought four horses into the business, the alliance between circus and drama was completed and a period of increasing prosperity inaugurated. In such ways the large proportion of the whole field of variety entertainment brought into focus by Philip Astley was reproduced and carried about the country. " Old Wilde " is a single and rather humble instance of a large grouping of shows which by this amalgam of theatre and circus was perpetuated but which, in its momentum, absorbed many themes of variety entertainment.

The classic example of the showman's career, within living memory, is that of " Lord " George Sanger, who in his autobiography is able to boast proudly that he rescued Astley's from the bankruptcy into which it had fallen after the régime of E. T. Smith, and the experiments in legitimate drama conducted there by Dion Boucicault. The output of Sanger was magnificently true to the traditional craft, and though remembered primarily in connection with his huge circus menagerie, reproduced all its characteristics and ideals with an exactitude which included, in the use of historical pageantry, Charles Dibdin's mediæval enthusiasms.

By such means was kept in the foreground very considerable elements of variety which were handed on to the music hall and brought it into line with a wider tradition. The tale must now be taken up within this narrower field, and on ground unaffected by the influences in this chapter.

CHAPTER VII

"*Evans's Late Joys*"

" And when the Opera is out,
And all the girls are home,
Our swells light up the social pipe
And unto Evans roam."

THE keynote of Evans's was the determined anti-feminism of the mid-Victorian Bohemian. Although at its height, rather self-consciously a revival of the eighteenth-century coterie, Evans's was, in fact, the reflection of a very different kind of club life from that which assembled, as did the famous " Catamarans," such men as Theodore Hook, Richard Brinsley Sheridan and Monk Lewis. These free-living and outspoken personalities were now exchanged for the circle of men who founded the Arundel and Re-Union Clubs ; their membership drawn from such blameless stock as E. L. Blanchard and his cronies. These men eagerly supported Evans's, whose innocuous revels, lasting into the small hours of the morning, were a refuge from the responsibilities of home. For life at Evans's was exclusively male : only at a late date did the management reluctantly admit a feminine element. Still, it was a refuge which involved no loss of moral status ; and its greatest popularity was achieved by fostering a reaction against the freedom of the Cider Cellars and the singing of W. G. Ross, who was never allowed to enter its doors. The enthusiasm so freely expressed for the adoption at Evans's of an older form of entertainment, though important as a factor in music-hall development, was, on the whole, a superficial one ; the background of glees, madrigals and the like performed by cathedral choir-boys, helped in providing a pleasant illusion of " the good old days " over which an easy sentimentality might range. But there was very little spontaneity in the matter, and several commentators reveal, between the lines, the fact that more than a little boredom was engendered by this aspect of the place.

Still, there were many compensations. The comedians and " buffo " singers of the time were well represented by John

Caulfield, John Penniket, J. W. Sharpe, John Binge and others, while Evans's moreover could claim an almost proprietary right in the hero of the hour, Sam Cowell. And of the old guard there were Labern, Harry Sidney, Charles Sloman, and others, who played an important part in the life of the place.

George Augustus Sala, in his *Twice Round the Clock*, speaks a trifle vaguely of Evans's as having grown out of one of the more notorious of the " night cellars." This is hardly a fair statement of the case. Certainly, the house (the basement floor of which formed the original site of Evans's supper room) had been a tavern since 1733. But a tavern definitely of the higher class. Prior to this date it had, as a private house, passed through distinguished hands. Both Sir Kenelm Digby and Admiral the Earl of Orford had lived there, and the latter had immortalized his tenure in two delightful ways : by adding a fine carved stairway which survived to the present century, and by bestowing the name of " Piazza " upon the foundlings frequently deposited upon his doorstep, the picturesque name being chosen in honour of the chief architectural feature of Covent Garden.

The conversion of the house to a tavern was carried out in the grand manner and under the patronage of a number of peers of the realm, whence its banqueting room became known as the Star Chamber. Advertisements, moreover, stated that the house contained accommodation and stabling for " one hundred noblemen and horses."

At the end of the century the property was acquired by one Joy, a circumstance which gave rise to facetiousness when, later, the lamps at the door bore the inscription " Evans's late Joys." Evans himself, who took the tavern towards the end of the Regency, with its aristocratic honours still upon it, had been a chorister at the opera. In the existing basement room he at first directed singing evenings according to the gentleman-amateur tradition of the eighteenth century. Later, the full glories of the place were to be celebrated in the hall built over the ground at the back of the house.[1] The element of professionalism, provided in part by Evans himself, who is reported to have excelled in two songs, *The Englishman* and *If I Had a Thousand a Year*, gradually encroached, and when, in 1844, Evans retired and the business came into the hands of his musical director, Greenmore, also formerly a singer in the theatre, the house began to present a fully-organized entertainment, of a character not to be found elsewhere in London. Circumstances —among them the sense of tradition inherent in the place, and

[1]John Hollingshead gives 1854 as the date of the building of the larger rooms, He adds that the garden to the Earl of Orford's house had contained two cottages. one of which had been tenanted by John Philip Kemble.

the characteristics of both Evans and Greenmore—combined in giving it that rather artificial smugness which was reflected from the platform. Contemporary writers, in enthusiastic acceptance, jostled one another in urging the claim that here, at least, might be enjoyed good English music, as elevating to the mind as it was enjoyable to the senses. The fact was, that the moment was an admirable one for this gesture of an improving and high-minded conviviality. It was yet another symptom of the prevailing craze for linking up every undertaking with some sort of moral or social "purpose." How far that craze had taken root can only be fully appreciated when it is remembered that the pious works of Exeter Hall and of the Temperance and Total Abstinence movements was invading even such forms of popular entertainment as the nigger minstrels, giving a fantastic oddness beyond all belief to the performances inspired by imitations of poor Jim Crow of Cincinatti. Evans is said to have been a red-faced old-fashioned kind of man, and Greenmore was such another. He is described, moreover, by Hollingshead as "prosy." One suspects that he was, in fact, a bore. "A host of the older school," says Gilbert A'Beckett of Evans, whom he met the year before the latter retired. "He strutted about the room, beaming," says Clement Scott of Greenmore; which means that both men indulged in that form of personal assiduity which even now pleases some people. Greenmore came to be known affectionately as old "Paddy Green." He carried a snuff-box, acted the crony to his regular patrons, and called them his "dear boys."

True to the mediæval principle that a buffoon should form part of the amusements of a gentleman, there was provided, not as once would have been the case, a hermaphrodite or a hunchback, but a harmless butt, in the person of the now elderly Van Joel, of whose earlier exploits at Vauxhall Gardens we have already heard something. At Evans's this gentleman divided his time between the performance of his celebrated bird imitations and the vending of cigars at the supper tables. With what enthusiasm would they have welcomed the late-lamented Simpson of Vauxhall at Evans's. Still, the old guard was not without its representatives. There were Thackeray, Ballantine or Lord Exmouth to lend the touch of an old-world grace and culture. It is true that these gentlemen might also be seen on other evenings at the Cyder Cellars or the Coal Hole, and Burnand, arriving at the former haunt when, as a rather frightened boy, he was tasting the sensations of a first "night out," found the distinguished group of *habitués* assembled round the smoke-room fire. Still, the moral status which was imperilled by their association with these places was reaffirmed by the utterance of public rebukes and, as the whole world knows (it is impossible to read any reminiscences

of the period without meeting with some reference to the matter), an early incident in *The Newcomes* contains the famous condemnation of Ross's performance of *Sam Hall*, implied in the incident of Colonel Newcome's outburst at "The Cave of Harmony."[1]

George Augustus Sala, and Ewing Ritchie, in quite differing ways, provide a complete eye-witness's account of the proceedings in Covent Garden. Midnight, "when all the girls were home," was the correct time at which to arrive. In Paddy Green's days, when the larger room had been built, entering down the two or three steps which are still to be seen, one made one's way through the smaller room to the Hall, where at long tables groups of gentlemen were seated, taking supper and listening, or half listening, to the efforts of the entertainers on the large platform at the end of the room, which was flanked by Corinthian pillars, backed by a large apse, and supported a grand piano and a harmonium. Much has been made of the food consumed at Evans's, and it is important, for appreciation of its atmosphere, to remember that the place was essentially a cabaret in which entertainment was incidental to refreshment. There is a concensus of opinion that the food supplied was good, and that the prices charged for it were high. The style of the menu was that of the high-class chop house. Favourite dishes were poached eggs on steak and devilled kidneys seasoned with red pepper. The baked potatoes in their jackets inspired poems in their day, and the brown ale, porter, stout and brandy, served to the clients in those happy times, at all hours of the night, enjoyed their full share of literary appreciation. There are records of a "calculating waiter" who bluffed the more unsuspecting customers by the rapidity with which he concocted a fictitious reckoning, and who, like Joel, was enshrined as an institution. Then there was Skinner, the surly porter, identified by some as the waiter himself. Without such privileged Aborigines the place would have been lacking in an element of its cherished, if artificial flavour.

Sala, Clement Scott, Gilbert A'Beckett, Burnand Edmund Yates, Ballantine, George R. Sims, and the rest have written of the "homeliness" comfort and good-fellowship of Evans's, of its attic wit, and of its camaraderie and there can be no doubt that in the best years they enjoyed themselves there. The mental picture afforded by the many descriptions of the place is not unpleasing. The lofty hall, with its chaste neo-Grecian embellishments, the tables humming with conversation—(this in spite of the adjuration printed on the green-covered programme booklets that "Gentlemen are respectfully requested to encourage the vocalists by attention: the café part of the room being intended for conversational parties")—and old Van Joel doddering round

[1]But perhaps he was thinking of Joe Wells?

the hall selling the cigars which all commentators take relish in describing as bad, and telling the purchasers that, upon a date not yet fixed he is giving a benefit concert, and will they kindly purchase a ticket?

In this setting a miscellaneous entertainment was given. It was in two parts. In the earlier section the boys from the Savoy Chapel sang their glees and part songs. The words for these were printed in the green books mentioned above, together with antiquarian notes (forerunners of the Queen's Hall analytical programme), and A'Beckett is proud of the remembrance that Paddy Green was in the habit of showing him these works in proof, and of asking him for a critical opinion. The performance of boys and a solo or two by Binge or S. A. Jones constituted this introductory concert. The choral singing, which included a number by adult voices, often comprised platform performances of scenes from operas, an innovation claimed by Evans's, and imitated by Charles Morton at the Canterbury Hall. The adoption of this convention was subjected to a certain amount of ridicule in contemporary journals and is disrespectfully remembered by subsequent writers.

The real fun began considerably later in the evening, when Sam Cowell and the other comic vocalists arrived. Cowell, who was an American by birth, and came to London by way of Scotland, was the actual agent of Evans's triumphant success. This ripe vocalist and comedian, who died at the age of forty-four, has left behind him a vividly remembered personality, and undoubtedly ranks, with artists such as Dan Leno and Arthur Roberts, among the greatest exponents of entertainment. As is always the case, a remarkable gift of facial expression emphasized his sense of comedy, and both these characteristics have been inherited, together with a strong family resemblance, by his daughter, Mrs. A. B. Tapping, and by his grand-daughter, Miss Sydney Fairbrother. His voice was round, clear, and well produced. His power of mimicry was considerable, and, an actor before everything, he penetrated the characters he presented while retaining that mysterious "plus" of personality without which no entertainer can make his special type of effect.

His first appearance in London occurred when he was thirty-one years old, and his first engagement at Evans's followed upon an appearance in E. L. Blanchard's burlesque on the Great Exhibition of 1851, called *Nobody in London*. Like his great contemporary, Robson (who immediately preceded him as a concert entertainer), he made extensive use of the comic narrative-ballad. A number of these were written for him, such as the

[1]He sang in opera at the Surrey and Olympic Theatres and at Covent Garden, but not, as Emily Soldene suggests in her memoirs, with Robson at the Grecian. He joined the Grecian later, under Conquest.

Hamlet, Macbeth and Othello burlesques ; others were revivals and current successes, such as *Alonzo the Brave*,[1] *Villikins and His Dinah*, and *The Ratcatcher's Darter*.

The latter song, so famous in the form in which Cowell sang it, the lyric by the Rev. E. Bradley (as Cuthbert Bede, the author of *Verdant Green*), and the tune occasionally attributed to Cowell himself, was probably, as Renton Nicholson in his autobiography avers it was, a re-hash of an earlier song.[2]

With this song together with a typical ballad called *Billy Barlow*, Cowell achieved the height of his vogue. I have not been able to discover an authorship for *Billy Barlow ;* the earliest edition of it to be found at the British Museum, dated *c.* 1852, only refers to an arrangement by C. L. Sanders. The song's value lay in the creation of a character, slender enough in cold print, but easily brought to life in performance, and made the mouthpiece of a commentary on passing events. The song embodied no new device, and in no way, except, perhaps, by a happy turn in the traditional melody, has it any intrinsic value, but in Cowell's hands it brought a new name into everyday speech. The universal nature of the " Barlow " vogue is reflected in its use among the penny gaff and street performers, and it even provided an addition to the caste of *Punch and Judy*.

With other songs in Cowell's repertory I have dealt elsewhere : the most characteristic picture of him is undoubtedly his appearance in the " Billy Barlow " costume, which consisted of the tattered remnants of a workman's dress, the cord of a dressing-gown tied round the waist, a clay pipe in hand, and one eye badly blacked ; the whole crowned by the famous brimless hat.

It is supposed that Greenmore, his reactionary nature ill-disposed to the triumphs of the modern comedian, was more than a little jealous of Cowell's overwhelming success. Cowell was of a prodigal nature, and not given to punctuality, so that on many occasions the house was kept waiting for him. Nevertheless, his appearance, however late, was invariably greeted with an ovation. On one occasion the irate Greenmore, infuriated by the audience's leniency towards its favourite, smote the table with his fist, and thundered, " You've made Mr. Cowell your God, gentlemen, but by God, he shan't be mine." Cowell did not live to enjoy his popularity for long. In 1860, by which time his appearances at the Canterbury Hall had established the fortune of that house, he returned to America. On this tour his health gave way, and in 1864, having come back to England, he died at a friend's house in Dorsetshire.

[1]E. L. Blanchard records in his diary that he wrote this song in 1847 for his old friend, J. B. Howe.

[2]Nicholson states that he remembers hearing it at Harmonic Meetings in Covent Garden in the 'twenties.

Of almost equal importance to Evans's and an artist of universal popularity was J. W. Sharpe, a mercurial comedian whose style has been compared by Chance Newton to that of Arthur Roberts. Sharpe, whose work was also identified with White Conduit House, the Cyder Cellars and Vauxhall Gardens, was even shorter-lived than Cowell, and died in 1856 at the age of thirty-eight, in the Dover Workhouse, as the result of exposure and semi-starvation. Ewing Ritchie, for whom it may be claimed that he was the James Douglas of his day,[1] does not fail, in his *Night Haunts of London*, to remind us of this unfortunate occurrence, and implies some responsibility on the part of Evans's for Sharpe's tragic downfall. In his chapter dealing with the Song and Supper Rooms, after having spoken of the deleterious effects, both physical and moral, of a form of entertainment associated with late hours, smoking, and the consumption of alcohol, he arrives at the following peroration : " You tell me the comic singer is a happy fellow, that he gets six guineas a week,[2] that he lives in a nice little cottage in the Hampstead Road. I know better than you : the man I write of, after having been the attraction of the Cave of Harmony for years, after having been feasted by the nobility and gentry, after having led a life of pleasure on the most extravagant scale, will go down, yet young, as a beggar, to one of our seaport towns, and after craving in vain a refuge from the winter's cold and a crust of bread, will die in the workhouse, and be buried in a pauper's grave. How many of the gay young fellows around us will have a similar termination to their career ? I never can pass the Cave of Harmony without thinking of the Comic Singer as I last saw him—in the very flush of health and life, stimulated by wine and applause, little dreaming of the workhouse in which he was so soon to beg for room to die."

Sharpe, unlike Cowell, Robson and other great comic singers, was not associated with any one particular song, or even type of song. Although I can discern no trace in his published repertoire of anything even hinting at indecency, he certainly had some reputation for being *risqué* and his appearances at Vauxhall Gardens in 1847 provoked the comment that the management was now engaging singers of the " fast school." The charge was probably justified by the artist's introduction of gags and stage business, and herein, maybe, lay the resemblance to the style of Roberts. Sharpe (and this is a frequently found characteristic of the earlier comedians) indulged at times in a vein of dramatic sentiment, and one of his songs composed by James Bruton, the vocalist, and arranged by M. Corri, deals, in the manner of the

[1] I am indebted to my friend, Mr. W. L. Hanchant, for this interesting simile.

[2] Sharpe is actually credited with earnings as much as £80 on his total weekly appearances.

temperance songs of a later date, with the evils of *The Bottle*.

The songs in his repertoire most often quoted are two by John Labern : *Who'll Buy My Images* and *Pity the Downfall of Poor Punch and Judy*. Many of his songs were the work of this composer, who is a rather considerable figure among the song writers of the period. Parody, an extremely popular form at the time, constituted a large proportion of his work. Songs of this type performed by Sharpe included *A Dainty Plant is the Cabbage Green*, one of a number of burlesques on the clergyman's song in *The Pickwick Papers*, which had been originally set by Thomas Haynes Bayly. Another and better-known version of the same theme was *The Lively Flea*, which W. G. Ross helped to popularize. A further parody was that on Henry Russell's *There's a Good Time Coming*, composed to the lyric by Dr. Charles Mackay. In the *Cadger's Ball*, also by John Labern, one seems to sense something of the actual quality of the singer, but it is difficult to get evidence of a style from the songs as a whole. Sharpe's indebteness to Labern is the one definite factor.[1] His early life is obscure : an appearance in the 'thirties at White Conduit House is on record. Rather unusually in the case of a comic singer whose work spread over the 'forties and 'fifties, I can find no trace of any connection with the theatre. Perhaps he hardly earned so high a place as he by tradition holds in the hierarchy of comedians; it is possible that the romantic associations of his reckless life and the very name, Jack Sharpe, together with the hint that he resembled Arthur Roberts, acts unduly upon the imagination ; but there is also to be taken into account E. L. Blanchard's and E. W. Mackney's testimony that he was the greatest comic singer of his day.

Sam Collins, who was known at all the concert rooms, was another important artist at Evans's. His real name was Vagg, and he began life as a chimney-sweep. The peripatetic method of his former trade appears to have clung to him in his early professional career, for he is described as having tramped from one singing room to another. his clothes tied up in a bundle and carried on a stick over his shoulder. Collins earned his considerable reputation by translating the stage Irishman to the concert rooms ; his best remembered song is *The Rocky Road to*

[1]Labern was himself an entertainer of some note, and appears to have sung without accompaniment. He was born *c.* 1815 and died *c.* 1880. A portrait of him in a miniature edition of his songs dated 1865 is indited, " I remain, dear Sharpe, yours very truly, John Labern." The portrait exhibits a refined and interesting face. Two MS. notes, written on the fly leaf of an earlier edition of the songs, are in separate hands, and read as follows :—

" Labern was music collector at Chappell and Beale's (Cramer). In 1873 he was keeping a newspaper shop and snuff, etc., at top of New Road, two or three doors from Tottenham Court Road. He and Beuler were the best comic song Writters [*sic*] of the Period."

Dublin, though it is unlikely, as H. G. Hibbert has pointed out, " that he ever trod that road." That he was a prudent and successful member of his profession is shown by the fact that at the age of thirty he had acquired an interest in the " Rose of Normandy " concert rooms in Church Street, Marylebone, from which he created the Marylebone Music Hall, and which, in 1861, he leased to William Botting in order to extend his investments to the Landsdowne Tavern in Islington Green, which he opened in the following year as Collins's Music Hall. The house had been developed on similar lines a few months previously by the proprietor Montgomery, but until Collins took it, it had proved a notable failure. Even then, the new manager risked a serious *débâcle* by being obliged to wait for over six months for the transfer of the Music and Dancing Licence. Collins's fame undoubtedly rested to a large extent upon personal popularity: exploitation of the conventional songs of the Irish type, such as *Limerick Races*, was of great familiarity in other spheres; and apart from these, such lyrics as *Pity the Downfall of Uncle Sam* hardly suggest a distinctive method. On his death in 1865 he bequeathed his Islington property to his widow, who engaged Harry Sydney, a close friend of her husband, as manager. And it was Harry Sydney who penned Collins's epitaph, to be seen in Kensal Green Cemetery, which runs as follows:

> A loving husband and a faithful friend,
> Ever the first a helping hand to lend;
> Farewell, good-natured, honest-hearted Sam,
> Until we meet before the Great I AM.

The house, ever since associated with his name, has been open with very little interruption since its foundation; in recent years it has achieved success with a permanent repertory company, with Chas. A. Baker as its leading actor, an artist whose death was a great loss to the simpler kind of melodrama. After a somewhat futile attempt to revive the " old-time music hall," with a chairman—for which the veteran Leo Dryden was engaged—it again began functioning as a variety house under normal conditions.

Harry Sydney, who is especially remembered by Gilbert A'Beckett as singing *A Quiet Sort of Man* and *Let the World Jog Along* at Evans's, was as popular there as he was in later life at Collins's. These, and *A Rolling Stone Was Never Known to Gain Much Moss*, are said to have been his most popular songs. The short and effective rhythmical chorus of *A Rolling Stone* may have explained its vogue, but the words (Sydney was his own librettist) are particularly dreary. It has been said of him that he was " the one vocalist among the many music hall artists who ap-

proached the closest to the rhymsters of old. His songs were always records of passing events effectively tinged with satire." This statement begs many questions, but it serves to point the fact that he was popular as a topical vocalist who pleased the old guard by his methods and personality.

When Charles Morton built the Oxford Music Hall in 1861, Sidney was engaged by him and made regular appearances there during the first management. Collins's, which he called "the little Gold-mine," no doubt owed a great deal to his chairmanship, and not long before his death in 1870 he acted as manager for the Philharmonic Hall, Islington, during the time when Morton, having taken over the "Spittoon," as this hall was then affectionately called, was marking time before securing a regular theatre licence there.

Collins's was later sold to a man called Watts, whose wife, a stage artist, took benefit nights at the house, at which Harry Sydney assisted. In gratitude, the Watts' offered the use of the hall to Sydney's widow on his death, and a performance was organized on her behalf. Frederick Strange (the restaurateur who later managed the Alhambra), Paddy Green, and others, also raised subscriptions. Both Sydney's popularity and his improvidence are indicated by these facts.

Similar in type, but with more definite characteristics, was Harry Clifton, whose work was especially suitable to the more old-fashioned concert room, and who figured at Evans's. Clifton was a prolific and successful writer of lyrics; he is also credited with the composition of many of their melodies, but here his claims have a full proportion of that nebulousness associated with many music-hall composer-vocalists. Like Sidney, he specialized in motto songs, and brought this form to a high pitch of popularity. Some of these have remained with us, and the phrases have acquired an added solemnity: *Wait for the Turn of the Tide*, *Pulling Hard Against the Stream*, and *Paddle Your Own Canoe* are perhaps the most famous. Combined with that strong element of wish-fulfilment which is embedded in so many popular songs of all periods, is the hardly less important element of stoicism, together with that quality which the authors of the valuable book called *The Variety Stage* at one time call "camarderie" and at another, "bonhomerie." Both qualities may be found in Clifton's songs, and are effectively present in the following stanza:

"Then love your neighbour as yourself
As the world you go travelling through,
And never sit down with a tear or a frown,
But paddle your own canoe."

Wait for the Turn of the Tide, *There's a Good Time Coming* and *Pulling Hard Against the Stream* strike an optimistic note, tinged with Christian resignation :

" Then do your best for one another,
  Making life a Pleasant Dream.
Help a worn and weary brother,
  Pulling hard against the Stream."

And *Wait for the Turn of the Tide* has the following :

" Then try to be happy and gay, boys,
  Remember the world is wide,
And Rome wasn't built in a day, boys,
  So wait for the turn of the Tide."

There's a Good Time Coming had been anticipated by the song, already mentioned, of Charles Mackay, and this was shortly to be parodied, with the same title, by G. W. Hunt.

Songs such as *Work, Boys, and be Contented* and *Always Put Your Shoulder to the Wheel*, must have given great satisfaction to those members of his audience who were employers of labour ; but it is a part of the strange psychology of music hall audiences that this kind of sentiment is invariably well received in the gallery.[1]

Evans's, in addition to its choral work, was rich in ballad singing by individual artists. Among these may be quoted the little tenor, Binge, Leffler, Joseph Plumpton, and John Caulfield. The last was for a time Evans's choirmaster, as Jonghmanns was later for Paddy Green. Jonghmanns was a prolific composer and a singer of merit : his son followed him as a vocalist and musical director. There was, in addition, E. L. J. Hime, who is remembered gratefully by several writers. He composed a number of songs, among which a motto song called *Look Always on the Sunny Side*[2] was an especial favourite. There is no reliable record of Sims Reeves having sung at Evans's, though he may very well have done so, as he is known to have appeared both at the Grecian and the Canterbury under the assumed name of Johnson.

The reluctance of the management to include in its programmes such comedians of the newer type as the Great Vance, finds record in a conversation between Paddy Green and William A'Beckett, in the course of which he says, " Paddy hated innova-

[1]Other characteristic titles from among a large number of these songs are *Never Trouble Trouble Till Trouble Troubles You* (F. Williams), *One Story is Good Till Another is Told*, and *Hit the Right Nail on the Head* (Alexander Lee).

[2]To the music of Stewart Farquharson, Esq., D.C.I., F.S.A., with whom he also wrote *Annie and Ronald, I'm lonely in the House now* and *I Dream of Thee*..

tions. When the Great Vance was engaged for a turn (at a high salary), my old friend was in despair, and he never really cared for acrobats."

An important feature, however, was the "blacked-up" or nigger minstrel comedian, and the minstrel troupes which had arrived from America. Some details of these companies may not be out of place at this juncture, though Evans's was not the first house to offer the English variant of this product to a concert-room audience.

J. A. Cave, as a "young fellow," is noted by Edmund Yates as having introduced the banjo at the Coal Hole. He must be accounted one of the earliest of English imitators of T. D. Rice, and claimed to be the first of English banjoists. Cave's work in this line did not begin until well into the 'forties, and, as has already been stated, it is by no means clear that Rice's triumphs at the Adelphi and Surrey Theatres (1836-1838) resulted in any immediate plagiarism. The vogue of English negro impersonation rather dates from the arrival in this country five years later of the Virginia Minstrels, a company organized by an artist called Whitlock, which gave its initial performances at Bartlett's Billiard Rooms in New York in 1843.

Rice's influence was naturally felt principally on the regular stage through the medium of the burlettàs written by Leman Rede and the performer himself. These served to establish the negro in the English theatre as a comic rather than a sentimental figure.

To Cave, then, and to the troupes who followed the Virginia Minstrels, is to be attributed the introduction of the nigger to the concert-room stage. Soon afterwards was to appear E. W. Mackney (the Great Mackney), followed by a host of comedians, from Vance onwards, who, having ventured their early fortunes in the negro character, deserted it later during the overwhelming demand for the "Lion Comique."

The Virginia Minstrels, consisting of Dan Emmett, the great coon song writer, Frank Brown, Dick Pelham, and Billy Whitlock, arrived in England in May 1843, and gave their first performances in Liverpool and Manchester.[1] In June they arrived at the Adelphi Theatre in London, where they gave entertainments in collaboration with Anderson, the "Wizard of the North." They were exploited by this impresario with astute showmanship. It is to be noted that this, the first of the Nigger Minstrel Troupes, gave their performances in realistic plantation costume. In spite of the presence of Emmett, the company achieved no outstanding

[1]It is of interest to note that a Pandean minstrel band was playing at Vauxhall before 1840. This was probably the band heard by Miss Ivins in her visit to the Eagle reported by Boz.

success : the Press was polite, describing the entertainment as " distinctly odd and amusing," but at the end of the season the company broke up.

The real furore began with the arrival of the " Æthiopian Serenaders," two and a half years afterwards. This company consisted of five artists headed by the banjoist Pell (sometimes credited with having originated that instrument). Immediate success attended their opening season in the new year of 1846. They charmed principally by their gentility, and this impression was heightened by the fact that they appeared in conventional tail coats and white waistcoats. The *Era* has the following comment on their début : " The entertainment provided by the ' Æthiopian Serenaders ' is on a far higher plane than others. Their predecessors dressed in plantation costumes, but in this case we have a quartette of gentlemen " (the critic has not counted correctly) " dressed in the height of fashion, discoursing most elegant music. Their songs are of a melodious and artistic nature. Several of the company possess quite good voices, and the comedians manage to get the utmost fun out of their business, without resorting to vulgarity in any form. This company will prove a decided attraction."

It did. Within a year, Germon, Starrwood, Harrington, White and Pell were performing at Vauxhall, and finally the doors of Evans's were opened to them. It is not difficult to imagine their success here. The magnificent repertory of Emmett's and Collins Foster's songs—*The Swanee River*, *Old Man Tucker*, *Massa's in the Cold, Cold Ground*, *Buffalo Gals* and the rest—might be enjoyed to the full to the accompaniment of such elegant respectability of costume. The thing had now become *de regle*. It is true that George Augustus Sala, writing in 1857, mentions the Serenaders with great casualness as " individuals of the Ethiopian way of thinking, accoutred in the ordinary amount of lamp-black, Welsh wig, and shirt collars, and provided with the usual banjo, accordian, tambourine, and bones . . . in the habit of informing the audience that things in general are assuming an appearance of ' Hoop de Dooden Do,' " but it is known on unimpeachable testimony that these artists brought tears to the spectacles of William Thackeray, and it should be remembered that by the year in which Sala wrote, the vogue was already sufficiently familiar—the Æthiopian Serenaders having been followed in hot pursuit by the Buckley Troupe (which popularized *I'd Choose to be a Daisy if I could be a Flower*)—quite a domestic affair, consisting originally of four members of an English family which had migrated to America in the 'thirties. The composition of the song mentioned, and of many others, was the work of the patriarchal R. Bishop

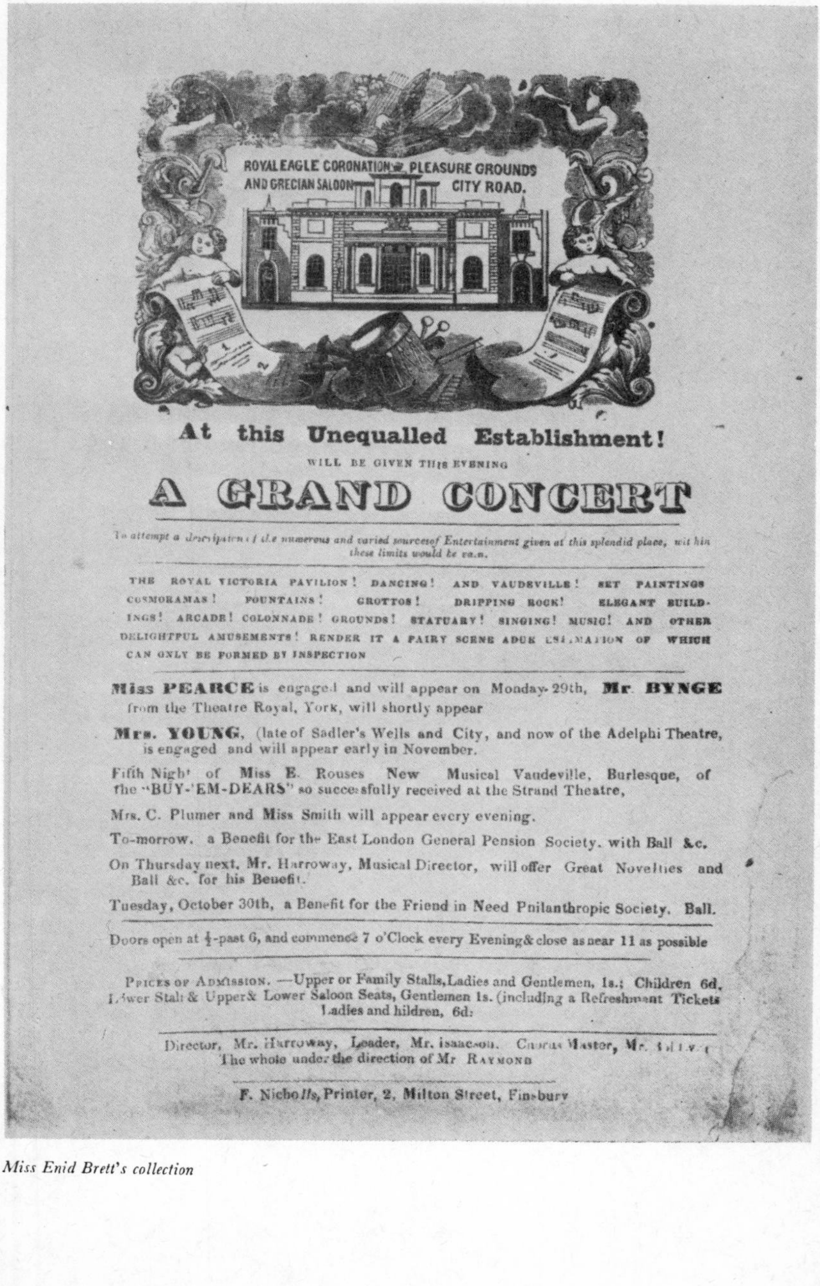

ROYAL EAGLE CORONATION PLEASURE GROUNDS AND GRECIAN SALOON CITY ROAD.

At this Unequalled Establishment!

WILL BE GIVEN THIS EVENING

A GRAND CONCERT

To attempt a description of the numerous and varied sources of Entertainment given at this splendid place, within these limits would be vain.

THE ROYAL VICTORIA PAVILION! DANCING! AND VAUDEVILLE! SET PAINTINGS COSMORAMAS! FOUNTAINS! GROTTOS! DRIPPING ROCK! ELEGANT BUILDINGS! ARCADE! COLONNADE! GROUNDS! STATUARY! SINGING! MUSIC! AND OTHER DELIGHTFUL AMUSEMENTS! RENDER IT A FAIRY SCENE ADUE ESTIMATION OF WHICH CAN ONLY BE FORMED BY INSPECTION

Miss **PEARCE** is engaged and will appear on Monday 29th, **Mr BYNGE** from the Theatre Royal, York, will shortly appear

Mrs. YOUNG, (late of Sadler's Wells and City, and now of the Adelphi Theatre, is engaged and will appear early in November.

Fifth Night of Miss E. Rouses New Musical Vaudeville, Burlesque, of the "BUY-'EM-DEARS" so successfully received at the Strand Theatre,

Mrs. C. Plumer and Miss Smith will appear every evening.

To-morrow. a Benefit for the East London General Pension Society. with Ball &c.

On Thursday next, Mr. Harroway, Musical Director, will offer Great Novelties and Ball &c. for his Benefit.

Tuesday, October 30th, a Benefit for the Friend in Need Philanthropic Society. Ball.

Doors open at ½-past 6, and commence 7 o'Clock every Evening & close as near 11 as possible

PRICES OF ADMISSION. —Upper or Family Stalls, Ladies and Gentlemen, 1s.; Children 6d, Lower Stall & Upper & Lower Saloon Seats, Gentlemen 1s. (including a Refreshment Ticket) Ladies and hildren, 6d.

Director, Mr. Harroway, Leader, Mr. Isaacson. Chorus Master, Mr. [illegible]
The whole under the direction of Mr RAYMOND

F. Nicholls, Printer, 2, Milton Street, Finsbury

Miss Enid Brett's collection

GRECIAN SALOON,
EAGLE TAVERN
CITY ROAD.

The First Public Concert Room in England!!!

This peculiar and elegantly fitted up Establishment, where the Public have an opportunity of enjoying a CONCERT, comprising selections from the popular Music of the Day, interspersed with old-established Favourites; a Musical Vaudeville Dancing, &c., to the charms of which, are added Comforts, not to be equalled in Europe, will continue to offer its unrivalled Amusements until further notice.

☞ The very extensive improvements, additions and alterations which are actively proceeding, to render the Grounds, attached to the Saloon, as unique as money is capable of rendering them, and which, when completed will accomodate from 6000 to 8000 Persons, (with protection from Unfavourable Weather) and exceed any Public Garden in England! for compactness, elegance, comfort and accomodation, (at a price of admission capable of being obtained by all classes of Society) will be shortly thrown open to the Public, of which due notice will be given,

Continued Triumphant Success of the Dancers from the Queen's Theatre.

This Evening, "The QUEEN'S CHERRIES"
Tomorrow, "The TWO MINIATURES"
"The KISS AND THE ROSE" is in active revival and will be presented on Saturday.
On Wednesday May the 9th, a Benefit in Aid of the "City Road Benevolent Association" held at the New Fountain Tavern.
Two new Vaudevilles are in active Rehearsal.
Selection of Music from the last New Opera of "The GIPSEY'S WARNING" will be immediately brought forward.

PRICES OF ADMISSION.—Upper or Family Stalls, Ladies and Gentlemen, 1s.; Children 6d.
Lower Stall & Upper& Lower Saloon Seats, Gentlemen 1s. (including a Refreshment Ticket, Ladies and Children, 6d:
Children in arms cannot be admitted unless they are paid for.

Doors open at half-past Six, and commence Seven o'Clock every Evening, and close as near Eleven as possible.
Parties who have paid for the Saloon can have Pass Checks to the Upper Stall seats, at the Bar, on payment of 6d. Family Stalls can be taken nightly, to contain from Eight to Twelve Persons.

Musical Director, Mr. HARROWAY, R. A. M. Leader, Mr. ISAACSON. Chorus Master, Mr. BALDWIN. The whole under the direction of Mr RAYMOND.

F NICHOLLS PRINTER, 2, MILTON STREET FINSBURY

Miss Enid Brett's collection

Buckley. This troupe was probably the first to give the semi-dramatized presentation of negro songs, a modern instance of which was Charles Cochran's production, *Blackbirds*, at the London Pavilion. The entertainment was contained in three parts : the first called *Darkies in City Life* (in the programme of 1860, quoted by Mr. Harry Reynolds, the Overture to *Zampa* was performed as a solo on the bones (" a feat never attempted before by any other performer ") ; the second part was devoted to a sketch (one imagines a broad farce), and a " musical selection" from *Il Trovatore*, the artists appearing throughout this part with blackened faces ; and the third part consisted of " variety," which included a " Burlesque Fling," a Melaphone solo, a comic pas de deux, a plantation jig, a banjo trio, a violin solo, and, to conclude, a sequence of plantation festival songs called *Dixie's Land*.

The practice of giving a sketch—not, I think, included by the Æthiopian Seranaders—became an important part of the minstrel programme, and, if one may judge from recollections of niggers such as those on the Margate sands, presided over with such fierce autocracy by " Mr. Bones "—was reproduced by all the troupes down to the humblest itinerants. These sketches, eagerly awaited by all juvenile audiences as the *bon bouche* of the show, were performed " in character " (giving them a peculiarly delicious quality) ; that is, the actors put on " scratch " wigs and armed themselves with two-leaved sticks with which they freely and frequently hit one another over the head. The dialogue of these sea-shore minstrels was a matter of " gags," and the method was no doubt traditional. These were by no means the only alfresco practitioners of the craft for, after the arrival of the Christy Minstrels in 1857, there came a spate of wandering troupes which invaded the streets of London, the provincial towns, the fairs, and the countryside public-houses.[1] The " Ethiopians " figure more prominently than any other type of performer in the pictorial cover of a song of the 'fifties describing the cacophanies of street music, and their band is shown as of the most orthodox kind. These strange people still linger in obscure doorways, and are to be seen on bank holidays trudging round the villages and the outer suburbs. An interesting statement given to Henry Mayhew and recorded by him, indicates the general degree of popularity enjoyed by the minstrels in his time. The performer in question related that he first sang in the streets just before Queen Victoria's coronation, and, if a correct statement, this is significant and points to a large body of Rice's imitators, of whom records are lacking. After joining up with a troupe

[1]They were also to be seen on the twopenny steamboats which plied the Thames from London Bridge.

they sought pitches in Regent Street, Oxford Street, and " the greater part " of St. James's—the City being a banned area. Dan Emmett's *Buffalo Gals* proved to be their most popular song. A mention of the artist Juba, by another informant, as a " first class—a regular A1", is a reminder that he was the first actual man of colour to make an appearance in English minstrelsy. The tendency did not go uncriticized. When by the 'nineties the true negro artist had begun to assert himself in entertainments of this kind, the custom is bitterly deplored by Joseph Hatton in an article in the *Idler*, who saw in the innovation an instance of the movement towards realism which, in his opinion, was based on a misunderstanding of theatrical art. " To-day," he writes, " the music hall negro must be a real negro "—rather oddly, at a moment when Eugene Stratton, Le Gros, Mackney and Chirgwin were on the boards together.

The street troupes, as did the busking actors of a slightly earlier time, obtained engagements at the lesser concert rooms. Mayhew's interlocutor appeared at the Albion in Ratcliffe Highway and The Ship and Camel in Bermondsey. On these occasions a strange variant of the " poses plastiques " was performed by the niggers. These consisted of tableaux of the negro life of the plantations. " We illustrate the adventures of Pompey or the life of a negro slave. The first position is when he is in the sugar brake, cutting the sugar-cane. Then he is supposed to take it to be weighed and, not being weight, he is ordered to be flogged. . . . The next position is when he is being flogged . . . and afterwards when he murders the overseer. Then there's the flight of Pompey, and so on, and I conclude with a variety of sculptures, from the statues, such as the Achilles in Hyde Park and so on." None of these vagaries are, however, to be attributed to the "Æthiopian Serenaders" who gladdened the audience of Evans's and whose appearances there, together with vocalists of the J. W. Sharpe school, constituted the principal note of variety to be found at that establishment.

It has been said that acrobatic and conjuring acts were to be found there ; I have found no account of any. But there probably were ; and colour is lent to Sala's statement, if it be true, that " in the intervals of Performance " a tableau curtain was lowered. Such a device would have been practically a necessity in the presentation of acts involving elaborate paraphernalia. But one may doubt the accuracy of his statement.[1] Elsewhere the term " platform " is invariably used, and A'Beckett, in writing of Boat-race night at Evans's, describes the raiding of this platform by the University " bloods " and their insistence that

[1]The mention of a curtain is in G. A. Sala's *Twice Round the Clock* ; but Sala was writing in Italy, where the atmosphere is notoriously romantic.

Harry Sydney shall share bottles of champagne with them there : a really Elizabethan proceeding. Possibly the artists even sat on the platform while the concert was in progress. This would explain Ritchie's statement in his " Cave of Harmony " chapter : " we are at the end of a long room ; at the other is a raised platform, on which is a Piano, and in front of which some half a dozen gentlemen are seated—these are the Performers."

No better general summary of the physical features of Evans's can be given than that of Ritchie : " Let us stroll twards Covent Garden," he says convivially, " and enter that doorway indicated by the glare of gas ; come with me down those stairs, and into that room, the door of which the waiter obligingly holds open. . . . You find yourself in a room holding some hundreds of gentlemen ; look around . . . there are no poor people here. We have heavy swells, moustached, and with white kid gloves—officers in the Army—scions of noble houses . . . with every moral sensibility dead, who have sat for years listening to the same songs and the same outpourings ; . . . of course, the majority in the room are clerks, and commercial gents, and fellows in Government situations, learning here the extravagance which in time will compel them to commit frauds and forgery. . . . The Cave of Harmony is not a cheap place to sup at. The chop and baked potatoes are excellent but dear . . . and the chances are you will meet a friend who will persuade you to make a night of it and stroll West with him, where you will see Vice flaunting more finely and with greater bravery than in any other capital in Europe."

Ritchie's implications that Evans's was primarily a haunt of the would-be fast is a conscious suppression of the whole truth ; revealed by his inclusion of literary men among its *habitués*. The fact is that Evans's successfully maintained its position for a decade as an important scene of cultural life on its convivial side. One feels that a similar institution to-day would be much affected by the tankard-and-pipe section of the writing community, and call for just such a setting—a floor not, indeed, vulgarly sanded, but supporting the stout oak settle with its burden of English pewter, and walls re-echoing the songs of the days when England really was, as Mr. Herbert Farjeon put it, " what she used to be." Among those authors who took the place seriously, Thackeray is undoubtedly the most important. Hollingshead, who attributed Thackeray's fondness for Evans's principally to his love for the seventeenth century (one may remark that it was the strangest expression of that enthusiasm), describes the famous author's connection with the house as follows : " Thackeray had a small following at the Garrick Club, and heading there night after night, he made the underground singing saloon . . . the most

popular smoking-room of the Club. The choir of boy choristers, who were surpliced in the day at a great Roman Catholic Church, and sang in evening dress at night in an atmosphere of baked potatoes, devilled kidneys, mutton chops, gin, beer and tobacco, were special favourites with the great author. He suffered from a painful internal disease, and the music relieved him."

At what moment Greenmore found it necessary to adopt such a daring innovation as the admission of women to the floor of Evans's there is no precise information. It occurred, however, in the late 'sixties, some years after the conclusion of the first step towards this policy, the construction of boxes in the balcony shielded by a grille behind which ladies (accompanied by gentlemen) were allowed to view the proceedings without themselves being seen. No charge was made for admission to these boxes; it was a privilege accorded by the manager to persons of social distinction, and during the evening he would pay his guests the compliment of bringing them nosegays. In this decade there were two causes at work to undermine the popularity of the house .One was internal—a growth of *ennui* settling on the place —and the other was the enormous stride in esteem of the modern music hall. Yet another factor was sufficient to close the place entirely. An Act of 1872 made provision to render the holding of a licensed public entertainment illegal after 12.30 at night. This gave the final blow : the essence of Evans's programme being that it took place in the small hours of the morning. It was probably then that, by a reckless stroke, a decision was made to open the doors to both sexes. Gilbert A'Beckett has the following anecdote of the first nights of the new régime : " It was expected that the hall would be thronged with all sorts and conditions of persons. But the persons in question preferred more congenial haunts and did not turn up. The only female present was the homely wife of a farmer, who was having supper with her husband, and who seemed greatly surprised at the interest that appeared to be taken in her movements by a number of lads young enough to be her children." But shortly afterwards the number of women visitors must have greatly increased, for the place became morally suspect, was refused a licence, and died. By this time, Paddy Green had retired and was given a benefit matinée at the new Gaiety Theatre, which realized £700. With the death of Evans's the old order, artificially revived, fairly passed away, leaving the field for the now fully developed music hall, which, as early as the beginning of the 'fifties, had been a menace to this stubborn survival.

CHAPTER VIII

Charles Morton and Others

More than once there have occurred in this book prophetic references to Charles Morton, whose New Canterbury Hall, raised on the bowling green of the Canterbury Arms at the junction of the Westminster Bridge Road and the Upper Marsh, was opened while Evans's was still in its first vigour. The eventful moment in Morton's career occurred in 1851. He had taken the Canterbury property three years previously, establishing regular sing-songs in 1849 ; after having served his apprenticeship as a publican in various parts of London. At two of the houses with which he had been connected, he had organized Harmonic Meetings and exhibited a betting list. At a house in Southwark he was in close proximity to the thriving " Surrey " Music Hall, familiarly known as " The Grapes," and his mind was no doubt directed to music hall management by visists to this house. With some accumulation of capital and valuable experience in the direction of sing-songs, he took a lease of the Canterbury Arms and at once set about the realization of his ambition, that of creating, by degrees, a separate music hall establishment of equal importance to its neighbour in the Southwark Bridge Road.

The Harmonic Meetings held at the new house, at first on Mondays and Saturdays, and later with the addition of a Thursday evening to which women were admitted, led in 1850 to the building of a one-storied hall whose foundation stone, we are told by Emily Soldene in her altogether delightful book of reminiscences, was laid by two children—Lily Morton, the proprietor's daughter, and Marie Grey, the daughter of his landlord. The concerts continued to prosper in these surroundings, and in the following year Morton began the raising of the edifice (by building above and beyond the initial house), which made such a strong impression upon the Press and the public of his day and which almost, but not quite, silenced the disapproval of Ewing Ritchie.

At the new second Canterbury, where the shows continued during the rebuilding operations, Morton appears to have adopted a combination of the policies of Evans's and the Surrey

Music Hall. From Evans's, Morton borrowed two very important features: their principal comedian, Sam Cowell, and the idea of a picture gallery. The latter (in conjunction with the former) had more to do with the enormous success of the Canterbury than perhaps any other measure. The thought of a picture gallery in a music hall in Lambeth, among the homes of the poorer classes, fascinated everyone. Augustus Sala called it "the Royal Academy over the water"—and, though a facile epigram, it became a famous one. Next year, dear E. L. Blanchard, who had such humility of spirit, that one wonders that anyone took any notice of him, wrote in genuine awe that he had visited the new Canterbury Hall, "a house with accommodation for over 1,200 people, and with a picture gallery that cost thousands of pounds." Actually, the pictures were from one stock and were supplied by Gambart's of Berners Street, on sale or return, though most of them were subsequently purchased by the management. They included works by Sir A. Calcott, Daniel Maclise, Benjamin Haydon, and Rosa Bonheur. The most important, or rather the largest of them, Haydon's *Curtius leaping into the Gulf*, had been exhibited by the painter—the friend of Keats and Leigh Hunt—in a room in the Egyptian Hall, at a time when Barnum was presenting the celebrated dwarf General Tom Thumb in the same building. "Curtius" dogs our footsteps in music hall history, for he was heard of at Gatti's in the Westminster Bridge Road—a hall which was opened about ten years later than the second Canterbury, and whose original building still stands.[1] The picture, however, is unhappily no longer there. Morton's pictures undoubtedly stamped themselves upon the age. Enthusiastic references to them appeared in the Press; Punch became quite lyrical about them; Clement Scott gave them a full measure of publicity; and critics such as Dutton Cook, whose mission was with the theatre of literature, wrote that he had heard that there was one music hall which was not unmindful of the educational needs of the masses.

These well-meant outbursts served to obscure less edifying features of Morton's venture, such as the fact that the system of "wet money," or payment which entitled the purchaser of a ticket to a proportion of drink, had been adopted, though this method had been successfully abandoned at the Surrey. But there were more surprises in store. In addition to the engagement of Cowell, the glee-singing practised at Evans's was extended by Morton to the giving of operatic selections in what would be described as "concert performances." And in this connection a

[1]The picture was later to be seen in Gatti's Restaurant in Villers Street. Some years ago it again appeared in an auction room, an occasion which promoted a characteristic Sunday reminiscence by Edward V. Lucas.

great *coup* was achieved by the acquisition of the score of Gounod's *Faust*, hitherto unperformed in England. The work had been heard in Paris by Mr. Gye of Covent Garden, but he had discovered no virtues in it except the "Soldier's Chorus." With superior musical appreciation, the work was secured for the Canterbury and the parts of Gretchen and Mephistopheles were sung by Miss Russell, the niece of the composer of *Cheer, Boys, Cheer*, and Albert Lawrence. Much credit was achieved by Morton for the action he took, but it is perhaps somewhat discounted by the fact that he had discovered that, owing to some failure in registering the work according to the rules of international copyright, it was available for production in England without the payment of a royalty. On the other hand, it is only fair to suppose that the management of Covent Garden were equally alive to this situation, and we may, perhaps, assume that Morton had an enthusiasm for Gounod.

Sensation was, then, piling upon sensation at the Canterbury. But in painting the picture one must not overlook the truth of Hibbert's statement expressed in rather acrid terms, that Morton owed his sensational success less to the "half a dozen vocalists standing in a row in preposterous evening dress" than to "a comic singer or 'vocal comedian' seduced from the song-and-supper rooms at the West End—Sam Cowell." Even so, Hibbert might have added the wet money and the betting lists. To take the other view, however, much may be adduced from the cumulative effect of the various elements of what may be described as Morton's respectability campaign. Basically his problem was to lure the wealthier type of patron across the water in the wake of his favourite comedian. To attain this end a romantic glamour was the first consideration, a glamour combined with a sound reputation for pioneer work in promoting rational amusement. Morton's scheme was a revolutionary one only in respect of its geographical position.

And from this element of innovation he secured the maximum amount of publicity and moral *kudos*.[1] The commercial astuteness of the policy was paramount since, simultaneously raising the tone and the prices of his establishment, the rent and overhead expenses were virtually undisturbed. The triumph of the methods by which the enterprise was conducted, the com-

[1]It was a considerable achievement for Charles Morton and for music-hall prestige when *The Times* accepted his advertisement of the Canterbury following upon the judge's favourable comments on the place during the hearing of the case against him in respect of his production of extravaganza there.

In spite of the reference from Clement Scott in the note on page 21, it is probably a mistake to imagine that, up to the moment of the passing of the Theatre Act of 1843, the most important theatres had, as fully as the saloon theatre, followed the practice of selling refreshments in the auditorium.

bination of magnificence, picture-gallery and operatic music in the Westminster Bridge Road, did even more than guarantee commercial success it achieved for Morton the enviable if entirely unearned reputation of being the actual creator of the music hall itself. Commentators seem almost unanimous on this point. " The Canterbury—the first music hall established in the metropolis," is Walford's comment in his *Old and New London*. " Charles Morton, afterwards the Father of the Halls," writes Chance Newton, and he is echoed by George R. Sims. H. G. Hibbert alone stands for the truth.

Then there is Clement Scott, to whom we are originally indebted for the phrase, " Father of the Halls." It is perhaps a little unfair to disinter that well-meaning man's elegy to Morton written for the celebration of the manager's eightieth birthday (for Morton completed the patriarchal impression by living to a great age). This affair took place in the then luxuriously modern Palace Theatre which Morton was at the time conducting as a music hall (though it had been built a few years previously for the housing of English opera). This rhymed address, spoken at the conclusion of the complimentary matinée in Morton's honour, by Mrs. Beerbohm Tree, is, however, so complete an epitome of the nineteenth-century verdict that it may be as well to quote it in full. (The references it contains to a conflict with theatrical vested interests are discussed later in the chapter.)

On Mr. Morton's Eightieth Birthday.

What has he done for us, Grand Old Man? In his record of eighty years?
He has fought for liberty! Planted Truth! With trouble, maybe with tears!
With its ebb and flow, the tide of Life has "beached" here safe and sound,
But the struggle was tough, and the straits were sore, till his feet touched solid ground.
His Harbour Light was a vista view of things as they ought to be,
The Pleasures of England *should* be pure, and Art it *must* be free!
He took with pluck, this parable up, at Duty's high call,
And swore he would lead to Paths of Peace, the degenerate Music Hall!

Sixty or seventy years ago, in the days of the " drinking den,"
The jokes they made and the songs they sang, were sorrow to Englishmen.
If you doubt my word, take Thackeray down, and Colonel Newcome call

To tell the tale of the days of " Ross," and the shudder at vile " Sam Hall."
But he dreamed of the Madrigal, Grand Old Man, and the English Catch and Glee,
And murmured, " Pleasure it should be pure, and Art it must be free."
So he opened a " Sing Song " bright and gay, Vice took to its heels and ran !
Said the women, " Oh ! Governor ! Let us in ! " " You shall come," said the Grand Old Man.

But the dogs in the manger howled and snarled, as they gnawed Protection's bone !
You are giving the patient Public Bread ! For you here's a Paving Stone !
So they dug old Acts of Parliament up, and tinkled the legal bell,
And said, " Dear Charles ! If you want the Law there's the Dock and the Police Court Cell.
You have threatened our Privilege, Grand Old Man, with your rubbish of Purity,
The *Play's* the thing that the Law allows, so just climb down ! D'you see ! "
But the Grand Old Man still fought for Art, and the public so deserving,
And degenerate Dog in the Manger lays, collapsed, with Henry Irving.

Then they left the Grand Old Man alone, safe, planted firm on feet.
And now, if they pine for nastiness, they must go down another street.
They have swept it out of the Music Halls ; and Variety lifts her head
With the aid and fame of a Literal Man, now the Dog in the Manger's dead !
So I ask a cheer for that Englishman—one more for his eighty years.
He has borne them bravely, borne them well, you will own when he appears,
Sunny of face and snowy of head ! Of life he has still a span !
But wait one second, I won't be long, I'll fetch you the Grand Old Man !

The later story of the Canterbury Hall may be briefly placed together. The prolonged engagement of Sam Cowell was quickly followed by another happy selection of an artist scarcely less

popular, E. W. Mackney, or " The Great " Mackney, as he was called, the celebrated negro impersonator, song-writer and instrumentalist. A year or so earlier, Mackney had secured an engagement at Evans's and the success he had achieved there had attracted Morton's attention. Much of Mackney's repertoire was common to the Ethiopian tribe, as, for instance, Dan Emmet's *Such a Gittin' Upstairs*, one of his most popular songs. For the rest a semi-topical song of his own called *The Whole Hog or None* has perhaps first place.

Besides adding the fashionable J. W. Sharpe and the respected Sam Collins to his programmes, Morton did much to establish the reputation of Tom Maclagan. The chief characteristic of this comedian was his versatility, for he was no less renowned as a mimic than as a singer of comic and sentimental songs. Maclagan was in the true sense a singing actor, and after having completed successful seasons at the Canterbury, became a very great favourite as a resident vocalist-comedian at the Britannia, where he was heard in his famous song, *Captain Jinks of the Horse Marines*.[1] As a Caledonian of the purest blend, the pronounced accent must have given an individual touch to his many appearances in grand opera.

Both the Jonghmanns and both the Caulfields, father and son, were connected with the Canterbury during Morton's management. Caulfield's wife was also an important feature in the scheme of entertainment, for she developed a style of song which earned for her *genre* the title of " lady serio-comic vocalist." It is probably the designation rather than any note of real innovation which has caused the commentators to claim her as the first comedienne who appeared at the music halls. But there is this difference between Mrs. Caulfield's work and that of her predecessors, that her repertoire was perhaps the first to include versions of the male comedians' favourite songs, as, for instance, that by which she is especially remembered, *Keemo-Kimo*. *Bobbing Around*, another very well-known song of Mrs. Caulfield's which she has been given the credit of introducing to the public, was not her creation, but was brought to England by another woman, Mrs. Florence, who arrived with her husband from America in the early 'fifties. Both became established favourites in this country. The " ladies' versions " of comic songs became a general custom ; there was even a female *Champagne Charley* in the person of Louie Sherrington. For all this assumption of the mantle of the comic singer, there was a long distance between the Mrs. Caulfields and the later music-hall comediennes such as Marie Lloyd. Indeed, the

[1]The song was written by Harry Rickards, who probably sang it as well as his own *Captain Cuff*. The lyric of *Captain Jinks of the Horse Marines* is by Maclagan, and the tune is a slight variation of the melody of *My Lord Tom Noddy*.

Caulfield family belonged essentially to the more polite theatrical tradition and their graduation for the Canterbury, at the Haymarket theatre, is a survival of the old order of things. Apart from the operatic selections, no extensive call was made upon feminine artistry at the Canterbury—far less, indeed, than at the older establishments such as White Conduit House, and, it is fairly safe to say, as at such genuine tavern concerts of earlier origin as the Doctor Johnson and the Surrey.

Throughout Morton's management, something of the primitiveness of an earlier century, borrowed in part from Evans's and partly due to its recent emergence from the stage of weekly " harmonic meeting," clung to the programmes of the Canterbury. This gave to the sudden assumption of magnificence a quality of dramatic effect. Indeed, Morton's policy was consciously to make the transition appear as violent and revolutionary as possible. He chose to ignore the process of development which had been going on elsewhere, and boldly issued a pamphlet which, I am afraid, saddles him with full responsibility for the make-belief in which the reputation of the Canterbury is involved. I have been fortunate in securing a copy of this now rare document, and it will be seen from the following passages how slyly Morton assumes the character of a reformist-innovator :

" The proprietor of the Canterbury Hall hopes that he has been enabled to improve upon the remote civilization of *King Cole*. He gives a little more than a ' pipe ' and a ' glass ' and ' fiddlers three.' To speak more seriously—the unprecedented patronage which has rewarded his efforts to provide a first-class vocal entertainment for the people, emboldens him to hazard the reasons why he believes those efforts to have been successful. In the first place he knew that the eye had to be consulted, as well as the ear. The magnificent and brilliantly-lighted Hall, in which the Concert is held, exercises no little influence upon the minds of his audience. . . . In the carrying out of the vocal programme, it has been the constant endeavour of the proprietor, by popularizing the best music, to form and refine the public taste. . . . The comic element must not be lost sight of. The proprietor has aimed at rendering this portion of the programme unexceptionable. As on the stage, fun may be too broad, so humour in the concert-room has often degenerated into licence. . . .

" And now a word to his patronesses. Perhaps they do not reflect on the service he has done them in establishing the Canterbury Hall ; but this question he would be bold enough to ask them. When husbands, who now frequent the Canterbury Hall, used to tell their wives that ' they were going to hear a song,' or ' had been to hear a song ' . . . had the poor wives the slightest

inkling as to where their truant spouses were going or had been? Did not the announcement of an intention of 'hearing a song' too often ring the knell of many an evening's enjoyment to the poor woman sitting at home? Need husbands be mysterious, or wives suspicious, any longer? . . . It is a disgrace to English civilization that toiling wives and sisters should be circumscribed in their enjoyments. There is the familiar canine prohibition, 'no dogs admitted.' 'No ladies admitted' has been the chivalrous phrase in which Englishmen of the nineteenth century exclude the gentler sex from rational and refining recreations."

This passionate plea for the rights of womanhood could only by the wildest stretch of imagination have had reference to the most timid of the sex. Women of perfect respectability had for years past found their way to the Rotunda, the Surrey, the Doctor Johnson, Wilton's and elsewhere, to say nothing of the taverns with gardens attached to them from which they had never been absent. In conjunction with the pamphlet, Chance Newton's comment (and Newton was Morton's greatest apologist) reads strangely. It is to the effect that Morton, when his house threatened to become crowded with women visitors, often caused the "House Full" boards temporarily to be put out, his reason for doing so being the diminishing effect of women's presence upon the sale of alcohol.

These were incidents of the early days. But they laid the foundations of his fortunes. Within ten years Morton was able to abandon the suburbs and upon the profits of the reformed sing-song to build the Oxford Music Hall in triumphant opposition to Weston's house in Holborn, with its long bars and pretty barmaids, and its spacious promenade, from which women were by no means excluded.

With the arrival of Emily Soldene at the Canterbury the selections from grand opera began to be extended and the dangerous enterprise of opera bouffe presented theatrically, as in the days of the saloon theatres, was embarked upon. Dangerous, because such productions were a clear contravention of the provisions of the Theatre Act of 1843. The first piece attempted was called *The Enchanted Hash;* it was a one-act musical extravaganza. Proceedings were at once instituted against Morton, a prime mover in the attack being Alfred Wigan at the Olympic.

The grounds of the prosecution were limited to the fact that the piece contained dramatic dialogue; Morton countered the injunction by producing the piece in dumb-show, the dialogue being spoken, however, from the corner of the stage in the form of "explanatory text." Morton then attempted a condensed musical version of *The Tempest*, and was again fined for the delinquency. By this time, however, the battle was virtually won;

the legal defeat was trifling and involved a merely nominal penalty. The judgment was accompanied by an apology from the magistrate at being compelled to impose it. The triumph quickly spread; *The Times*, which had hitherto refused Morton's advertisements, now began to print them, a privilege which they had never extended even to the Grecian. This noble struggle for the rights of the stage in respect of two vaudeville sketches and a musical comedy excerpt from Shakespeare, which, together with some further brushes with the managers of the legitimate theatres, explains the latter verses of Clement Scott's amazing poem. The *impresario* was, of course, but Clement Scott's pretext for his impassioned campaign on behalf of theatrical free trade, the struggle for which, after the Theatres Act, became limited to the question of whether dramatic elements should be allowed on the music hall stage. The agitation was undoubtedly benevolent in intention and indeed ethically unassailable, for all such restrictions are accompanied sooner or later by some measure of corruption, but Scott's attitude throughout, which was a representative one, was firmly based on the conviction that anything in the nature of a play must of necessity be superior to other forms of entertainment, and that the fight for the sketches involved a sacred principle of art.

On Morton's sensational victory, a remarkable managerial achievement when the locality and antecedents of his hall are borne in mind, we may at present abandon the Canterbury. Morton's management of the house came to an end in 1867, six years after the founding of the Oxford Hall. There were no especial signs of a new order prior to this date. George Leybourne and the famous batch of "Lions Comiques" did not appear at the Canterbury until William Holland, self-styled "The People's Caterer," took the hall. It was during his régime that Blondin made his first appearance in a London music hall.

For the moment it will be best to confine the narrative to the decade which preceded Morton's fresh adventure. The opening of the Oxford Hall in 1861 serves as a convenient landmark in music hall development.

Before this date, Mrs. Caulfield remained a lonely figure in the world of serio-comics, though the star of Annie Adams was nearing its ascendant. The great comediennes such as Jenny Hill and Bessie Bellwood had not yet risen to fame—the former was a child, performing the double task of entertaining the frequenters of a small sing-song and washing up their mugs and glasses. Sydney, Sloman, Penniket, Cowell, and Sharpe still held the field.

But the decade was one of considerable activity in the enlargement and economic development of the halls, though it was not until immediately after 1860 that the avalanche fell. Then it

was that the new orientation of music hall finance began to influence development, for groups and syndicates had been forming and capital in larger sums had become available.

During the 'fifties, meantime, a number of the lesser houses arrived at music hall status. Among these, the most important was Edward Weston's reorganization of the Seven Tankards and Punchbowl tavern in High Holborn. The new manager also took over the abandoned premises of the Holborn National School, and on the site arose the auditorium of Weston's Music Hall in 1852. There is no doubt that this invasion of the West End of London shortened Morton's tenancy of the Canterbury—it most certainly hastened his decision to build a new hall in Oxford Street. Weston formed a partnership with the licensed victualler Sweasey, and with William Holland, a partnership dissolved in 1867. Later the hall was retitled the Royal, and since rebuilt, but with an uninterrupted history it is now known as the Holborn Empire.

The Philharmonic Hall in Islington was founded in the 'fifties. Its promoters were Frederick Saunders and Edward Laçey. The house did not greatly prosper under this management, when it alternated variety with melodrama upon lines not far removed from those of the " gaff." In 1851 Morton arrived on the scene, and by a wave of his magic wand converted the dreary little place into a thriving centre of opera bouffe with a production of *Genevieve de Brabant* with his Oxford Hall star, Emily Soldene, in the character of Drogan.

To the same period belongs the reconstitution of the Eagle Tea Gardens in the Mile End Road. These had been known earlier as the Tiverly Gardens, Eagle Tavern. Owned in the 'forties by a man called Ward (not, I think, identical with the Ward of the Surrey), the house came into the hands of William Lusby, who at first paid considerable attention to the alfresco attractions of the place and renamed it Lusby's Summer and Winter Garden.

Subsequently under the simpler name of Lusby's, it housed all the music hall stars of the 'sixties. Its later history includes a rebuilding when Crowder and Payne took over the house in 1867. After a fire it was again renamed the Paragon, under which title it survived for many years.

A house of greater antiquity, but of which no definite information is available until the 'fities, was the Doctor Johnson tavern in Bolt Court, Fleet Street. In 1857 it was honoured with a visit from Ewing Ritchie, and we gather the impression that the City Concert Room, its official title at this time, had fallen on somewhat evil days. Evidently conducted in humble imitation of Evans's, the writer discovered it to be " thinly attended " by

about fifty or sixty gentlemen, " chiefly young ones." A variant of the Evans's method is supplied by the presence of a lady " with a very handsome blue satin dress, and a very powerful voice . . . screaming out something about Lovely Spring." There is also a performance of Labern's *The Lively Flea*, of which Ritchie expresses himself as being heartily tired—as well he might be, the song having been written at least twenty years earlier. He does not divulge the name of the singer of this venerable parody, but I have an uneasy suspicion that it was Charles Sloman. The hall did not survive into the 'seventies, but despite its depressed condition, leading vocalists appeared there during its last ten years of existence. Jenny Hill is said to have sung there before her discovery by Didcott. One of its latter gestures was to give Charles Sloman the post of chairman.

A hall which was created in the 'fifties was known as the New Music Hall in Hungerford Market. Founded on the site of a Mesmeric Saloon, it is advertised in 1855 in a manner which clearly indicated the influence of the Canterbury. The handbill states that the hall has been " redecorated and embellished in a most superb manner, representing the Battles of Alma, Balaklava, Inkerman, and Eupatoria." There are also " correct portraits of Queen Victoria, Elizabeth, Milton, Shakespeare, Scott, Nelson, and the Duke of Wellington." A permanent company of male and female vocalists was retained here, their names, however, are obscure. Glees were performed in the Canterbury manner, and the words of the songs were printed on special programmes. Once again, Ritchie can help us to bring the place to life : " One or two young swells," he tells us, " not in keeping with the character of the place, which . . . truth compels me to denominate as seedy, to say nothing of the damp tunnel-like atmosphere which not even the fumes of tobacco, grog, and gas could overpower." The details given us of the stage arrangements at the Hungerford Market Hall are of considerable interest. At each side of the stage was a " little box " : " on one side the ladies are penned, on the other the gentlemen ; a wise arrangement." These boxes were apparently used as dressing-rooms, or, at any rate, " quick-change " rooms, for we read of a comedian " diving into the little red-curtained crib " and reappearing as a new character.

The Effingham Saloon in Whitechapel, which may be classed among the products of the 'fifties, was conducted on lines approximating to those of a minor theatre. Bills of the time announce the well-known burletta of *Tiddlewinks*, into which has been introduced Harrison Ainsworth's song, *Nix My Dolly Pals*. The hall, however, was a receptacle of many variety acts. In the 'sixties it was acquired by Morris Abrahams and renamed the

East London Theatre. George Leybourne became a part proprietor of the house in the 'seventies, and used to drive there in his brougham to sandwich a hurried turn between two West End appearances.

The alternative name for Wilton's in Wellclose Square was the Old Mahogany Bar, and although the date of its opening is given in the *Era Almanack* as 1859, was already in existence two years earlier, for it is accorded an entire chapter in *The Night Side of London.* I have at the moment no definite confirmation that the house was on the site of John Palmer's Royalty Theatre, the likelihood of which is increased by the fact that it was not associated with licensed premises. Its auditorium, still to be seen as part of the Sailors' Mission, is a large one and may derive from the earlier theatre. When Ritchie visited the place the programmes contained an element of drama, which suggests the possibility of a Lord Chamberlain's licence. "Jack Tar," says Ritchie, "may be seen witnessing dramatic performances, not very artistic, but really, on the score of morality, not so objectionable as what I have seen applauded by an Adelphi audience. . . ." One does not know what enormity was witnessed in the Strand, but the comment suggests a glimmering of reason and humanity. The place came under new management in the 'sixties; in the beginning of the next decade it had improved its standard, and its programmes were of a moderate level of excellence. It is advertised among the list of leading houses in the *Music Hall Gazette* of 1870.

The neighbouring Ratcliffe Highway, rich in sing-songs, developed music halls in the 'fifties. Ward's was the most popular, and is probably the house of which a small woodcut is reproduced in this book. A clue is to be found in the lurid description of a tavern concert, which occurs in the temperance novel, *The Devil's Chain*, by Edward Jenkins, M.P., published in 1875. The physical features of the illustration may be identified in the author's description of the place. Emily, the hero of his novel, "disguised in a coarse woollen dress," enters, with trepidation, "one of the houses in Ratcliffe Highway which had a licence for liquor, music and dancing. The bar below was filled with sailors of every nationality, engaged in drinking, polyglot blasphemy and coarse courtship . . . up a few steps and through a door they passed into a room resounding with odd orchestral music— a lofty room with a ventilating skylight. The walls were decorated with paper in gaudy panels, in the middle of which were depicted highly-coloured tropical beauties, displaying their charm with Grecian naïveté but un-Grecian grace. By the door was the semi-circular bar, where the women were kept busy in drawing and mixing the liquors. Over the bar the orchestra

urged its doleful jollity of sound. On one side of the room were narrow tables and seats, just then crowded with men, chiefly sailors—and women, all of one class."

This house, together with the well-known Macdonald's and Harwood's Varieties (the former opposite the Britannia Theatre), were developed in the 'fifties. The City Road Eagle, also, had its rival in the concert room of the Green Gate Tavern (on the western side of that road). A description of this house accompanies the drawing of the place reproduced in this book. It did not prosper, and as a music hall is not heard of beyond the 'sixties, the public-house from which it derived still stands.

Many of the older tavern gardens in the centre of the town were settling down to an indoor prosperity about the same time. The Tiverley Gardens, the New Globe Gardens, and the Montpelier Gardens at Walworth being instances of a second career such as that of the Mile End Eagle. The list might be considerably lengthened, but would have little significance. In the important centres, halls naturally had a greater tendency to take root, but no important houses had yet appeared in the West End. In the 'fifties the London Pavilion was still a sing-song. The little Swallow Street Hall, off Piccadilly, was probably in existence. Though it never developed as a first-class hall, it was destined to house most of the important artists of the 'seventies and 'eighties. Music hall development in rivalry to the leading theatres did not come until Charles Morton's onslaught at the Oxford, on the supremacy of Weston's house in Holborn.

CHAPTER IX

The Great Period

CHARLES MORTON opened his brand-new Oxford Music Hall in November 1861, after encountering the fiercest opposition from his rival, Edward Weston, of the Royal, Holborn. In this achievement he may be said to have brought the older music hall era to a close. Here was a hall rising, fully accoutred, to conquer the West End of London, in defiance of the regular theatres. Considerable capital had been invested in the enterprise and a limited company had been formed, a method—first inaugurated by E. T. Smith, at the Alhambra—which was to be repeated in all directions during the succeeding decade. The inevitable decay of the garden taverns, following upon the rapid growth of London and the rise in value of ground rents, had brought into focus the new music hall developments. Islington Spa, Bagnigge Wells, White Conduit House, and the Yorkshire Stingo had all succumbed to the new advance before 1850 ; the Albert and similar saloons, before 1860.

The larger pleasure gardens had, on the other hand, survived. Cremorne was carrying on the tradition of Vauxhall, and, overlapping, there were the North Woolwich Gardens, and the St. Helena Gardens in Bermondsey. The former came under the control of a music hall proprietor, William Holland, famous for his management of the Canterbury and the Surrey Theatre. It shares with the Eagle a record of great vitality : they both closed their doors in the same year, 1881. These gardens in general were spectacular affairs, however, which had perhaps gathered fresh momentum from the Exhibition of 1851 ; it was the smaller gardens and saloons which had been eliminated. The Act of 1872, with its licensing restrictions, among them the fixing of 12.30 as a closing hour for all public entertainments, had also sounded the death-knell of the song and supper rooms, but even before that date the growth of the habit among men and women of taking their evenings' pleasure in one another's company had put that institution out of fashion. The function of " cabaret," moreover, was supplied by the conquering music hall, for the music hall, it must not be forgotten, in spite of its growth on

theatrical lines and its abandonment of intimacy, was still essentially of that order—that is to say, it was a place primarily devoted to public eating and drinking with the addition of a stage entertainment. Even in 1875, and after, an *Encyclopædia* describes the music hall in the following terms :

" Cheap-priced places of entertainment somewhat akin to the French Cafés Chantants, where refreshments are supplied and comic singing, dancing and acrobatic exhibitions form the leading attractions. . . . The entertainments, though usually harmless, are, with few exceptions, of an inferior, and often of a vulgar type."

This shows clearly that the business of convivial entertainment had passed in direct succession to the music hall ; and this aspect of its functions was so far realized by Morton as being essential, that although he no longer supervised personally the preparation of his clients' chops and steaks, nor served them, as he did at the first Canterbury, with his own hands, he supplied his new hall with an extensive restaurant area in the auditorium. A sign of the coming change was, however, visible in the fact that the non-supping part of the audience, though still within sight and sound of the stage, were retired from the main body of the Oxford Hall, which was usurped by the stall seats in use at the regular theatres. The music hall was already beginning to take the path previously trodden by the saloon theatre, in identifying itself as nearly as might be with the dramatic régime. This action of the halls in partially banishing the restaurant element from the auditorium thus began that change of policy, completed by the London County Council many years after, which eliminated altogether the institution of the public cabaret. This was effected finally through the L.C.C.'s very elastic use of " general powers " by the issue of a circular to all music hall managers in the early days of the 1914 War to the effect that, as the practice of drinking in the auditorium had been largely discontinued, it was advisable that the abstention should become universal.

Emily Soldene, whose early history is bound up in Morton's, gives a lively account, in her reminiscences, of the Oxford Hall in its first years. She describes it as " a magnificent structure in the Italian style . . . beautifully decorated with frescoes, gilding and lots of light. Bars down the side were dressed with plenty of flowers, coloured glass . . . brass-bound barrels and bottles." She adds that the most attractive feature of these bars were the barmaids.[1]

The opening of the hall, delayed by the machinations of the rival interests in Holborn, was celebrated by Morton in his usual

[1]Her recollection of the rows of little tables at which people smoked and drank must be qualified in the respect to which I have referred above.

grandiose manner by the engagement of the famous singers Rosa Paripa and Charles Santley. Sims Reeves had been approached, but had declined the offer, perhaps, with some memory of his experiences at the Grecian Saloon.[1] Morton was, however, determined that his new music hall should justify a literal interpretation of its title and that a sensational note should be sounded. The bill was, of course, not lacking in the more conventional music hall elements—a cornet solo and the performances of two comedians were included, though neither of the latter bore a name of the magnitude of Sharpe or Sam Cowell : under Morton the Oxford was not destined to provide a new star of the purely music hall type. Dancing, with the Daubans and the Wardes, operatic selections with Emily Soldene and Miss Russell as principal singers were popular features.

Such artists as Tom Maclagan (also seen in opera bouffe) and Harry Liston, both of whom had appeared at the Canterbury, were insufficient to compete as major attractions with the immortal family of lions comiques, in each case the creation of one or other of Morton's rivals. This phenomenon, expressive of the music halls new-born social ambitions, really only existed separately by virtue of the rich and suggestive phrase, said to have been invented by J. J. Poole and to have been applied in the first instance to George Leybourne, who shares with Marie Lloyd and Dan Leno, the supreme place in music hall history. The men to whom this title is by general consent most properly applied were Leybourne, Alfred Vance, Arthur Lloyd, and G. H. Macdermott, and none of these, as I have said, was the discovery of Morton. Each, in his turn, however, appeared at the Oxford, for as yet contracts included no "barring" clause which sought to secure the monopoly of a particular artist's work. The individuality of each member of this group was, however, imprinted on particular halls : that of Leybourne on the Royal, Holborn, and the Canterbury ; of Lloyd and Macdermott on the Pavilion ; and of Vance on the Oxford. Leybourne, the greatest of the four and the first to assume the full dignities of the cult, did not sing at the Oxford during the Morton management, and it was the need for a comic singer of the first magnitude to pit against the furore created by him at the Royal which probably led to Vance's engagement at the Oxford in 1866.

Unlike his rival, Vance belonged to the older theatrical tradition from which the earlier concert-room artists had detached themselves. He was born in 1840, and was by a year or two the

[1]Clement Scott has stated that Morton invited Sims Reeves to sing at the Canterbury, in his own phrase, "to sing to the people, however lowly, however humble." Some confirmation of this is given by his biographer, Mr. C. E. Pearce, but I can find no supporting evidence. It is a fact that Sims Reeves, under the pseudonym of Johnson, sang at the Grecian earlier.

senior member of the fraternity. His earliest experiences were those of a " circuit " actor under Edmund Falconer, a dramatic author and manager in the 'fifties of the theatre at Preston. Vance also played with the Northamptonshire group of theatres known as Jackman's Circuit. Later, in Manchester, he was unwillingly faced with the performance of a number of the leading Shakespearean characters, the town being informed of his appearance in these parts before his arrival. It is said, however, that on this occasion some compromise was effected with the management, so that it is uncertain whether the future creator of *Cliquot* and *The Chickaleary Cove* was ever seen in the character of Richard III. In Liverpool, during this period of his career, he found himself a member of a distinguished company which included Benjamin Webster, Barry Sullivan, Robson and Charles Matthews.

His first breakaway from the legitimate stage of the provinces was made by Vance when he adopted the well-worn scheme of a one-man entertainment, in which he danced and sang his way through the country, playing twenty separate parts at each performance. The method remained a favourite one with him, and on his reappearance in London after these tours he would give publicity to the fact that he had been patronized by " His Royal Highness the Prince of Wales and the aristocracy and clergy of Great Britain and Ireland." It was on the suggestion of J. J. Poole, then manager and musical director of the Metropolitan (or White Lion) in the Edgware Road, that Vance was brought to London and sang at this hall and the Philharmonic in Islington. This was in or about 1864. As this date synchronized with Leybourne's first London appearance, he may be said to have shared with the latter the work of popularizing on the London stage characters of the " heavy swell type which are the hall-mark of the lion comique."

The arrival of this kind of artist had become inevitable since Morton had begun to encourage a feeling for display in the music hall, and pint pots of porter had been exchanged for magnums of champagne. Both Vance and Leybourne strove to uphold the reputation for being the first in the field with this new and fashionable character-type. To Vance must be given precedence if one dates the movement from his famous *Slap Bang, Here We Are Again*—though that song had, indeed, little claim to originality. Leybourne, on the other hand, was undoubtedly a pioneer with his *Champagne Charlie*, which was answered by Vance with *Cliquot*, and again countered by Leybourne with *Cool Burgundy Ben*. There was very little resemblance between the two comedians, though they were continually plaguing one another in this way. Vance, with his theatrical technique, was by far the more ver-

satile. He was, moreover, an expert dancer. Leybourne based his style entirely upon the presentation of his own expansive personality and on the occasional use in ballad of a fine natural voice. Vance's repertory included coster songs and songs written in "flash" and Cockney dialect. The two most important of these were *Costermonger Joe* and *The Chickaleary Cove*. Of the latter it is claimed in one printing of the song that Vance was its author and composer; another edition cites W. Bain as the composer and Ernee Clarke as the author of the lyric. A number of songs are attributed to Vance; among them an "answer" to George Ware's *Dark Girl Dressed in Blue* called *The Fair Girl Dressed in Check*, and an early song in the "swell" manner (perhaps his first) called *The Style, By Jove*. There is also a song written in the Harry Clifton manner. *Act on the Square, Boys*, which had a considerable vogue. An opportunity for rivalry in another direction arose from his extremely popular *Walking in the Zoo*, to which Leybourne replied with *Lounging in the Aq*. An entire change of theme was provided by *Come to your Martha*, in which the singer impersonated a bathing-machine woman. The sum of Vance's advantages and disadvantages as a music hall performer were to be found in this versatility, which was a weakening influence in his music hall work. For the day of the pure entertainer had arrived, and though artists were still to reach the music hall stage by way of the theatre, they were, for the most part, to limit their work, as in the case of G. H. Macdermott, to the exploitation of a single element of personality, whether natural or assumed. It was his lack of concentration which, from the music-hall angle, renders Vance a less significant artist than Leybourne, whom history remembers and will continue to remember for this reason.

This incomparable singer arrived on the music hall stage by way of the "free-and-easies" of the Midlands, having begun life as an artizan—an engine-fitter in Newcastle, according to the *Birmingham Daily Mail* for September 16th, 1884; according to Chance Newton, a hammer-man at Maudsley's in London. Considerable obscurity surrounds his early career: H. G. Hibbert states that the Midlands were his "jumping-off ground." All authorities give the Canterbury under William Holland as the place of his first London engagement of major importance. This occurred in or about 1865, and according to Hibbert once more, Leybourne, after having earned money as an entertainer in the manufacturing counties ("some foolery with a mechanical donkey of his own invention" is mentioned), came to London on a holiday, which was prolonged by engagements in the outlying halls. This is rather an improbable statement of the facts. The *Birmingham Mail* has it that at Wolverhampton and elsewhere, Leybourne had for some time been earning £3 a week as a singer,

as there is little doubt that these Northern appearances had for some years predated his London career. The *Era* for July 16th, 1909, states that Harry Hart, one of the most redoubtable promoters of music halls, who, in turn, was connected with the Raglan, Theobalds Road, the Salmon, Southwark, the Montpelier, Walworth, the Sun, Knightsbridge, and the Bedford, Camden Town, gave Leybourne his first actual appearance in London at the first-named of these house. A year or two of growing popularity resulted in the Canterbury engagement, which occurred about 1868.

Holland, with Morton and E. T. Smith, belongs to the group of men who took the music halls, as it were, by the scruff of the neck and " made " them. The engagement of Leybourne was one of those happy instances of the magnetism of personalities. The two men were born to co-operate. The term " lion comique " as has been suggested, had probably a separate origin. But the richness of the term is fully in harmony with Holland's methods by which he threw over Leybourne a remarkable glamour. The effort was not a wasted one : Leybourne had a nature which warmly responded to Holland's showmanship. He was a remarkably handsome and superbly proportioned man, the possessor, as has already been said, of a fine and magnetic voice and with a natural stage presence expressing itself with that ease and " inevitableness " of gesture which is an inbred quality. Leybourne, who, by now, it is reported, had received offers at a considerable salary in the provinces, was engaged by Holland at £30 a week. He at once became the rage and the arrival of *Champagne Charlie* redoubled his popularity. The astute manager, realizing to the full the possibilities of Leybourne as the music hall type of the "jeunesse dorée," then supplied him with a carriage drawn by four white horses in which he stipulated that the singer should drive from one hall to another. The excellent opportunity provided by this for a mimicry in burlesque was not overlooked by Leybourne's rivals. According to Chance Newton, it was Harry Liston who ridiculed his rival by appearing in the streets driving a cart drawn by four donkeys, but by an elderly man with whom I had the pleasure of a chat in the bar of the Winchester in the Southwark Bridge Road, the action was attributed to Walter Laburnum, whose marked resemblance to Leybourne would have given point to the joke. He, moreover, recalled that, whereas Leybourne's coachman and Tiger were dressed as jockeys, those of Laburnum were arrayed in the peaked caps worn by shoeblacks.

A pen-and-ink drawing by Alfred Bryan, the caricaturist of the *Entr'acte*, shows Leybourne in all his "near-gentlemanly" splendour dressed in a handsome fur-collared coat, his delicate

hands ringed, a cigar poised. The clothes were as important a part of his public personality as the equipage in which he rode, or the bottles of champagne which he distributed nightly in the theatre bars. But Leybourne, in spite of *Champagne Charlie*, was by no means a one-song man. He excelled in a group of songs devoted to romantic and adventurous themes, such as *Zazel, Zazel*, *The Flying Trapeze*, and *Up in a Balloon*. At times he gave " character " performances, as in *The Mouse-Trap Man*.

Numerous " ladies' versions " of the songs were purveyed by the female serio-comics ; and Nellie Power, whose vogue at the Royal, Holborn after the accession of Sweasey and William Holland, was only second to that of Leybourne himself, added to their popularity by her performances. Nellie Power may be cited as a predecessor of Vesta Tilley, though with less of the genuine quality as a male impersonator than her contemporary, Bessie Bonehill. In spite of the innovations of Mdme. Vestris many years earlier, the wearing of realistic male costume by women had not reached the music halls in the 'seventies. On a song cover of this decade, Nellie Power is depicted as wearing the tights, spangles and tight-waisted corsage of tradition, the whole crowned by one of the fashionable curly-brimmed bowler hats. As with Leybourne, the Royal, Holborn forestalled the Oxford by its presentation of another short-lived sensation, J. H. Stead, *The Perfect Cure*. The title is derived from an immensely popular song, accompanied by an eccentric dance, this artist's sole claim to a posthumous reputation. The lyric of the song was the work of Frederick Perry, and the air, attributed to John Blewitt, as Chance Newton has reminded us, was a variant of a forgotten classic called *The Monkey and the Nuts*. Stead was primarily a dancer, and the song was merely the excuse for the execution of a number of contortions and especially of a leap performed by jumping with both feet at once. This, if we are to believe the statement of *Household Words*, he was able to achieve 1,600 times in succession. He performed the song in a very unattractive clown's costume and conical hat, which had the effect of exaggerating the dancer's height. It is impossible at this distance of time to account for the immense vogue of the *Perfect Cure* ; no clue is provided either by the verses or the music of the song, which are completely devoid of interest.

The rivalry of the Royal and the Oxford continued through the 'sixties without producing at either place any extension of the music hall art. Morton's one innovation, the operatic selections, were faithfully reproduced at the Holborn house, and performances from scenes of *Massaniello* were given. Both houses also produced a certain proportion of ballet. Apart from these features, the programmes conformed more or less faithfully to the concert-

room tradition. It was elsewhere that developments were being made, in the new field opened up by the establishment of the Alhambra Music Hall in Leicester Square.

This house had been inaugurated by E. T. Smith as early as 1854, upon the collapse of the Panoptikon. The versatile manager, whose varied career, it will be remembered, included the direction of Cremorne Gardens and who, as a publican, had, in 1850, achieved notoriety by dressing his barmaids in "Bloomer" costume, acquired the Panoptikon building, together with its remarkable contents, and having sold its organ to St. Paul's Cathedral, and disposed somehow of the scientific apparatus, provided the place with a stage and opened it as a Theatre of Varieties on a policy which included operatic selections in the Morton manner, and an exhibition by the celebrated prize-fighters, Sayers and Heenan. After Smith's tenancy followed a briefer adaptation of the house and a period of stability was achieved by Frederick Strange, a caterer who had held a refreshment contract for the Great Exhibition, and who, with considerable success, invested capital in the Alhambra and formed a limited company. An important feature of his management was the introduction of Léotard, the gymnast, to London audiences. The grace exhibited by this artist, who was credited with having originated the special use of the swinging bar known as the flying trapeze, created a furore and the Alhambra henceforward established a traditional association with this type of performance.

Léotard was of French birth and parentage. He was a man of domesticated habits, and his family attended him in all his appearances, even when he was earning the vast salary of 70,000 francs a month at the Cirque Franconi in Paris. They came with him when he visited England. He is remembered by Hollingshead as possessing charming manners and a modest disposition. The sobriety of his nature was reflected in his costume, which differed from the highly-coloured acrobatic costume of tradition. Léotard died at the early age of thirty-seven; according to Hibbert, of smallpox, and to Hollingshead, of consumption. As the founder of a school, he is to be regarded as one of the most important figures in the history of acrobatics.

Under Strange's management (1864-1869) the Alhambra achieved a recrudescence of the theatre of variety in contradistinction to the music hall, and its object appeared to be the partial revival of the saloon theatre of the 'thirties despite the restrictions of the 1843 Act. This policy, attempted in a new and luxurious setting, proceeding, by a logical process, to the production of a ballet of action, soon transferred the scene of the war waged upon this piece of legislation, from the Canterbury Hall to Leicester Square. It is not surprising, therefore, to hear, after

the storm provoked by Morton's attempt at extravaganza at the Canterbury, of the implacable opposition offered by the managers to Strange's production, in the centre of theatrical London, of an opera ballet with music by Auber, which had a few months previously formed the central feature of a spectacle at Drury Lane.

At this stage of the fight, an invaluable ally for the cause of free trade was found in John Hollingshead, whose activities provoked the establishing of the parliamentary committee on Theatre Licensing of 1866, which actually issued a majority report in favour of unrestricted performances. But neither this committee nor the later one which sat in 1892 succeeded in defining the limits of a stage play, and under the unchanged legislative conditions this lack of definition was to cause almost uninterrupted dispute. On Hollingshead's arrival at the Alhambra in 1865, another infringement of the law was attempted by the production of a harlequinade called *Where's the Police?* A prosecution at once followed, and a heavy fine was in this case imposed. It is not to be wondered at that the attack by the legitimate theatre managers was waged fiercely from a combined front, since Strange and Hollingshead were together reinstating the saloon theatre under their noses. Any trace of music hall intimacy had been discarded. The row of respectably garbed opera singers was halved, and a large permanent corps de ballet formed. Another link with the earlier saloon theatre was made by the introduction of aquatic effects, and a remarkable resemblance to the scenic methods of the 'thirties, preserved for us by the designs made for the toy stages, was to be seen in the production of an operatic ballet called *The Spirit of the Waves*. That the pantomime ballet, *Where's The Police?* was in effect a revival of the old dumb-shows based on the Italian masks constituted a strange reversal of the situation as it existed when the status of the minor theatres was in dispute before the passing of the Act, and shows how much closer was the net in which it was sought to imprison the music hall. Luckily for the art of ballet, which was gradually being discarded by the operatic stage, the net proved to be a fragile one. Under the heading of "divertissement," the ballet achieved status as a non-dramatic form and flourished until the arrival of revue both at the Alhambra and the Empire, as an integral part of music hall output—even though the question of the legality of narrative action remained in abeyance. Meanwhile one may picture the fury engendered by the usages of the Alhambra. In this entirely theatrical atmosphere, the long tables laden with food and drink were retained and covered the entire stall area of the house, while on the stage, supported by the findings of the 1866 Committee (though no legislation ever found its way into the Statute Book), a policy was pur-

sued in direct contravention to the spirit of the Act.

The peculiar nature of the Alhambra building, with its Panoptikon rooms convertible into restaurants and supper bars, made it possible for Strange's hall to excel any of the others in providing facility for drinking and lounging. A booklet issued by the company and compiled by William White, a former lecturer on physics at the Panoptikon, makes enthusiastic references to the fact that " in every direction, neatly fitted-up bars and stalls, presided over by the most civil and obliging demoiselles, offer inducements for the lounger to indulge himself in what a facetious friend denominates 'Perkins.' " The principal supper-room was on the left of the vestibule. The Saloon, constructed so as to give a view from one side to the stage, was the prototype of the Promenade at the Empire, and was used for the same purpose. The unique room of the theatre was, however, the " Canteen," provided by the solicitous management for the use of the performers and staff, but which our friend Ewing Ritchie discovered (and in his essay on the Alhambra he indignantly passed on the tip to all whom it might concern), was accessible to members of the audience by the exercise of a little " influence." Of this rather equivocal institution he further expressed himself in the following unmeasured terms :

" The most objectionable feature of the place is the ' Canteen.' . . . The Canteen is an underground cellar with a refreshment bar and benches and tables of the plainest and rudest description. Looking through a dense haze of tobacco smoke, you will see some forty or fifty ballet girls standing chatting or seated in company with their male admirers. A ballet girl need not be an objectionable character . . . As a rule, the difference between her and other girls of the same rank of life, is that she looks a little more shabby, and that her clothes are a trifle dirtier ; but in the Canteen she appears in her conventional dress as she is displayed on the stage with flashing eye and beauteous form. If she is virtuous she cannot be expected to remain so long, as the Canteen is opened for the convenience of herself and her admirers . . . . No wonder that the girls are bold and brazen, intent chiefly on a liberal display of personal charms . . . but there are those to whom the fact that a girl belongs to the ballet renders her additionally attractive ; to such the long, dingy Canteen, with its bare boards and benches and whitewashed, walls is a great attraction."[1]

[1]This and other attacks is countered by the *Handbook* in the following words : " There exists, despite all that has been said or written by ignorant or spiteful critics to the contrary, an exceedingly well-conducted Apartment, where, at a reduced Tariff, the whole of the Staff are accommodated with the refreshments which their frequently painful labours create a demand for. This snuggery is under the perpetual surveillance of the principal Officers ; and, under certain proper modifications, open to visitors."

While the Alhambra's claim to supremacy in ballet was for a number of years uncontested, it also gathered fame for its presentation of acrobatic displays. Following on the performances of Léotard were the unforgettable exploits of Blondin which, in turn, were followed by his imitator, Farini, who together with his son " Lulu " were major sensations of the 'seventies. The account of the latter artists, however, more properly belongs to the story of the Westminster Aquarium.

Though the great Blondin is chiefly remembered in England by his performances at the Crystal Palace and the Alhambra, it was William Holland who, at the Canterbury, introduced this acrobat to London. Never since the days of Jacob Hall or Madame Saqui (who at the age of seventy-one ascended the high-rope in Vauxhall Gardens), had the country been so moved by the performances of a tight-rope walker. Like his great contemporary, Léotard, Blondin was a Frenchman—the name being not, as has been stated, an assumed one. He was born in 1824 and was the son of one of Napoleon's officers. At the age of six he became excited by the performances of some travelling acrobats, and his father placed him in the Ecole de Gymnase at Lyons. Thence he made his first appearance on the boards as an equilibrist, with the title of " The Little Wonder." A turning point in his life was the offer he received from the Ravel family of acrobats, with whom he first visited America, which became his country by adoption.[1] Here he conceived the major feat of his life, the crossing of Niagara Falls upon a rope. This was achieved by him for the first time on June 30th, 1859, when he was thirty-five years of age. The intrepidity and supreme showmanship which he brought to this attempt at once made him world-famous. The event was witnessed by twenty-five thousand persons who had been brought to the falls by every possible means of conveyance. They were regaled by the performance of wonders far more complicated than the simple crossing on a rope hung at an altitude of a hundred and sixty feet above the basin of the falls. Midway across, Blondin lay on the rope at full length and then turned a back-somersault. The journey took him five minutes to accomplish, and to the strains of a band playing the *Marseillaise* he landed safely amid scenes of overwhelming enthusiasm. He then made the return crossing. This time he took a chair with him and, balancing it on the rope by two of its legs, he sat in it ; and on one leg, stood on the seat. In England the story of the feat was discredited, and popular incredulity was increased by a report

[1]A glimpse of the Ravel Family's activities in America is given in N. M. Ludlow's " Dramatic Life as I Found it " (St. Louis, 1880). The author gives the titles of a number of " entertaining pieces " (presumably comedy ballets) which they performed at St. Charles in 1846. The titles include *Blare and Babet*, *Godenska* and *Vol au Vent*. They also gave Bedouin Arab Feats and *Glimpses of the Vatican at Rome*.

which got abroad that Blondin was a purely imaginary person. These rumours were dispelled when he repeated the performance in July and August of the same year, adding a number of new and extraordinary features to the performance, which included a crossing of the falls blindfolded, and bearing a man upon his back (the name of the hero who accompanied him has unfortunately been lost). He also stood on his head upon the rope, " surrounded by a protracted blaze of fireworks." On this occasion the acrobat carried out his performance " in the character of a Siberian Slave." His last crossing of the Niagara was made on September 14th, 1860, in the presence of Albert Edward, Prince of Wales. On this occasion he achieved the unparalleled feat of crossing the Falls on stilts. He also politely offered to carry the Prince over, but this was declined, it is said, only on the urgent advice of the Duke of Cambridge, who was also present.

In April 1862 Blondin arrived in London under an engagement to appear at the Crystal Palace for twelve performances for an inclusive fee of £1,200. Blondin's appearance at the Crystal Palace was fiercely attacked by Charles Dickens in *Household Words*, who took up his favourite journalistic pose of public moralist and castigated the enthusiastic multitudes on the score of morbid curiosity. His performances on these occasions were embellished by further marvels. He appeared on the rope in the character of a " chef de cuisine " and cooked himself an omelette in mid-air on one of Walker's patent self-feeding stoves ; he also played the march from William Tell, on a fiddle, dancing and somersaulting the while. The scene at these first performances is romantically described by Linnaeus Banks, who wrote a monograph on the great acrobat which was published in the following year. " What with the glorious sunshine," he said, " streaming in through dome and transept, the flags of all nations drooping gracefully from the galleries, the fountains radiant with many hues . . . it resembled a picture from the Arabian Nights Tales." And this setting served to underline the fabulous nature of the feats performed on the rope stretched from balcony to balcony. The whole of London was glutted by these miracles. It reacted with a blaze of Blondin worship, and the usual spate of souvenirs—garments, trinkets and fal-las—bearing the name of the hero was poured forth. The governors of the Crystal Palace netted a profit of over ten thousand pounds. As a thank-offering they presented Blondin with a gold medal, " in token of his courage and talents, being the only gift of this sort offered by the Directors to any individual, since the memorable presentation to Her Majesty on the occasion of the opening of the building."

After a provincial tour, during which, at Sheffield, an eighteen-months-old lion cub was wheeled in a barrow across

the rope, Blondin made his first appearance in a London Music Hall, the Canterbury, and this was followed by his engagement at the Alhambra. Previously, however, he had made an excursion into the dramatic field, by appearing in a melodrama called *The Child of the Wreck*, written by his manager, Coleman. In this work, played in " a newly-erected and elegantly appointed stage in the centre transept of the Crystal Palace," he sustained the part of a monkey and was said to have revealed 'mimetic' powers of the highest order."

At the Alhambra, at which his first appearance was under the management of William Wilde, the circus proprietor, Blondin repeated the awe-inspiring performance of the Crystal Palace and provided a thrill for jaded pleasure-seekers by carrying passengers on his back at five pounds a time. He thus established that connection with London entertainment which was not broken until his death in 1890, which occurred at his villa home in Northfields. This great artist had in his later years gradually decreased the number of his public appearances in favour of recreations which included chess-playing, horsemanship, agriculture and mathematics. The existence of a Niagara Avenue marks the site of his now demolished English home and gives testimony to the depth of the feelings which he inspired.

The Alhambra, having stimulated the production of ballet in England on a spectacular scale, played its part, under the vigorous direction of Hollingshead, in presenting a dance which scandalized the professional moralists at the close of the 'sixties and helped to bring upon the music halls a stigma reflected in the refusal of so many licences in the following decade—this was the celebrated Can-Can. Though Hollingshead infers in his memoirs that it was he who actually introduced the dance to the London stage, this is not entirely substantiated by an inquiry into the facts.

In 1867, a pantomime produced at the Lyceum by E. T. Smith, Strange's predecessor at the Alhambra, had been enlivened by the inclusion of Finette, who danced the Can-Can in the production and earned the approval of the Press for her version of this variant of the revolutionary Carmagnole. Hollingshead mentions this engagement as having been inspired by himself, but in the previous year an operatic production which should have included the dance had been presented at Drury Lane with this omission, and there can be no doubt that the astute Smith was on the watch for an opportunity to make the omission good. In the following year, Clodoche, a brilliant amateur who had evolved the Can-Can as an entertainment for his friends at the Parisian *bal masqués*, made his first appearance in England with his now professional troupe, at the Princess's Theatre then under the management of E. T. Smith.

Meanwhile, in the spring of this year, Finette had made her first appearances at the Alhambra in a ballet called *Mabille*. The Clodoche performances were repeated in 1869 at Covent Garden, and in the following year at the Philharmonic Hall (under Morton). At the latter house the Clodoche troupe had been preceded by the engagement of Sara (who suffered the nickname of " wiry Sal "), and who had trained with another group of Can-Can specialists, the Colonna troupe. This artist interpolated the dance in the 1870 revival of an abbreviated version of Hervé's *Le Roi Chilperic*. Sara was followed by the entire Colonna group at the Philharmonic, hut it was not until the late summer of this year that the Can-Can was danced at the Alhambra by the Colonnas in a ballet called *Les Nations*. In the following month the music hall licence was cancelled. This incident roughly synchronized with the Clodoche appearances at the Philharmonic, and brought to a climax the rage which had seized not only the West End of London but had found its way to the outlying houses such as Giovanelli's Alexandra theatre attached to the casino at Highbury Barn. The Alhambra, by this time under the management of John Baum, suffered the loss of its music hall licence for fourteen years, during which time it continued a policy of dramatic ballet under a theatre licence. In 1884 its music hall status was revived.

The same year marked the foundation of the Empire Theatre on the north side of Leicester Square which was destined to carry on and further the new movement in the music hall. The site of the house was acquired under a mortgage and built under the management of a limited company with H. J. Hitchins as its general manager. The ground on which the new theatre stood had behind it a long history of entertainment and pleasure-seeking, of a Bohemian and international character. It is impossible here to discuss in any detail the conglomeration of entertainments which had, before 1870, partially absorbed the sites of Leicester and Savile Houses. Some mention has already been made of the needlework exhibitions of Miss Linwood in the 'thirties—those works for which thousands of pounds were offered (and refused) by the " simple-minded exemplary schoolmistress," who preferred to make a presentation of her *chef d' œuvre* to Queen Victoria. Confusion has often been allowed to creep in where references have been made to the entertainments on this site. Leicester House, partially demolished at the end of the eighteenth century, when its grounds were built over in the making of Lisle Street, was reconditioned early in the nineteenth century, and it was in the reconditioned house that the Linwood and other exhibitions were held.

From the respectabilities of pictorial needlework until 1865

when it was pulled down, Savile House, as this rebuilt site was called, became, in the words of Augusta Sala, "the greatest booth in Europe." Of the shows, the "poses plastiques," in imitation of those popularized by Renton Nicholson, played an important part. Sala, in his entertaining *Gaslight and Daylight*, gives a vivid story of a visit he paid to one of these performances. "The subject was Adam and Eve in the Garden of Eden. Adam by Herr Something, and Eve by Madame Somebody . . . The most amusing part of the Entertainment was the middle thereof, at which point, two warriors, arrayed in the uniform of Her Majesty, appeared on the Turn Table, and claimed Adam as a deserter from the third Buffs." For the rest, the place had all the characteristics of an indoor fair. Agagin, in the words of Sala, who summarized the matter admirably, "Serpents, both of land and sea—panoramas of all the rivers of the known world; jugglers, ventriloquists, imitations of the noises of animals, dioramas of the North Pole, and the gold diggers of California; somnambulists (very lurid) . . ; giants; dwarfs; sheep with six legs; calves born inside out; marionettes; living marionettes; lectures on Bloomerism; expositions of 'orrery.' . . . One touch of showmanship makes the whole world kin in this omni-showing house."

Savile House, too, had its "Shades" of a character to remind Sala of the night cellars of the eighteenth century; but it was in the remains of the adjacent Leicester House (the Leicester Square frontage of the nineteenth century covered the garden-ground of the original mansion), that the life of the Café Chantant was centred, previously to the fire which put an end to the separate identity of the two houses. In the early 'fifties, over the garden frontage just mentioned was developed the "Parisian Café." A fire then rendered the site derelict for fourteen years, after which a theatre, the Alcazar, was projected but abandoned for a larger scheme by which, under the name of the Denmark, in honour of the Princess Alexandra, a theatre was to be combined with a club and a winter garden. Neither of these projects was achieved and after a period of panorama and the like, a house with a very short history known as the Pandora was opened. The promotion of the Empire Theatre was the result of the seizure of the property whilst languishing under the unsuccessful régime of the Pandora, by Nicols, the proprietor of the Café Royal. Here unsuccessful ventures in opera bouffe, first under Morton, who revived *Chilperic*, and later under Hollingshead, occupied a year or so. Then the music hall licence was applied for and finally granted eight years after the opening of the house, and variety entertainment in the West End of London entered upon the height of its "flash" period. When the form of licence was

By courtesy of British Museum

Miss Enid Brett's collection

GROUNDS OF EAGLE TAVERN—GRECIAN SALOON IN BACKGROUND

changed, a new company holding the premises with George Edwardes as managing director fitted the seats in the auditorium with glass-holders and the place began to flow with champagne. The "Promenade," an extension of the old concert-room "saloon," rapidly became a predominant feature of the house, the traditions of the immediate neighbourhood lending it the picturesque colour aptly conveyed in the phrase "Cosmopolitan Club of the World."

The Empire was not suffered to flourish long before it became a cynosure of Puritan eyes. The Promenade was the storm centre, and within two years the clouds, which had been gathering since 1870, burst. In October 1892 the renewal of the music and dancing licence was, for the first time, seriously opposed by a committee of ladies, headed by Mrs. Ormiston Chant, whose demands for a reconstitution of the auditorium was based on the scandalous extent to which it was alleged traffic in prostitution was being carried on in the Promenade. The Management countered the suggestion with a vigour which went beyond the limits of discretion, threatening ruin and consequent unemployment as the result of any tampering with this feature of the house. The question of the conditions of licence, at first debated by the Theatres and Music Halls Committee of the London County Council, resulted in a recommendation (slyly whittled down in co-operation with an obliging architect), that (1) the Promenade be abolished, and (2) that no drink be sold in the auditorium.

The suggested amendments then came before the main body of the Council. The hearing was followed eagerly in the Press, and the proceedings afforded an excellent if rather equivocal advertisement for the management. Clement Scott, somewhat irrelevantly, made the matter a platform for his campaign of "free trade in the theatre" and excelled his previous efforts in *Daily Telegraph* articles which he called *Prudes on the Prowl.* For the opposing views, an eminent Q.C. appeared on behalf of the Empire Theatre, and Mrs. Chant herself voiced the attitude of her committee. The latter based her arguments on an attempted refutation of the plea that the theatre would be endangered financially by insistence on the alterations, and on prophecies of an improvement in public morals resulting from the abolishment of the Promenade. Her opponent confined himself to a defence of the rights of private property.

One ray of light was shed by John Burns, who spoke as a member of the Council. He accused the Empire management of lying, and he reminded Mrs. Chant that "it was not by harrowing prostitutes that prostitution can be diminished," but only by removing the economic conditions by which it is aggravated. A

Colonel Rotton then arrived on the scene to add to the gaiety of the meeting. He pointed out that " as for the Empire, the evidence was either in favour of it or against it. (Laughter). He was always pleased to give an opportunity for laughter, but . . . to shut up a place like this would be absolutely to conduce to the immorality already so rampant in the streets of London." And by way of giving point to this impressive pronouncement, he immediately followed up his line of argument in the following manner : " He would like to say that ladies quite as pure, quite as moral, quite as anxious for the well-being and morality of London had been to the Empire constantly (a councillor : to the Promenade ?), and they told him that they had never seen anything to which a modest and pure-minded person could take the slightest exception. (A councillor : To the Promenade ?) To the Promenade ! These constant interruptions were unfair, considering that he was giving an interesting statement . . . He had been to the place himself," . . . etc.

The votes went in favour of insistance on a slender bulwark designed as a concealment to the promenade bar, and an immediate outcry in all directions was the result. In point of historical fact, absolutely no material change resulted from the entire business, for the life of the Promenade continued quite undisturbed by the new regulations. The only tangible result, indeed, was one of those light-hearted riots known affectionately as " rags " which in England have always been a popular vehicle of public opinion. The scene centred itself in the auditorium in the vicinity of the lath and canvas screen placed, according to the architect's requirements, round the dress-circle bar. Quite early at the performance in question, a feeling of unrest was noticeable in the audience by the recurrence of wild outbursts of applause. When Eugene Stratton came on the stage to sing his coon-songs, he was humorously shouted down and was forced to retire. Then an attack was levelled at the screen. " Well-dressed men," reported the *Evening Standard*, " some of them almost middle-aged, kicked at it from within, bursting the canvas . . . The attendants watched in helpless and amused inactivity. Mr. Hitchins attempted argumentative remonstrance . . . The crowd then went out into the street, brandishing fragments of the screen." In all it was calculated that the crowd was swelled to the number of about twenty thousand. It may be added that one of these gentlemen was a famous Prime Minister.

The atmosphere of high jinks which characterized West End life in the " naughty 'nineties " had been fostered in the previous decades by an institution which by transmutation added another music hall to the West End. This was the assembly room or " casino " known as the Argyll Rooms. Its history is relegated to

obscurity by most historians of London. Wheatley, for instance, remarks that " the place gained an unsavoury reputation and has no history worthy of relation." Still, the growth of the casino, which may be attributed partly to the decline of the tavern as a social centre, played a part of some importance in social life. The Argyll Rooms dated from the 'sixties. They occupied a site at one time a tennis court attached to a gaming-house called Piccadilly Hall, and the name Argyll Rooms appears to have been a purely arbitrary one. In any event it has no connection with those earlier Argyll Rooms in Regent Street which were the scene of Fulke Greville's Pic-Nic Society, though the similarity of the title has led to confusion.[1] The proprietorship of the rooms, first constituted as a dancing academy and ball room by the son of the clown Laurent, passed by inheritance to Robert Bignell. Under his management, the unwelcome attention of the newly formed London County Council was focussed on the place, and in 1878 its dancing licence was rescinded.[2] After a short period Bignell reopened the place as a music hall under the name of the Trocadero.

Success did not at first result from the change of policy, in spite of the commerce of its enormous bar which exceeded the stall area of the house. Then Charles Coborn, with the manuscript of his famous *Two Lovely Black Eyes* in his pocket, secured a fortnight's engagement there in the absence of Bignell on holiday in July 1886. Coborn, whose autobiography reveals him as an idealist with an unconquerable personality, has described very vividly the success of his song, which created a furore perhaps unique in music hall history. For his engagement, limited by the original arrangement to fourteen days, was prolonged during fourteen months, and during the entire period *Two Lovely Black Eyes* was sung with unexampled success. Previously he had sung the song for a few performances at the Paragon in Mile End. The neighbourhood had at once become infected with its refrain and Coborn has left it on record that he saw " parties of girls and lads of the coster fraternity, all of a row, arm in arm, shouting out my chorus at the top of their voices." The Trocadero is enshrined in the memory of this famous song (a parody of a forgotten ballad), the second line of whose chorus is, I think, rightly acclaimed by the author as the *clou* of the whole matter.

[1]Probably Thornbury is contrasting Fulke Greville's Argyle Rooms with Bignell's in the following comment : " They indeed were aristocratic and bad ; the present Rooms, it appears, are equally vicious but not equally aristocratic."

[2]Dancing was, of course, the major attraction : a small element of other entertainment was offered later. A bill of 1870 announces Solo Euphonium, Signor Monca, and Solo Cornet, Mr. Graves. The charges for admission were on a music-hall basis, admission to the body of the hall was 1s., to the balcony 2s.

When that line entered the author's brain (in a train making the rather uninspiring journey from Aldgate to Shepherd's Bush) his joy was not a misplaced one, for it carried much of the success of a whole career.

The equally celebrated *Man Who Broke the Bank at Monte Carlo* is of a slightly later date and was not sung at the Trocadero. This song was sent to Coborn by the author, Fred Gilbert, whose prolific output as a writer of lyrics ranged from broad comedy to the sentiment of such things as *Little Willie's Grave*. Coborn's performance of these two songs was the peak of his career, though during a long period of prosperity in which his name ranked with the greatest stars of the time, his repertory was a very varied one. In *Another Kind Love* and *Our 'Armonic Club* he identified himself completely with the lower classes, and it was the veracity of these studies and their fullness of detail which made him seem essentially the comedian of the proletarian music hall, though he lived through and contributed so notably to its transition to High Life.

In Coborn one sees how nearly the two aspects of the music hall approached one another. His adoption of the "swell" type in *The Man Who Broke the Bank* was not made without some misgivings and its success, outstanding though it was, did not eclipse the vogue of *Two Lovely Black Eyes*, by which he discovered a common denominator for the audiences of the Mile End Road and Piccadilly Circus. If the Trocadero stood for anything it was perhaps this welding of flash life with the simple methods of the concert room. The aristocracy was well represented among the *habitués* of the place. Mr. Coborn remembers one remarkable evening when he counted, out of curiosity, seven peers and baronets sitting round one little table. "I do not remember them all," he says, "but I do remember Lord de Clifford, Lord Lurgon, Sir Edward Sassoon, Lord Garmoyle (son of Earl Cairns—his dearest friends christened him 'gumboil'), and Sir George Chetwynd."

In the manner of the Empire and the Alhambra and, like the latter house, forming a link with schemes of Victorian social purpose, was the Westminster Aquarium. In a somewhat modified degree, the scheme for the Aquarium was, as Mr. Erroll Sherson puts it, to form a Crystal Palace in the centre of London. It was preceded by the erection of a similar place at Brighton in 1873. So late a flowering of the movement (the Westminster house was inaugurated in January 1876) was not likely to make a very determined effort in the educational direction. The Mr. Wheatley who tells us that the history of the Argyll Rooms is unworthy of comment finds little consolation in the Westminster Aquarium. After informing us that it "is a building of great extent, occupying the whole of the north side of Tothill Street,"

and that its architect was Mr. Bedborough, he continues, "it was projected as a Summer Lounge and Winter Garden as well as Aquarium and a place for high-class music and refined entertainment ; but its chief attractions have been firing women from cannon, dancing Zulus, swimming ladies, and like elegant and 'stimulating' exhibitions."

This is a sufficient indication of its general characteristics. In its use of aquatic spectacle and circus it is an historical link between the theatre of Astley and his imitators and, later, places such as the London Hippodrome and the vast Empress Hall of the Earls Court Exhibition. A hint of its rather uncertain ideals may be gathered from the list of its first directors which included Sir Arthur Sullivan, Bassano, the photographer, and William Whiteley. Wybrow Robertson was the actual promoter, who shared with Henry Labouchère the major financial interest.

The house comprised not only the elaborate Summer and Winter Garden, but, separately constructed, a theatre, standing on ground where, in 1834, an earlier theatre had been erected. Labouchère took sole control of the theatre and his first production there was an adaptation of *Bleak House* called *Jo*. The subsequent history of the Aquarium Theatre after its decline, and the purchase in 1903 of the whole Aquarium property by the Wesleyan Methodists, is not without interest. After a failure as an "Afternoon Theatre," it was leased by the celebrated Mrs. Langtry, and was very elaborately redecorated with banners, purple silk draperies and an art-needlework tableau curtain. In the reconstituted house Ellen Terry produced Ibsen's *The Vikings*, with Gordon Craig's settings, and here also Lewis Waller was seen in two of his most famous parts, *Henry the Fifth* and *Monsieur Beaucaire*.

No Aquarium handbook exists to commemorate its original high-minded purposes, but one gathers that the fish and the exhibits did not long play an important part in the curriculum. Robertson and Labouchère having quarrelled, it came under the sole management of the former, and, shortly afterwards, the acrobat G. A. Farini was called in as a consultative manager. Then there began that long series of sensational attractions with which its memory is associated. The experimental nature of these shows produced endless journalistic comment, and may almost be said to have created social history. Besides the exploits on the wire of Farini himself, together with his son who passed from the phase of "infant prodigy" to a period of masquerading as a beautiful girl under the name of Lulu, they included the notorious acrobatic displays of Zazel and Zaeo, the boxing kangaroo, a Zulu kraal, a bearded lady, and a talking walrus. Among these, first place should be given to Zazel. She was shot

from the mouth of a cannon. The trick, simple in mechanism, produced a widespread protest on the score of its alleged danger, and an extensive advertisement for the Aquarium resulted. Farini was even more successful in his presentation of Zaeo, whose business it was to leap from a great height into a net. The apparent danger of the feat, together with the scantiness of the costume in which it was performed and the audacity of the poster by which it was advertised, provoked a scandal, which, it has been alleged, had been vigorously spread by the management.

The performances took place on a stage at the end of a railed-off part of the building. Within the enclosure seats were sold, but beyond people might assemble as they pleased, and a view of the shows might also be had from the balconies which ran round the walls. Gradually this element of the place, originally one of its "side-shows," became the major attraction and the music-hall comedians found their way there.[1] Meanwhile, the reputation of the Aquarium as a place of public resort had suffered. The Zaeo affair had probably been fomented merely as an element of the Purity Campaign, indeed, a libel action brought by the directors, of which the story is told in Findlater Bussey's *Sixty Years of Journalism*, indicated the fantastic degree to which the place had come under the ban of the moralists. The suit centred round a marionette performance, and Bussey's book may perhaps be quoted : "One day, at a time when I was unaware of the suit of the Aquarium Company, my friend, Mr. Wilkinson . . . asked if I had not frequently seen the marionette display? I, of course, replied that I had. 'Well,' said Mr. Wilkinson, 'have you ever noticed anything improper or indecent in it?' 'Certainly not,' I replied ; 'but what scene in the little show are you referring to?' 'That,' answered my friend, 'in which clown and pantaloon go through a series of tricks—I am now referring especially to the butterfly business.' I remembered that there was a scene in which a yellow butterfly was dangled, here and there, across the stage and ineffectually chased by the imitation pantomimists, until at last it settled on the floor, and the clown, thinking he had caught it as he threw himself down where it seemed to be, called out, 'I've got it, Joey.' 'Where?' said the pantaloon, coming across to look.' There,' replied the clown, throwing up his foot and giving his companion a kick under the chin. The next thing I knew of the matter was revealed in my being served with a subpœna to give evidence at the

[1]A specimen programme of the morning session at the Aquarium in its heyday begins as follows : 9 a.m. National Fisheries Exhibition. Free. 10 a.m. to 1 p.m. Free Varieties. Marvellous Performance, over 100 artists. Performing Animals. Pantomime Sketches. Illusions. Ballets. Serio Comics. Strong Man and Woman. Conjuring. Ring Trapeze. Gymnastics. Triple Bar Acrobatic and Mid-Air Performances. Musical Eccentrics, etc.

approaching trial. I was one of the first witnesses examined in the case, and in answer to Mr. Dickens, Q.C., who appeared on behalf of the Aquarium Company, I stated that I had not only seen nothing of an indecent character in the performance, but had taken my wife and my married daughter to witness it, and that during the afternoon entertainments I had frequently seen Members of Parliament and clergymen with their wives and children in the stalls, evidently enjoying the exhibition. The trial ended in a verdict for the plaintiffs, with £500 damages and costs. Against this Mr. Parkinson appealed but without success, and in addition to the £500 damages had to pay the cost of both suits."

The Aquarium's final management, that of Josiah Ritchie, felt the effects of the prosecution and in its last years the Aquarium, although saved from complete insolvency, did not prosper. Important rivals in showmanship, such as the Kiralfy's spectacular productions at Olympia, were appearing on the scene, and under the combination of competition it closed in 1903.

The cycle of important central music halls existing before 1890 is completed by the London Pavilion. Its concert room period has already been touched on ; it remained as an important rival in the larger times of the Empire and the Alhambra. No account of this hall is complete without a mention of the contiguity of Dr. Kahn's anatomical museum which formed a part of the converted swimming baths from which the auditorium adjacent to the original inn was formed. The Trocadero had its museum as a next-door neighbour also, but in the case of the Pavilion the gallery of the house suffered truncation from an intrusion of one of the walls of the museum.

In the case of both the Trocadero and the Pavilion it is perhaps timely to remind the reader of the non-existence, before 1885, of the existence of Shaftesbury Avenue. For a mental picture of the houses, one must think of them in the terms of Great Windmill Street frontages. Not until after that date did the classic façade of the Pavilion arise to serve as a symbol for the pleasure haunts of London in a thousand posters and guide books. From 1878 until then the hall was under the direction of Edwin Villiers, who, as a comedian of the theatre in his early years, did not win the admiration of H. G. Hibbert. He had previously been part proprietor of the South London Music Hall in London Road. His manager in the first years at the Pavilion was Sam Adams, later manager and proprietor of the Trocadero ; a man to whose personal charm and popularity both Chance Newton and Charles Coborn have given testimony.

Most of the leading London music halls achieved a separate personality ; and though one associates the Pavilion's near neigh-

bourhood with its legacy of "Bon Ton" inherited from the Argyll Rooms, yet the atmosphere of the Pavilion was engendered by the homeliness and intimacy of the years of sing-song activity at the associated tavern, the Black Horse. The scene is dominated by the procession of individual artists who have given immortality to the house. Of these the first great name, and for the fortunes of the house the most significant one, is that of Arthur Lloyd, rather strangely described because of his long life, by more than one commentator, as the last of the lions comiques. Actually, he was on the scene about the same time as Leybourne and Vance. Like the latter, he was trained as a legitimate actor. His father was a Scotch comedian of some local importance, and Arthur Lloyd's first professional experience was gained in the stock company in Edinburgh of which his father was a member. His success in songs performed between the dramatic pieces and a marked facility for writing tunes and lyrics suggested a transfer to concert-room work, and he accordingly made a beginning by appearing at the "Whitebait," a musical tavern in Glasgow. His arrival in London in 1862 or 1863,[1] where he secured an engagement at the Islington Philharmonic Hall, was quickly followed by his first great song success, and the consequent appearance at the London Pavilion (quite recently reconstituted under this title by two Jewish restaurateurs, Loibl and Sonnenhammer) was the turning-point both in his own career and that of the new music hall. Under the influence of his personal triumph the house rapidly achieved a reputation, and its status was further raised by the adoption of a policy, instigated by Lloyd, under which the refreshment ticket method of admission was abandoned for a system of priced seats.

The song which was in the main responsible for these occurrences was called *Not for Joseph;* it was written and composed by Lloyd himself and, on publication, achieved an unprecedented sale. It was based on a study of an individual character, that of a 'bus driver named Baxter (the full name is given in the first line of the song), a man who was in the habit of referring genially to himself in the third person. The idea was one in complete harmony with the music hall of the time, based as it was on a piece of familiar observation. The raciness of the subject and the richness of Lloyd's power of character impersonation render its success understandable. He excelled in this quality of intimacy allied with close observation. To choose an instance at random, the opening couplet of a forgotten song:

"Just by the Angel at Islington,
Close by the clock that always is wrong,"

[1]According to Macdonald Rendle, Lloyd was for a time apprenticed to a hatter in the Strand.

gives an indication of the personal style which resulted from his alertness to detail.[1] At the same time, the shrewdness which enabled him to coin a hundred quotable phrases was not accompanied by the warmth of personality which is the pervading quality of a great artist. A number of his early songs were elaborate character studies, often of musicians and instrumentalists. He developed, also, a lyrical vein, as in the celebrated *Pretty Lips Sweeter than Cherry or Plum.* Then there were cockney studies, such as *Immensikoff*, and nonsense songs, of a type popular in his day, such as *Chillingo-Wullabadorie.*

Lloyd's face, which launched a thousand song-covers, was expressive—heavy, yet lit by a smile with a charming dimple in the cheeks. Concannon's portrait of him singing his German Band song is full of suggestion of the character of the man.

Little of Lloyd's private life has become the subject of comment. Off the stage he was apparently not an entertaining person. One hardly looks for a private life from a man who appeared to divide his entire time between writing and singing such an overwhelming number of songs. He was essentially Scotch, a family man who brought up a large number of children. His work was not limited to the music halls. As in the case of other leading comedians, he gave a recital entertainment, and toured with it. This bore the innocuous name of *Two Hours of Genuine Fun.* Like his successor, Macdermott, Lloyd was moreover a playwright, a four-act drama by him called *Bally Voyan* was performed at Newcastle-on-Tyne in 1887.

Lloyd's successor at the Pavilion (though Lloyd survived him) was the "Great" Macdermott. This man, whose original name was Hastings, began life as a labourer and then went to sea for some years. Abandoning the deck for the stage, he appeared in the 'sixties at the Grecian, and before venturing on the halls had himself made an adaptation of Dickens' *Edwin Drood* (Britannia Theatre, 1872), in which he played the part of Grewgious; he had also written a romantic drama on the legend of Henry II and Rosamund. At the Grecian his professional association with its "resident dramatist," Henry Pettitt, had a very important bearing on his career. Pettitt had written a song which Macdermott acquired called *The Scamp*, a charming affair with impudent references to Brigham the Mormon and Odger the Tichborne claimant. The tune was by Lance Major, and the success of the song was never in any doubt. It secured Macdermott his engagement at the Pavilion, where, in the later 'seventies

[1] I cannot resist another couplet. A song, written round the phrase "Just to Show there's no Ill Feeling," gives rise to:

"Yesterday she gave me twins,
Just to show there's no ill feeling."

and during the succeeding decade, he stole the thunder of Arthur Lloyd.

Macdermott's posthumous fame is not associated with a great number of songs ; they are overshadowed by the one shattering success scored by G. W. Hunt's patriotic ballad, which earned for its author the title of "Jingo" Hunt. The occasion of the song was that threatening of Constantinople by the Russians, so confusing to those who had been taught to regard the Turkish Empire as a menace to civilization, but which was seized upon by the man in the street as the occasion for a display of imperialist feeling. Macdermott, with his square jaw, magnificent enunciation and stentorian voice, was just the man to represent this section of the community. The song was felt to be an inspiration by Hunt, who arrived on Macdermott's doorstep with it early one morning. His confidence was not misplaced : its second line, "But by Jingo if we do," added a new word to the language. The phrase was exploited in every direction, notably in the pages of *Punch.* It was translated, moreover, into almost every known language. There is really no more to be said about it than that. There is little suggestion of distinction in the achievement. It was merely a "journalistic" tag of the first magnitude, adapted to the music hall. Hunt, a little man weighed down by a big moustache, had this knack, and it is said that both he and Macdermott took the song very seriously as a contribution to foreign policy.[1]

A later feature of Macdermott's career is less edifying. When the divorce proceedings against Charles Wentworth Dilke were being heard in 1885, he joined the hue and cry after the ruined politician with a song the burden of which was

"Charlie Dilke upset the milk
Taking it home to Chelsea,"

and so much was this intelligent lampoon savoured at the moment that one reads of special "Charlie Dilke" nights being held at Romano's restaurant in the Strand.

[1]Pettit wrote a burlesque of the song ("Waiting for the Signal") for Herbert Campbell. This exhibits a healthy reaction in sentiment :

"I don't want to fight,
I'll be slaughtered if I do.
I'd let the Russians have Constantinople."

Other lines recall feelings freely expressed at the conclusion of the European War :

"Newspapers talk of Russian hate,
Of its ambition tell.
Of course they want a war because
It makes the papers sell.
Let all the politicians
Who desire to help the Turk
Put on the uniform themselves
And go and do the work."

With his excellent voice and powerful personality, Macdermott was an acceptable addition to the ranks of the lions comiques. His theatrical ability was not strained by his work there, though as a character actor his range appears to have been varied for, in addition to the appearances as Grewgious, there were others, as Peggotty in a dramatization of *David Copperfield*. Though he is allowed but little humour by his contemporaries, in a number of his songs one can sense a particular vein of impudence which at times has a somewhat sickening quality. This was well served by such writers as N. G. Travers and Geoffrey Thompson. Strangely enough, Macdermott supplied the nursery with one of its favourite slogans in the song, *Whist! Here comes the Bogie Man*, of which he was the author. In *Dear Old Pals* he sounded a note of sentimental fervour, and perhaps the kindliest picture one can retain of him is conveyed by the chorus of this song, in which the peculiar flavour of tipsy fellowship is fully conveyed :

> " Dear old Pals, Jolly old Pals,
> Clinging together in all sorts of weather ;
> Dear old Pals, jolly old Pals,
> Give me the friendship of dear old Pals."

The Lloyd-Macdermott régime passed on to the 'nineties, and then gave way to the most powerful influence of the modern music hall, that of Dan Leno. As usual, this new influence (in externals, at all events) had no element of actual novelty. The position was rather the other way round. In Dan Leno's triumph the new-fangled Lion Comique was routed by the old timeless comedian. At the earliest, the Lion Comique is traceable to the convivial concert-room singer of the preceding century ; the comic actor-entertainer, on the other hand, has never been entirely without representatives, even among the lions comiques themselves. The direction of the comedians was that of a gradual sharpening and narrowing down of technique towards the presentation of a simplified type, or, at any rate, a single aspect of personality. But in the case of Leno, there was more in it than that. The individual quality of his genius gave a conscious direction to a new kind of co-operation in laughter with his audience. This was the abandonment of the laughter of ridicule, the laughter directed against the common enemy (minions of the law, clergymen, Puritans, tax-collectors and the like), and the replacing of it by a laughter of sympathy and even of introspection.

The organized music hall had been ushered in by many fine actors, and this specialization involving the selection of a type had, to a greater or lesser degree, been achieved by Cowell, Maclagan, Liston, Sharpe and others. It might be argued that

the art of negro impersonation (as instanced by Mackney) was a complete acceptance of the method, and that the quondam actor of old comedies, James Fawn, who began before Leno, by making a " corner " in studies of inebriety, was doing the same thing. There is, of course, no dogmatic line to be drawn. But the objective of these artists was a far different one from that of Leno and of the output which he influenced. In the other cases, for the most part, it was one of purely external entertainment. With him, characterization took on a character more bound to real life, however wildly fantastic its presentation might be, and when hard on his heels, Dunville, Chevalier, Little Tich, and even Robey came on the scene, rein was given to free expression and, a vital factor, the halls were released from the artificialities which are so well implied in the ridiculous descriptive title of " The Jolly Nash." This entry into intimate burlesque-comedy marks the return of a fresh vitality, and the music halls enter on their final and greatest period.

The names bracketed with Leno through the height of his career are dazzling and numerous—among the men, Lauder, Chevalier, Tich, Dunville, The Macs, Elen, Roberts ; among the women, Bessie Bellewood, Bessie Bonehill, Jenny Hill, Marie Lloyd, Katie Lawrence, Vesta Tilley . . . pages might be filled in merely cataloguing important names.

Let us for the moment confine ourselves to the greatest of them all. Dan Leno, born in 1860, did not appear on the London music hall stage until 1885—that is, not as an individual artist. Even then he suffered partial failure, for his clog dancing, his most popular accomplishment in the Midlands, on which he had expended tremendous energy and patience, quite naturally was of little interest to a southern audience. By birth Dan Leno was a Londoner ; his birthplace, No. 4 Eve Court, St. Pancras, is now absorbed by the L.M.S. railway terminus. Leno himself has expressed in unforgettable words the thought with which his buried birthplace inspired him in the little book of sketches and stories he published in 1901. " Here," he says, " I spent my happy childhood hours. Ah ! What is man ? Wherefore does he why ? Whence did he whence ? Whither is he withering ? . . . Then the Guard yelled out : Leicester, Derby, Nottingham, Manchester, Liverpool ! "

The name under which the infant Leno was registered was George Galvin ; there was, however, a family " nom de théâtre," that of Wilde. At the age of four, or thereabouts, he changed his name again, for he then acquired the name of Leno from his stepfather, to whom in his book he refers as " Dad " and of whom he says, in an article on pantomime written in 1897, that " he will be remembered as one of the foremost clowns and character

comedians of the time." History, I am afraid, does not remember it: nor is there anything surviving in the public life of his actual father except a meagre tradition that as "singing and acting duettists" the parents were in the habit of making appearances at the Rotunda in the Blackfriars Road. It has been truly stated by Hickory Wood that Leno had but little choice in the matter of a calling, that he was inevitably an actor, and that, by the time he was old enough to think for himself, he was probably surprised to discover that any other profession existed.

After a short period of being left in a chest of drawers while his parents were out at their work, he was taken with them, and at the age of three years and some months, attired in a pair of ladies' stockings ("I blushed, I can tell you," says Leno), was brought on to the stage to support the character of "Little George, the Infant Wonder, Contortionist and Posturer." This occurred at the Cosmetheka Hall, Bell Street, Paddington, given by Leno (probably misprinted) as the Cosmo Theatre Hall. His début is described by him in the following words: "I didn't sing or patter, but mostly looked at the audience and wondered what they were wasting their time there for, and I didn't get very good money for that." Although launched in a theatrical career, his amount of responsibility is, perhaps, a little overstated by Wood. It is true that, when his father died, the situation was a difficult one, but Mrs. Galvin soon remarried and the new father, William Grant, whose stage name was Leno, acted as *deus ex machina* to the family fortunes. His recollections of this new "Dad" are given by Leno in some detail. First, he recalls three or four pantomimes in which they appeared together, including one in which the son performed as a contribution to the "Variety Entertainment" a clog dance and an Irish jig; and another in which his part was that of a wolf, the skin for which so fascinated him that he refused to take it off and slept in it for several nights. I give a further quotation from an 1897 article by him. "In those days my Dad and I were prepared to play anything, anywhere, at a moment's notice. I recollect a manager once, Mr. Teddy Lyons of Stockport, asking my father's advice as to what he should produce. It was Easter time, but my father replied without the slightest hesitation, 'Produce a pantomime.' We got into Stockport on a Saturday night, worked all day Sunday on the piece, and produced it on Monday."

The mention of the "Irish comedian" song is significant, for it was in this character that Leno first made an individual appearance on the halls at the age of eleven. He had now become "Dan Patrick Leno: Descriptive and Irish Character Vocalist," and he specialized in an entirely un-Irish song called *Pity the Poor Italian.* This song, with its traditional title, may be regarded as

Leno's first success with the public. In it he struck a note of pathos, here explicit, but under the surface a quality of so much of his work. The early years of the 'eighties were spent by Leno in perfecting his technique as a clog-dancer. The will to dance was an essential part of his nature, the choice of clog-dancing was merely the result of his environment. In 1880 he won the first open contest for a world championship in clog-dancing held at Leeds, and this success was ratified and never afterwards challenged at Oldham in 1883, the year of his marriage. He had not yet abandoned troupe work and was, in addition to his individual appearances, still performing with his family in sketches, burlesques, and "gorgeous spectacular entertainments." But the urgency of his personality was rapidly carrying him beyond these humble boundaries, and in 1885 he came to London with his wife; and at a salary of £5 a week took engagements, in the interval between provincial visits, at the Foresters' Hall (Cambridge Road); the Middlesex; the Queen's, Poplar; Deacon's, and other suburban halls. Journalistic appreciation came this year from Chance Newton, who had met Leno in the provinces and who would have us believe that he was among many who "with great difficulty persuaded Dan to take to what we felt to be his trump card," comic singing and pattering. This statement should be accepted with reservation. He had been singing and pattering all his life, and there is no reason to suppose that he was unaware of his value as a comedian. But his dancing had, in the north, been the means by which he had wrenched himself from the destroying poverty which had even condemned him to busker's work at street corners, and he had come to rely on it. There was an instinctive wisdom behind this adoption of specialization: without it the state of semi-starvation might have been indefinitely prolonged.

In his first London appearance there is no sign of a lack of self-confidence. His "turn" included two songs: one, in the character of a woman, called *Going to buy Milk for the Twins*; the other, a memory of "Dan Patrick Leno" called *When Rafferty Raffled his Watch*; the turn concluded with his champion clog-dance, and here his judgment was, for London, wide of the mark. He quickly abandoned the clogs which had brought him to London. Newton has left a description of the *Twins* song which may be quoted. "He appeared as a sort of nursemaid—a cross between Dickens' two 'servant' specimens, Tilly Slowboy and Miggs. That Lenonian and ceaselessly dancing damsel carried a huge kitchen pail on each arm and, breaking off into much extraordinary patter, periodically dashed into the startling refrain."

In the following year George Conquest gave Leno his first

London pantomime engagement at the Surrey Theatre. The engagement was made jointly with his wife and the combined salary was £20 a week. He had therefore achieved financial status by the age of twenty-six. The rest of the story is, on the surface, a triumph. In 1888 he was engaged by Sir Augustus Harris for the Drury Lane pantomime, written in that season by E. L. Blanchard, and he played there for fifteen consecutive years. The conquest of the London Pavilion audiences occurred a year or two earlier : in the building which has described itself as the "centre of the world," he became the symbolical figure for English low comedy, as at Drury Lane he stood in the place of Grimaldi as the national clown. He was even further exalted. One of the first gestures of Edward VII after his accession was in November 1901 to command his appearance at Sandringham. This visit led to a report that the King had, in his favour, revived the office of Court Jester. His death occurred in 1904, after a series of breakdowns, which, however, did not interrupt his annual appearances at Drury Lane. He sang for the last time upon a stage at the London Pavilion.

The figure of Dan Leno is significant both as a link with the past and with the future. It is impossible to avoid the association of Leno with Charlie Chaplin. It is both a physical and psychological resemblance. Their traditions and early environment are of the same kind : both found their education for the stage in the London streets and their technique was grounded in their experience of the cheapest and rowdiest of music halls. Max Beerbohm's comments on the art of Dan Leno might be read, by the generation which does not know Leno's work, as applying to the later artist. For instance, he says, "Leno's personality was of that finer kind—the lovable kind. He had, in a higher degree than any other actor I have ever seen, the indefinable quality of being sympathetic . . . The moment he capered on, with that air of wild determination . . . all hearts were his."

In the records of his life and in the subsequent relationship in which he stood to his audiences, Leno bore equally strong resemblance to his great predecessor, Grimaldi. To a host of people he became the essential expression of Christmas pantomime. These people belonged for the most part to the respectable middle-class, who had never seen him at the Pavilion in his too big frock-coat and top hat. To their children, Arthur Collins, the manager of Drury Lane, sent affectionate messages containing reference to Dan Leno as though he were a particularly funny uncle. In the halls a comparison with his great contemporary, Arthur Roberts, reveals the qualities by which he established contact with his audiences. Roberts stood for the embodiment of the social dash cut by the music hall in the days of splendour ;

Leno, though born into the same period of supremacy, stood for the understructure of life from which it emerged, by means of a comic transmutation of its dark privations and necessities expressed through a technique sharpened by knowledge and suffering. Dan Leno is the supremely comic figure emerging from a tragic conflict. " I have earned a good deal of butter to my bread," quotes Hickory Wood from a conversation, " but I wish the butter had been spread more evenly." In every physical feature there were traces of the conflict ; in the strained face, the small husky voice and the sudden wild bursts of movement : most of all in the deeply bitten-in sympathy of his character studies. His material was the sum of all the small things in the life of his class. It was full of babies' bottles, Sunday clothes, pawnshops, lodgings, cheap holidays and the like. There was no change in this material after he had ceased to be affected by all these problems. He remained, as Grimaldi remained, a member of his class, and was innocent of basing any behaviour on the assumption that he had left it. When he went to Sandringham he was appalled at the thought of meeting Royalty face to face : the breast-pin which was presented to him on this occasion figured in all his subsequent photographs. He hated the social demands of his position as leading comedian of the " National " Theatre. Drury Lane on Boxing Night, with its rows of critics and fashionable first-nighters, was an agony to him. A remark he made on the matter is an illuminating sidelight of his nature : " I never feel at home with my part till the first matinée "—and here his face would light up—" when the kiddies are in front." It will be clearly seen that he was unfitted to make the social transition demanded of stars belonging to the post-war period, even of those whose origins are identical with Leno's. The identification with Charlie Chaplin must therefore cease with the latter's early career.

Dan Leno has left behind him many traces of a technique, but the fundamentals are few. Much of his inventiveness has been reproduced in subsequent music hall work ; the use, for instance, of a long monologue introduced and terminated by a verse or chorus. His eyebrows, with their inflection of pained surprise, perpetuated in the even more famous eyebrows of George Robey ; his method of whirlwind entry on to the stage and so on. But the essentials have not reappeared ; there has been nothing since comparable with his creation of the bosom friend, Mrs. Kelly, whose identity he was at such pains to establish with the audience.

The difference between Leno and the lesser men was his greater fidelity to life. His concern with life was not bounded by his stage work ; he was in no narrow sense a specialist. All

his life he had been given to talking and writing down a kind of commentary, expressed in nonsense, but nonsense quickened by a sensitive intelligence. The habit of caricature, acquired in this manner, was an unconscious training for his stage work and supplied him with material for many of those rambling dissertations with which his songs were enriched. Two small instances of these written comments may be given ; small, but significant ; his description of the Tower of London as " supplying a long-felt want," and the pen-picture of two plumbers confronted with a bath : " The short one got up and stroked it and patted it with his hand as if he were telling it to be a good bath." There is, moreover, reproduced in Hickory Wood's *Life*, a pen-and-ink sketch (one of a number of sketches made on an envelope addressed to a friend), exhibiting his father leaning on a public-house bar, and bemoaning the decease of " poor George Leybourne "—a most illuminating little drawing !

Before leaving this greatest of music hall figures it would be well to modify the impression of him which it is easiest to render, as an instance of the " under-dog " become articulate. One should put in perspective the range of his active interests and a predisposition to much practical and worldly activity. Like Leybourne and other leading comedians, he was for a period a theatrical manager, though a rather unfortunate one. In partnership with Herbert Campbell, Harry Randall and Fred Williams he founded the Grand, Clapham, previously the Muntz Hall. Then followed the establishment of the Croydon Empire and the Granville at Walham Green, and the Palace, Camberwell. Later the Grand, Clapham, was replaced by a larger hall in the neighbourhood. All except the Granville failed and were disposed of by the group. Leno was particularly proud of the architectural beauties of the Granville, which was designed by Frank Matcham, who, among very many other houses, also designed the London Coliseum. They described the house as the Drawing-Room Music Hall.

Dan Leno had a marked talent for draughtsmanship. He conceived and executed over a period of nine years a panorama —the grown-up's toy which was losing its popularity when Leno was a child. History does not relate whether it was designed with a view to lighting effects and realistic foregrounds, but it probably was, for it was sold to Lieutenant Cole, the celebrated ventriloquist, and afterwards bought back by the artist, who kept it " in full working order " in his house.

Then there was Leno's house-pride expressed in a way to which justice only can be done by quoting a delightful anecdote given by H. G. Hibbert :

" I was ushered into a wonderful drawing-room, all yellow

and green plush and bronze figures and marble vases and flower-pots on bamboo tripods ; so dimly lighted that I fell headlong across the skull of a tiger still attached to the skin forming the hearthrug. Dan came from his hiding-place behind a screen. ' They mostly does that,' he said."

Leno's talent for drawing found expression in many pleasant thumbnail sketches and in the making and staging of figures and scenes for toy dramas with which to amuse his children. This pride in his talent also extended to a branch of his professional work—the designing of character wigs. " One of the hardest branches of my pantomime work," he says, rather pompously, " is the designing of novel and original wigs to my characters. These are made up by Mr. Clarkson from my own sketches, but directly I have used them in public once, they are immediately copied and circulated round the provinces. This I consider unfair to the original designer, who ought to be entitled to the exclusive benefits of his own inventions."

When Leno died, his funeral was one of the public events of the year. A spacious oration was spoken at the graveside, and the daily papers did not fail to note the inscriptions on the many wreaths sent by professional friends, among them the touching " Sleep well, old pal," from Marie Lloyd.

In the present survey of the growth of the central London halls, there remains for mention the latest and least personal of them, the Tivoli in the Strand, which was opened in 1891 on the site of a German Bier Keller known by the same name. By this time the promotion of music halls had become a part of normal theatrical enterprise, the licensed victualler being replaced by men of the type of Herbert Newson Smith. The original Tivoli syndicate included Edward Terry, and an inaugural dinner was held at which Oscar Wilde's popular brother, Willie, known intimately as " Wuffalo Will," presided. However, the con-derable puffing which the new hall received did not result in any measure of success until the redoubtable Morton was called in as manager in 1892. Morton set to work to create another Oxford Hall, and succeeded in all respects except that of giving the place an especial flavour. Its twenty-five years of life, however, contains the greatest period of music hall singing. Its end was hastened by the opportunity for a sale of the site, but actually it finally surrendered to the results in London of an occurrence, a year before its foundation, in the north : the registering in 1890 of the Moss Empires in Edinburgh for two million pounds. The Tivoli outlived our period, however, for the house was not demolished until 1916.

One of the first artists to appear on the Tivoli stage, immediately upon his achievement of fame as a music hall artist,

was Albert Chevalier, who was hailed as an innovator in cockney character. Actually he cannot be regarded in that light, being a latter-day example of a man of the theatre transferring his technique to the music halls. But Chevalier was born a little out of his time. For the actual democratization of cockney impersonation was, as we have seen, a modern note in the music hall comparable to the introduction of real negroes in negro impersonation. Chevaliers' traditional outlook is exemplified in his other activities—his theatre work, both as an actor and dramatist, was centred in the old melodrama, and his extra-music-hall activities included such conservative activities as the writing and publishing of parodies and burlesque lectures, and the habit of making recital tours.

Chevalier's habit of mind was that of an actor ; all his songs became in his hands elaborately built-up impersonations ; the style was broad, but on it was superimposed a minute attention to detailed effect. Arriving in the music hall at a time when the genuine cockney such as Hyram Travers and Teddy Mosedale had successfully asserted their popularity, Chevalier found himself pitted against a diametrically opposed school of actor, and this provoked a certain class prejudice against him inside the profession.

Although Chevalier's first appearances had been at the Pavilion in February 1891, it was at the Tivoli, under the enlightened management of Newson Smith, that his triumphs were secured. Here he was apparently on safe ground from the start. Even in London he had not at first been uniformly received, and he states that at his initial appearance at the Canterbury there was at first some interruption from the gallery during his singing (of all songs) of *My Old Dutch*. The technical perfection of his performance of this song was probably never repeated in the history of music hall singing. Yet it remained an actor's performance, the effect achieved by significantly observed detail rather than by a purely emotional appeal. The complete freedom from emotional *cliché*, not so successfully avoided in other songs, had, naturally, the effect of widening and deepening the overwhelming appeal of the song itself, which derived equally from the words and the music. The result was a perfect unity, a picture of life so faithful and yet achieved with such conscious art that there resulted the synthesis which all art strives for, (but the music hall art with, perhaps, more definite intention than any other), in which all class barriers are completely transcended. The song itself ranks conspicuously high. Chevalier himself wrote the lyric as in the case of most of his repertory. It is well balanced with a clear focus of interest. But the tune, which was the work of Chevalier's brother, who wrote under the name of Charles

Ingle, is one of the great inspirations in minor music. With Ingle, John Crook and Alfred West writing for him, Chevalier was particularly well served in the matter of tunes.

The Tivoli has served more or less legitimately for the citation of Albert Chevalier, since Newson Smith, as manager of the Pavilion when he made his first appearance there, was responsible, more than other men, for the establishment of his reputation, when he took the house over. It must serve less happily to introduce a discussion of another great name, since, apart from Chevalier, it has no special claims upon the recollection of any individual artist. Indeed, an occurrence in the early 'nineties rendered any such special association nugatory ; this was the formation at Newson Smith's suggestion of the "Syndicate Halls," a combination which, in the West End of London, linked together the Tivoli, Oxford and Pavilion. Henceforth the whole glittering array of late Victorian and Edwardian stars became the common property of these houses, and none more than the Tivoli pursued the simple policy of presenting these stars, week after week, in full array. The method held without variation through the remainder of Newson Smith's short life and later under George Adney Payne, up till the moment when the site was claimed by the Strand Improvement Scheme. The system, once asserted, was a facile one. It consisted in ringing the changes, with insufficient variation, according to Harry Randall, upon the leading comic singers of the day, and these alone.[1] The policy was undeterred by the new attack of the Northern Syndicates, which by the creation of the vast variety houses, the London Hippodrome and the London Coliseum, were working for the revival of the amphibious entertainment houses of the past and angling successfully for an infinitely wider public by clothing their halls in a garment of middle-class respectability. In London, therefore, the Syndicate Halls held the treasure of fifty years' development of music hall art. The movement outside—that of the Moss-Stoll-Thornton group—was, in essence, inimical to the music hall and was already threatening its existence. Not only were their halls far too large for any intimate relationship between the artist and the audience, but they were the outcome of changing social and economic conditions demanding a different type of artist ; the great singers of the time were seldom heard there and never to advantage. Only in the suburbs and the provinces did the new masters of the situation

[1]"There was a strenuous scramble among the rival combinations to obtain the cream of the profession. They outvied each other in securing them, and gave extravagant salaries to artists, handing them long contracts for their exclusive services . . . The consequence was that when you went into one of their halls, you saw a company of artists for a couple of weeks ; then they would disappear for a week . . . and back they would come again—the same old faces and the same old business."

attempt some fusion with the old order, and it was possible to hear at some local " palace " an artist of the calibre of Marie Lloyd.

With a discussion of Marie Lloyd this long chapter must end, for with her death the tale of the Edwardian music hall is completed ; from the most typical of origins she created a peak of achievement in the music hall tradition, and lived to see that tradition shattered.

Marie Lloyd, or Matilda Alice Victoria Wood, was born in 1870 in London. Her parents had professional connection with the stage, and from her early childhood her ambition was to become a music hall singer. This ambition was shared by her sisters, of whom there were three : all became professional entertainers, and one of them, under the name of Daisy Wood, achieved a considerable position. Marie Lloyd's romantic leaning to the stage as a child was described by her in the following words : " the dazzling lights, the gilded mirrors, the crowded audience—all these things had attractions for me, but the enchanting region beyond the imposing proscenium, with its background of classic terraces and shady groves, exercised a still greater fascination over my youthful fancy, and I determined at the earliest opportunity to gratify my ambition." There was that inevitable period when we hear that the child, even when left alone for five minutes or so, would " abandon her broom or duster " and proceed to " knock " an imaginary audience. Then, in the intervals of undertaking pupil-teaching in the local Sunday School and of assisting her mother in her dressmaking business, she made a first plunge into theatrical activity by organizing among her friends an amateur concert part to which was given the name of the " Fairy Bells Minstrels." At the age of fifteen she made her first (unpaid) appearance in public. This occurred at the Grecian Saloon, then on its last legs and under the management of a certain Broome. Here, under the romantic pseudonym of " Bella Delmere," she sang two songs, *My Soldier Lassie*, and a ballad by Hérold, called *Time is Flying*. She also danced an Irish jig. The Irish jig, she wrote, " went down ' immense,' as the saying is." On the following night she gave a trial performance at Belmont's Sebright Hall in the Hackney Road. The result was an engagement at fifteen shillings a week. Here the young artist met George Ware, a well-known vocalist and the composer *of The Dark Girl Dressed in Blue*, who later, as a music hall agent, earned the title of " The Old Reliable." Engagements were then procured for her by Ware at the Bedford and the Mogul, and finally, after a few months during which she sang at many of the smaller halls, including the Falstaff in Old Street and the Star at Bermondsey, came the appearance at the Royal,

Holborn, which established her reputation and was of a year's duration.

By this time Marie Lloyd was singing with marked success a song written and composed by George Ware in the year of her début, called *The Boy I Love is up in the Gallery.* This song had been previously performed, but without, one imagines, unusual effect, by Nellie Power. It seems likely from the evidence of cover designs, that the style of dress worn by Marie Lloyd for this song was taken from Nellie Power ; it certainly became traditional for, in the Sickert painting of Little Dot Hetherington singing the song, a similar dress is depicted. It consisted in the familiar short-sleeved frock with a large pinafore over it, and was used by Marie Lloyd for all the " romping schoolgirl songs " in which she felt particularly at home with her audiences and which she said " came most naturally " to her. After a stay of a year at the Oxford, the triumphant artist toured in the Colonies, and in 1891 took her place beside Dan Leno as principal girl in the pantomime of *Humpty Dumpty*, under Augustine Harris. She played also in the two following pantomimes, *Little Bo-Peep* and *Robinson Crusoe.* By this time she was developing that famous raciness of style which, though inseparable from her true personality, did something to endanger her prestige and which probably terminated her association with Drury Lane. This tendency is discernible in the brilliant lyrics of John Harrington, who, with George Le Brunn, the composer, was now producing the remarkable group of songs which played such an important part in her career. The fault, if it be one, may be attributed entirely to the exuberant sense of the power she exercised over her audiences and of the complete understanding which existed between them, an understanding deeply rooted in class-consciousness. Pornography it certainly never was. In its directness (for the innuendo of the printed page became under the influence of her consummate " flair " a direct hit) it was indeed the antithesis of this undesirable quality. But in her use of the method, she undoubtedly overstepped the limit of discretion. The readiness of her technique and the ease with which she was able to interpolate and improvise, were perhaps the chief temptations in her way. Of this effortlessness there is abundant evidence ; she cites an instance of it herself in a sudden lapse of memory overcome, to the delight of the audience, by the invention of a string of nonsense rhymes. Warnings against the tendency to Rabelaisianism eventually made their appearance in the Press, and these were echoed privately by her intimate friend, Chance Newton. Marie Lloyd was outraged and decided for a time to abandon the halls. In 1908 she accordingly went on a tour in a musical comedy of which Newton was the author, called *The*

Tea Shop Girl. In the following year she was back again, however, with an unrepentant repertoire which included the famous *Everything in the Garden's Lovely.* From the date until her death in October 1922, her connection with the music halls remained unbroken. Le Brunn, Harrington, with occasional interpolations by George Ware, Richard Morton, Joseph Tabrar and others, continued to provide her with songs which were the joy and pride of her enormous following, and which in many cases have provided phrases and catchwords which are a part of the language. These included *The Tale of the Skirt, A Little of What you Fancy, The Rich Girl and the Poor Girl, Buy me some Almond Rock, Oh, Mister Porter, One of the Ruins that Cromwell Knocked about a Bit, You're a thing of the Past, old Dear, Garn Away, Then You Wink the Other Eye, and* many more, equally famous.

Marie Lloyd's methods did not vary much with the years. The short-spoken prelude, the dancing between the verses of the song, remained.[1] Towards the end, when she grew rather stouter, though she never lost her nice cosy figure, she came to rely for some of her effect upon the elaborate dresses which she designed herself. Then the announcement on the posters would read, "Marie Lloyd in new Songs and new Gowns." Dressed thus in the height of fashion, she would sing songs, with very little action, in which was expressed a highly-developed sophistication. These latter-day songs were as perfectly timed and spoken as ever, but were far from being the pith of her work. This was revealed again at the end of her career by a song called *Dilly Dally,* which supplied one of those perfect moments, apt to occur in the life of a great artist, when the ripeness of a lifetime's experience is expressed in one faultless piece of creation. She sang the song at the Palladium just before her last tour in the provinces, and its subject was of the wanderings during alcoholic stress (occasioned by a family "removal") of one of those dear, moist-eyed old females . . . but the chorus of the song will speak for itself:

"My old man said 'follow the van
And don't dilly-dally on the way!'
Off went the cart with the home packed in it,
I walked behind with my old cock linnet.
But I dillied and dallied, dallied and dillied,
Lost the van and don't know where to roam.
I stopped on the way to have the old half-quartern,
And I can't find my way home."

[1]Marie Lloyd had evidently suffered earnest inquiries as to her artistic methods and scenes of rehearsal. To these she replies, in a newspaper article: "How I rehearse my songs? Well, I don't actually rehearse them at all. When I have learned the words and melody, I am prepared to go on and sing them right away." In

She never did anything better than this, though to the end she grappled with new material. The last song of all was *One of the Ruins that Cromwell Knocked about a Bit*. She had been advised not to appear, but had refused to give way. During the song she fell in agony on the stage, but the audience did not realize the truth. She died in the shuttered and balconied villa which she had built herself in the tram-ridden high road at Golders Green. It may be said that with her died that particular genre of English artist which it has been the purpose of this book to study.[1]

. . . . .

(Many instances have been given of Marie Lloyd's extremely charitable nature : it is so personal a matter that I have not sought to emphasize the fact. But with her this quality was not the merely superficial good nature so often attributed to stage artists. It was part of her religion. It was also linked with her intense class consciousness—a fierce upholding of the less lucky among those who had been born into her own world. Ray Wallace, who knew her well, and who still delights broadcast listeners with her brilliant imitations of the great comedienne, has told me of a first-hand experience of Marie Lloyd's charity. At the stage door of a suburban house at which they were both appearing a crowd of small children without shoes or stockings were hanging round the stage door when Marie Lloyd was leaving the theatre after her performance. She took the ragged little army under her wing, marched them to the nearest store and bought them all boots. The same group of children greeted them the next day, but alas, without the boots).

[1]I may perhaps be allowed to quote from Mr. T. S. Eliot's essay on Marie Lloyd. " Her superiority," he states, " was in a way a moral superiority. It was her undertanding of the people and sympathy with them, and the people's recognition of the fact that she embodied the virtue which they genuinely most respected in private life, that raised her to the position she occupied at her death . . . I have called her the expressive figure of the lower classes ; there is no such expressive figure for any other class. The middle classes have no such idol : the middle classes are morally corrupt."

commenting on the fact that she seldom made a slip or suffered a loss of memory on the stage, she recalls one such occasion, easily compassed by her supreme self-confidence : " I simply followed the orchestra with some nonsense rhymes," she says.

CHAPTER X

" *Uplift* "

LET us for a moment turn aside to survey briefly the details of that spate of Victorian improving entertainment, which in its day incorporated and even created some elements of the later music hall, and which, in the Alhambra, provided it with such an imposing edifice. At least three genuinely popular shows were the outcome of this frenzy for educating the public mind—the Minstrels, which very early in their career suffered this moral translation, Maskelyne and Cook's Home of Mystery at the Egyptian Hall, and the German Reed Burletta Theatre at the Gallery of Illustration. Moreover, beneath the surface of such titling as Eidophusikon, Eidouranium, Peristrephic Diorama and the like, which would appear to have made a Greek Lexikon indispensable to the equipment of the middle-class home, one may discern many sublimated forms of entertainment which are relevant to the subject of this book.

If many of these schemes were short-lived, their sites providing a happy hunting-ground for shows of a franker entertainment value, they did not cease to multiply over a considerable period of years. For the sake of convenience we may date the movement from 1826, the year of the foundation of the Polytechnic Institution. This amiable Society owed its existence to a pride in the Industrial Revolution, and at first the venture must have contained a sufficiently surprising element of novelty. The wonders of the diving bell and a variety of mechanical devices displaced the simple attractions of the Holophusikon with its jumble of stuffed birds, the Linwood tapestries and the Trepado (or cut paper) work at the Oxford Street bazaar.[1] Once the new enthusiasm had been instilled, the Polytechnic Institution developed a remarkably conservative body of support, with a loyalty so unvarying that the attraction of the diving bell, the wonders of which we find advertised in the *Era* in 1838, was still prominent exactly forty years later, though the reduction in price of admission may be regarded as a portent of change.

[1]In the handbook describing the Exhibition of Trepado work held at 73 Oxford Street, in 1829, are mentioned two pictures executed in this medium (cut paper used in imitation of line engraving) : *The Lord's Supper* and *A Portrait of His Majesty*.

In 1878, under a new committee,[1] the complete Polytechnician was invited to spend his day in the following manner : at noon he entered the Great Hall for a general inspection of models ; at 12.15 (in the small theatre) he attended Mr. Stokes' illustrations on memory, writing and music ; at 12.35 his attention was claimed by the new inventions, such as the typewriter and Hogg's ventilation. Then came the Compound Cycloidal Apparatus, followed by what must have been a well-earned interval for refreshments. At 2.10 p.m. he attended the illustrated lecture on the Progress of Royalty in India, and at 2.50 (fee 6d.) he was baptized in the Diving Bell. Then occurred a variation in the routine, a note of levity which belonged only to this later stage in the history of instructional amusement ; for his choice now lay between Mr. Taylor's Wonderful Boy (Plate Dancing, Clairvoyance, etc.), the Aerial Mercury, an illusion at which Mr. Grimsby Jopp, R.A.M., assisted with songs of his own composition, and (at 3.50) Duguar, the Prince of Jugglers. At 4.15 was given the musical entertainment of *Gabriel Grubb and the Goblins*, written and composed by George Buckland,[2] and illustrated by " magnificent views." To this was added an exhibition of Maclise's picture of *The Empty Chair*, some Dissolving Views, and a number of Chromatropes and Chorutoscopes. The whole business began again at 7 p.m., starting with the general inspection of models. Variations on this curriculum took the form of demonstrations of the Potter's Wheel in motion, the celebrated Polytechnic cement, and Bailey Brothers' marking ink. Then there was Mr. Laver's Fancy Stall (showing the new Air Rifle and Gas Lighter) ; on Wednesdays and Fridays only the Geological Piano ; and at 1.15 (just before the refreshment interval) a Lecture with the Pickwickian title of " The Inhabitants of our Ponds and Ditches."

From the Polytechnic to the Panoptikon ; to which a larger share of ironic interest belongs. The first conception of the building, so soon to be transformed into a vast Saloon Theatre, was attributed solely to Mr. Edward Marmaduke Clarke, a scientific instrument maker of 428 the Strand, author of a work entitled *Directions for Using Philosophical Apparatus* ; though a mysterious origin is suggested by John Hollingshead, who makes reference to the influence of a certain Pandemonium Paving Company, the identity of which I have been unable to trace.

[1]The Committee was headed by Lord Shaftesbury, who was supported by Miss Fossey, Mr. Larke, Miss Narraway, and Mr. Troake.

[2]It is of interest that this George Buckland made an adaptation of *Alice's Adventures in Wonderland*, performed at the Polytechnic Institution as a Christmas entertainment. The adaptation was done with the author's permission and was probably the sequel to Carroll's abortive attempt to secure a musical version from Sir Arthur Sullivan.

A pamphlet issued by the committee of management, headed by Marmaduke Clarke, gives information on the motives which inspired it on both the ideal and practical plane : " Experience has shown," it says, " that, with a rapidly increasing population, there has sprung up a growing taste for intellectual pursuits . . . the manufacturer by devoting a few hours weekly to the enunciations of the chemical Professor will be better prepared to meet that competition, which, tho' the very life of Commercial enterprise, is ever fatal to the indulgence of inactivity or ignorance . . . The edifice fulfils one's conception of some of the enchanted palaces described in Oriental fiction . . . It will not be supposed that so novel and extensive a design could have obtained its present condition of excellence without great and mental physical labour " . . . and so on.

The physical and mental labour was rewarded in 1850 by the granting of a Royal Charter and the enchanted palace began to rise on the east side of Leicester Square. Most of the preface to the committee's handbook is devoted to a eulogy on the building's architectural beauties. The choice of the Saracenic style of architecture, selected " as a novelty," which had been unkindly criticized at a meeting of the Royal Institute of British Architects, is vigorously defended, particularly the minarets, of which it is said that " independent of serving the office of ornaments, they are likely to become valuable adjuncts to the Institution, and instrumental of paramount benefit to the community at large." The precise nature of this benefit is not divulged.

The wonders of the building's interior, which is to be " no place for mere lounging and sight-seeing," are then described. As at the Polytechnic, they are to be revealed at two daily sessions ; the morning one devoted to scientific exposition only, and that in the evening tempered by an " artistic entertainment blending instruction with amusement." Importance having been placed upon the method of admittance by the new turnstile register, the exhibits are then enumerated. These include the Diving Apparatus, a demonstration of Hydrostation (or the ascensional force of balloons in water), E. M. Clark's electrical machine, Holme's Vacuum-Coated Flask, the Aurora Borealis Apparatus, the Thunder House, the Manufacture of Pins, the Gas Cooking Apparatus, Sculpture, Cork Hats, the Patent Ornamental Sewing Machine, the Euphatine, an Exhibition of Pyrography (i.e., poker painting), the Musical Narrator (a machine for recording improvised compositions on the piano), the Manufacture of Paper Hangings, and the Electro-Magnetic Apparatus. The handbook does not disclose the nature of the artistic entertainments to which some portion of the evening session was devoted. They probably did not differ materially from those at the Polytechnic ;

but whatever they were, they must have proved an insufficient relief from the formidable character of the exhibits. The end of the Panoptikon came four years after its ceremonious opening in 1854. The building, with its minarets, its gigantic organ, its ascending carriage and its scientific curiosities, then fell into the hands of E. T. Smith and London's largest music hall came into being.

The art of the one-man entertainment, which was so frequently requisitioned by the promoters of instructional amusement, as we know, considerably predated the Victorian age ; the methods of George Alexander Stevens finding imitators in the eighteenth century ; and upon independent lines beng practised by Samuel Foote and others. In the early years of the nineteenth century its principal exponent was the elder Charles Mathews ; but the man to whom mid-Victorian entertainers owed most was Charles Dibdin, whom we have as yet only encountered in connection with the Royal Circus. His influence is directly traceable in many of the entertainments of the eighteen-fifties, notably in those of Albert Smith and John Orlando Parry.

His entertainment, described as a " sort of musical lecture or soirée," Dibdin first evolved a performance of this type in 1788, and presented it under the title of *The Whim of the Moment.* The genius of this extraordinary man was here fully exploited, for he possessed versatile talents as an actor, composer, singer and author. It was said that few of his songs took him more than half an hour to compose. He had the same felicity with lyrics and dialogue ; which he presented with an easy naturalness of style described as " that of a person entertaining a party of friends in a drawing-room." Even his slighter pretensions as a graphic artist contributed to these attractive medleys, which made their appearance in a variety of forms and places over a period of twenty years, and gave occasion for many of his most famous songs. These entertainments, into which he introduced so many elements—even marionettes playing their part in one instance—gave him an outlet for the restless ingenuity which was the essence of the man. The method employed was always personal and idiomatic. O'Keefe, in his *Memoirs*, says that " his manner of coming upon the stage was in happy style : he ran on sprightly and with nearly a laughing face, like a friend who enters hastily to impart to you some good news." For the comic little dialogues and lively or pathetic tales of which the show partly consisted, he seemed " to trust more to his memory and to the impulse of the moment than to the written words before him. Though " singing with simplicity in a baritone of no great power or compass but of sweet and mellow quality," his pianistic arrangements were of a complicated order, for the instrument which on

some occasions he used, " combined the properties of the pianoforte and the chamber organ, and was so constructed that the performer could produce the tones of either instrument separately or both in combination. To this instrument was attached a set of bells, a side drum, a tambourine and a gong, which he could bring into play by various mechanical contrivances, so as to give a pleasing variety to his accompaniments."

Dibdin was forty-three years old when O'Keefe saw him. Henry Thorn quotes a description of his appearance and platform manner sent him by one who saw his performance at this time. The informant's name is not given ; the passage is as follows : " A handsome man with an open, pleasing countenance and of very gentlemanlike appearance and address. His costume was a blue coat, white waistcoat, and black silk breeches and stockings, and he wore his hair in the fashion of the day—full dressed and properly powdered. His manner of speaking was easy and colloquial . . . He was near-sighted, and when seated at his instrument he would bend his head close to the book for a few moments and then, laying it down, throw himself back in his chair and deliver his song without further reference to book or music."

The pleasant picture is completed by O'Keefe, who, having seen Dibdin's entertainment when in 1792 he was performing at the Lyceum Great Room in the Strand, asserts that " his peculiar mode of singing his own songs surpassed all he had ever heard." He adds that among his compositions, the music to *The Padlock*, *The Jubilee*, *The Waterman* and *The Quaker* was " most successfully productive."

Even so, very little which Didbin wrote for other people or which passed through the hands of publishers brought him any material gain. Of this he was always complaining. His *Professional Life* contains the most uninviting mixture of self-praise and bitterness towards the duplicity of nearly everyone with whom he had business dealings. It produces the strongest impression of a character oscillating between boastfulness and fear. The fact is that in the undeveloped quality of his genius, the *naïveté* and childishmess of his conceptions, which give to his artistic personality so much charm, are in themselves evidence of an arrestment which, meeting with the normal buffetings of life, reduced the man gradually to the somewhat pitiable figure presented in the *Autobiography*. One must look for the true Dibdin only in his achievement. His private life was a succession of irregularities and unhappiness. He was severely blamed by Garrick and others for his desertion of the woman who for a number of years was a wife to him, and for whose suicide he was held responsible. Here he suffered in a typical way for those

offences which are not permitted to encumber the lives of prudent and calculating people. If one is wise one turns from the picture of an embarrassed and irritable misanthrope to the delightful man who stepped so gaily on to the stage and charmed his audiences with homely and candid songs, decorated with the complicated simplicities of his curious entertainment.

As an entertainer, Dibdin takes the foremost rank, though he is only remembered as the writer of the famous sea songs. In this capacity his influence was paramount, but to him we also owe that salvation of the scientific and artistic " Exhibition," the light entertainer. Through him this movement was enriched by the work of John Orlando Parry and Albert Smith, who passed on the art to Corney Grain, Mel B. Spur, George Grossmith and Barclay Gammon.

Parry was among these the nearest to Dibdin's type, Albert Smith the most intellectually constituted. The former may have actually seen Dibdin perform, for he was born in 1810. There is a definite relation between them. Both received a certain amount of serious musical training—Parry under his father, the revered Welsh bard, later under Robert Boscha for the harp, and under Sir George Smart for his voice. Both were pleasant, though not powerful, baritones, and both had sung in opera ; Parry at John Braham's new St. James's Theatre in 1836, where he played for Dickens in his operetta, *The Village Coquettes*. Again both wrote and composed (though Parry not invariably) their songs, sketches and monologues ; and both occasionally made use in their performances of their talent for drawing. Parry, after appearing as an infant prodigy on the harp at the pleasure gardens, took to the concert platform as a singer in his early 'twenties, visiting Italy, where he found opportunities of discovering his talent for burlesque and mimicry. Then came some appearances in English light opera and these were followed by his ventures in entertaining in which the polite comic song, instanced by his early success, *Wanted a Governess*, was extended by interpolation and monologue into the full-fledged musical sketch. He continued to practise this method through a long professional career, the peak of which was his triumphant popularity in the complete single-handed section which he provided for the German Reed entertainments. To Parry, more than to Albert Smith, we owe the continued existence of this comic musical sketch with its snatches of acting, singing and parody. Smith was more correctly a literary man, observer, and journalist whose stage appearances were of a secondary character. He is an important link in the tradition, however, which he passed on to Corney Grain, an entertainer first and foremost. Smith is quite properly described in the *Dictionary of National Biography* as a lecturer, though he was

frequently other things as well. The faithful friend and plagiarist of Dickens, everything he attempted had on it the mark of astute journalism. It was in 1851 that the great inspiration of his life, his " Musical Lecture " on the Ascent of Mont Blanc, sent the whole of London to see him at the Egyptian Hall. Here he found an admirable medium for his varied accomplishments. The lecture was full of little anecdotes, snatches of song and observations on the oddities of the peoples encountered on this expedition. He sang a song about *Gagliani's Messenger;* about the Ship's Engineer, and so forth. Henry James when a small boy was taken to see Smith, and was much embarrassed to find himself in a stage box decorated to represent part of a Swiss Châlet as though he were himself a part of the entertainment. The vogue for these lectures was tremendous ; they were given consecutively for over a year. Albert Smith must have had some especially magnetic quality to carry to such heights of popularity material of this unpromising quality.

The success of the show created a fashion in the arts ; it was reproduced both in musical and pictorial forms ; there was even a waltz composed called *Echo de Mont Blanc.*

The phrase applied by Henry James is " big-bearded, rattling, chattering, mimicking Albert Smith," and in a comment quoted in J. T. Ley's book, *Dickens and his Circle*, mention is made of his " buoyant, happy spirit, his careless, irrepressible nature, and his keen enjoyment of the Bohemian side of the life of his day."

The German Reed Entertainments, which housed the talents of both Parry and Corney Grain, were in their most successful period given in a wing of Nash's house in Lower Regent Street, known at the time of their formation as the Gallery of Illustration, and they flourished for many years as a theatre-going outlet for the non-theatre-going public. Their founder, Priscilla Horton (afterwards Mrs. German Reed) was born in 1818 and made a début on the stage in 1828 at Covent Garden Theatre, where she played Ariel in *The Tempest* for Macready.[1] Her subsequent stage career included the creation of the part of Georgina Vesey in Bulwer Lytton's *Money.* The first entertainments were given in 1855 at the St. Martin's Hall, which three years later was the scene of Charles Dickens' first dramatic reading. Then came the period at the Gallery of Illustration where the German Reeds were joined by John Parry, who delighted the audiences with musical sketches such as *The County Commissioners* and *Berlin Wool.* By the 'seventies his powers were failing and after a breakdown

[1]Alfred Bunn, defending his introduction of Van Amburgh's menagerie into the spectacle of " Charlemagne " at Drury Lane, attributed the popularity of the current production of " The Tempest " to Priscilla Horton, singing of the Ariel song, suspended in mid-air.

he retired from the entertainments and a benefit was organized for him by Hollingshead at the Gaiety Theatre in 1877. A year or two later Corney Grain joined the company, and he and Albert German Reed became the principal supporting artists. Corney Grain's great popularity as an entertainer, his facility for joking without vulgarity, secured a successful continuance of the feature introduced by Parry. The entertainments flourished uninterruptedly until 1895, when (as a reverend historian of the entertainments phrases it), "in tragic sequence, recalling the first chapter of the Book of Job," the three popular favourites, Mrs. German Reed, Albert German Reed, and Corney Grain died; and the scheme of entertainment with which they were identified perished with them.

A word should be said here of the performances of Henry Russell, the father of Sir Landon Ronald, and composer of the celebrated *Cheer, Boys, Cheer*. Social and religious purpose plentifully abounded in the work of this popular singer and song-writer. Whole entertainments were devised by him to further the alleviation of some notorious evil or to fan some popular enthusiasm.

Russell was born at Sheerness in the same year as Dickens (1812), and exhibiting as a child a fine contralto voice, joined Elliston's company at the newly-named Surrey Theatre at the moment when that manager was endeavouring to establish a children's opera there. After studying in Italy under the patronage of Bulwer Lytton, he began his adult musical career as a concert singer in America; adopting at an early stage the methods of a single-handed entertainer to which he was always afterwards faithful and for which he found an audience in every part of the world. He began, too, to produce that stream of songs and "cantatas" (as his song-scenes were described by a contemporary), which he was in the habit of singing to his own piano accompaniment. Early successes were his setting of Dickens' *The Ivy Green*, and that happy inspiration of sentiment (arising, as he tells us in his reminiscences, from an incident of real life), *Woodman, Spare that Tree*. These and other songs brought him considerable fame as a composer, but it was not until he formed his association with Dr. Charles Mackay, poet and antiquarian, the author of *The Miller of the Dee*, that his fame was completely assured. Together they discovered a mission in life: to give expression in song to the advocacy of emigration inspired by the occurrences of the "hungry forties." *The Far West, or the Emigrant's Progress from the Old World to the New*, was a full-length entertainment, embellished with the pictures of Stanfield, and contained some of Russell's most famous songs, among them *Cheer, Boys, Cheer*, *To the West*, and *A Life on the Ocean Wave*. Other questions were in the same way given a lyrical prominence. The

By courtesy of British Museum

THE
HEAVY SWELL OF THE SEA.
The fellows look upon me with a jealous eye,
The ladies all adore me as I saunter by,
They titter and they blush, then after me they rush,
The newest of heavy seaside swells am I.
WRITTEN BY
T. L. CLAY
SUNG WITH THE GREATEST SUCCESS BY
COMPOSED BY
ALFRED LEE.
GEORGE LEYBOURNE.

By courtesy of British Museum

administration of the law formed the subject of *A Cry from the Courts*; *The Maniac* was inspired by the conduct of the private lunatic asylums; and such titles as *The Pauper's Drive* and *The Gambler's Wife* sufficiently indicate their content. In the two scenas, *The Ship on Fire* and *The Maniac*, Russell in effect laid the foundations of the work of the descriptive vocalists of the music hall, such as Jenny Hill and Charles Godfrey. Indeed, some of the heartiness of the music hall found its way into the Hanover Square Rooms when Russell was singing there, when its walls would re-echo the choruses which were taken up with enthusiasm by the audience. There was a refreshing *naïveté*, as well, about these concerts, which is illustrated by a story which Russell himself tells of an occasion when he was questioned from the auditorium on the subject of his song, *Woodman, Spare that Tree*. At the conclusion of the song, says Russell, " a gentleman rose up and in a very excited voice called out, ' was the tree spared, sir ? "

" ' It was,' I said.

" ' Thank God for that,' he answered, with a heartfelt sigh of relief."

CHAPTER XI

The Rest of Them

In this attempt to show the changing picture of the music hall, the smallest representation only has yet been made of the many artists who, especially from the 'sixties until the end of our period, call for attention.

It will be readily understood that in a book of this scope one must be content, even in dealing with that smaller number of really important names, to select only those which have a real significance. In this last chapter, therefore, an effort will be made, by such a selection, to convey the atmosphere of the latter period. Much survives from the singing rooms and from the other earlier forms of miscellaneous entertainment. Whatever change is noticeable is found to be associated predominantly with the rise of the eccentric comedian.

As we have seen in the previous chapter, the influence of Dan Leno was here so great, that one is tempted to attribute to him the creation of those features, which now, for the majority of people, represent the whole of the music hall. The creation of the modern comedian is the most important manifestation of the general movement towards specialization. One may quote many lesser instances. Women, for example, appearing in men's clothes ceased to do so sporadically, but became once and for all "male impersonators." In this respect lies the difference between Annie Adams or Bessie Wentworth, and Vesta Tilley. This art became again subdivided. There was the specialized female coon singer, whose male counterpart, deriving from Cave and Mackney, continued to be represented by artists such as Eugene Stratton and G. H. Chirgwin. Cockney songs ceased to be a part of the general repertoire of the comic singers, but became the monopoly of performers like Travers, Laburnum, and afterwards, with an even stronger emphasis, of Chevalier and Gus Elen. Here again the women followed suit; the supreme instances being Jenny Hill and Bessie Bellwood. The buffo vocalist, on the other hand, when not merged with the "lion comique," was a disappearing type. After Johngmanns of Evans's, whose long life included a period on the music halls, less is heard of this

kind of performer, though the tradition was to some extent prolonged in the patriotic songs of Jolly Nash and G. H. Macdermott. To the Irish vocalist, always a special feature of concert-room singing, though of theatrical origin, was added the Scottish comedian. Harry Lauder, it is surprising to read, began his career in London as an Irish vocalist with a song named *Call Again Kallighan* ; the return to his native idiom was achieved as an innovation, after his reputation had been made in this traditional manner. The " answers," parodies, and " ladies' versions " gave way to definite mimicry, or were abandoned for original work. The mimic, as entertainer, was, of course, no invention of the music hall period. His art had been inherited from the eighteenth century, or earlier—the great Garrick himself had practised it extensively, though in later life he had strongly disapproved of it. In the music hall it was given a special place (after its tentative use by artists such as John Moody and Tom Maclagan), by Arthur Playfair, Herbert Standing, and others.

Another popular specialization was that of the female duettists, usually presented under the title of " sisters." The practice owed much to the vogue created by genuine instances of relationship, such as the Vokes and the Vaughan families. A host of these sprang up from the 'seventies onwards, the most memorable of whom were perhaps the Bilton sisters, whose favourite duet was called *Fresh, fresh, fresh as the new mown hay* ; the three Sisters Levy, known as the Three Amazons, and the Leamar sisters, one of whom, Alice Leamar, was the creator in England of the American song, *Her Golden Hair was Hanging Down Her Back*. The vogue for instantaneous dancing became a feature of these " sister " acts. It notably remained in the work of the Dolly Sisters.[1]

The situation which rendered any dramatic performance on the music halls liable to prosecution naturally fostered a revival of the dramatic song-scena, a form of respectable antiquity : this found its most important exponent in Charles Godfrey, of whom some detailed mention will be made later. The same cause resulted in the artist who, since the eighteenth century, had been known as " pantomimist," putting the music hall to his own special uses, and numerous companies, notably that of Paul Martinetti and the Lauri family, specialized in presenting short dramatic ballets, sometimes with the interpolation of a certain amount of singing and dialogue.

There remained without change the vast array of jugglers, acrobats, conjurors, and illusionists. The great success of the performances of Blondin and Farini brought many imitators, and

[1] 1934.

always, or nearly always, the ancient prejudice lingering from the days of the nomadic tumbler of mediæval England, invested these performers with foreign names.

The greatest among music hall jugglers was Paul Cinquevalli —a German, whose actual name was Kestner. His reputation, originally gained as an acrobat, was made in much the same way as that of Blondin, by some audacious performances upon a high rope, in his case stretched above the river Bugg. His first appearance on the English stage was devoted to acrobatics, and as a boy he appeared in trapeze work under the name of the Little Flying Devil—presumably in memory of the great Redigé. When he turned his attention to juggling, his gifts of delicate finesse and humour were at once called into play. With æsthetic judgment, Cinquevalli set himself the task of perfecting feats which involved a strictly limited paraphernalia. One of his main studies was the complete mastery of the movements of a billiard ball. To E. V. Lucas his miraculous control, specially exhibited by the trick in which he made two of these balls move together between billiard cues, seemed to make all things possible. Cinquevalli made many highly-paid appearances in pantomime ; his first important London engagement was at Covent Garden during William Holland's tenancy. An interruption of his work was caused by the War of 1914, the knowledge of his nationality leading to a partial boycott, a boycott felt so keenly by him that it is said to have hastened his death.

Among performances based on exhibitions of strength, an important place was held in the 'eighties by " Samson," who was conquered by Eugen Sandow at a contest between them held at the London Aquarium. The latter, who still lives in the public mind, had a very keen sense of publicity, and was one of the most-photographed men of his time. He appeared at the London Hippodrome in 1902 at the height of his fame when the celebrated biceps figured in picture postcards all over the town. Here he appeared in a kind of rudimentary dramatic sketch, during which, bent backwards on his hands, he supported an enormous iron girder over which a procession of cavalry passed from one side of a remarkably shallow ravine to the other. The vanquishing of Samson and the rise of Sandow created a renewed interest in those athletic forms of entertainment which were borrowed from the fairs and circuses. These ranged from the display of boxing kangaroos (and even of boxing goats) to exhibitions of various kinds of human agility, especially of wrestling. The early nineteen-hundreds produced Hackenschmidt, Madrali, " the terrible Turk," and Yukio Tani, the first popular exponent of ju-jitsu.

Outdoor games adapted for theatrical entertainment were

also revived. In 1905 we read of bicycle polo matches played at the Empire between teams representing England and America. In all these performances women were represented. As early as the 'sixties the exploits of Blondin had evoked feminine competition, and an ill-fated woman exponent of high-rope walking who attempted to cross the Thames from Vauxhall Gardens, had been followed by others such as " Senvah," who appeared in 1868 at the Philharmonic Hall, Mdlle. " Victoria," the one and only female rival of Léotard," the sisters Vaidis (*c.* 1880), " Oura," who " flew in the air at the height of 150 feet," and Oceana, " The Wonder of the Day "—an exceptionally beautiful acrobat who enjoyed great popularity at the Aquarium. This rivalry re-occurred during the vogue for " strong men " and produced " Elspa, the Child Wonder," also known as " The Pocket Hercules." These features led the way to a revival of purely sensational performances of many kinds. Eventually, in 1901, the inclusion of a water tank at the London Hippodrome made possible later on, the performances of Annette Kellerman.

An instance may be given of the trick of " looping the loop," performed both in cars and on bicycles at the Hippodrome where, also, a one-legged cyclist took a leap on a bicycle from the roof into the water tank below.

Exhibitions of freaks also found their way to the music hall stage. In the 'nineties appeared the Siamese Twins, whose painful history can be found in the pages of H. G. Hibbert. In the same decade appeared the " Two-Headed Nightingale," a musical phenomenon of which the title is a sufficient explanation. The earlier exploits of Hervio Nano, the " Gnome Fly," had a reflection about the same time in the presentation of a fraudulent " Missing Link." Exhibitions of dwarfs and midgets had never been absent from the variety stage and appeared frequently in the latter period, though none had rivalled in popularity the renowned General Tom Thumb, the protégé of T. P. Barnum.[1]

This giant among dwarfs was born in New York in 1838. His name was Charles Stratton. At maturity he attained the height of thirty-one inches. His first appearance in England was in

[1]Barnum, the great entertainment promoter who presented *Tom Thumb* in England, was assiduous in his publicizing of the " General." Albert Smith recalled, in a description of a day spent with Barnum at Stratford-on-Avon in 1844, how the latter on leaving the Shakespeare birthplace in Henley Street left with the old lady a quantity of the little cards the General used to distribute at his levees, and begged her to tell the Shakespearean visitors that he was to be seen every day at Dee's Hotel, Birmingham. Barnum was a master in providing his American audiences with the extra entertainment material which has been described in this book as Victorian. Faced with licensing difficulties, he describes his vast assemblage of shows in New York as the American Museum—" something (says Albert Smith), " between Madame Tussaud's and the Polytechnic Institution." Barnum himself described the place as exhibiting " anything from Niagara to bell ringers."

1844,[1] and Queen Victoria commanded his appearance at Buckingham Palace. He was received by her and the Prince Consort in the Yellow Drawing-Room, where he obliged the company by singing *Yankee-Doodle*. The General married a midget whose name was Lavinia Warren.

His fame eventually suffered eclipse from the arrival of still smaller human beings.

The craze for all kinds of sensationalism brought another feature of the older miscellaneous entertainments such as wild beast shows to the music hall. These were revived at the London Hippodrome in the traditional quasi-dramatic setting. A favourite device was the use of a long water-chute down which the creatures were hustled into the tank which, with some painted scenery and property rocks, provided the setting of Hagenbeck's Polar Bears " sliding down a giant glacier."

But perhaps the Hippodrome's most effective *coup* in this direction was the presentation of the celebrated professional liar, " Louis de Rougemont," who accepted, as a challenge, the realization of one of his most famous fantasies, the harnessing and riding of a giant turtle. At the same time there was given a exhibition of genuine Chinese cormorants who were shown circling over the water and swooping for their prey.

Musical and acrobatic clowns from the continent flooded the music hall stage in the early 'nineties, largely owing to the activities of the agent. The most celebrated exponent of clownship within our latter period is Grock, who first appeared in London in the 'nineties. His immediate predecessor was Marceline, a master of comedy in dumb-show. The latter played for two years at the London Hippodrome, where he captured the imagination of all theatre-going children, and of E. V. Lucas.

In approaching the subject of displays of magic on the music hall, one must differentiate between acknowledged conjuring and the performers who exploited the credulity of audiences, a credulity which has sometimes been accorded even when no claim upon it has been directly made. Of this type the most celebrated instance is that of the Davenport Brothers. Here was a case of two quite normal tricksters who, by virtue of that complex existing in the public mind as a result of the conflict between natural superstition and nineteenth-century rationalism, produced a storm which culminated in a serious riot during their appearances at Liverpool in 1865. According to Houdini, who has left an interesting record of the brothers in his book, *A Magician among the Spirits*, the Davenports were more or less innocent of having put forward any active claim to supernatural powers. In

[1]In this year he appeared at the Egyptian Hall, and at the Adelaide Gallery, supported by " The Infant Thalia."

other words, they were perfectly normal conjurors who achieved their magical effects with the aid of a series of well-known rope ties. The phenomena apparently produced while the brothers were lashed to the sides of a cabinet, the doors of which were locked on them, had the effect of provoking bitter attacks from the opponents of spiritualism in reply to the equally passionate championship of its supporters, some of whom, on being allowed to enter the dark cupboard in which the miracles of bell-ringing and so forth were supposed to occur, announced that they had clearly seen spirit hands emerging from the darkness. Indeed, it is asserted by Houdini that thousands of people were thereby converted to the faith. The English career of the Davenports was brought to a conclusion by the Liverpool riots, in which it seems fairly clear that they were in part scapegoats of a larger controversy than that provoked by their rather innocuous mystery show, and they left the country under a cloud, denounced as impostors on every side and burlesqued by no less an artist than Sir Henry Irving.

Allied to the Davenport performances in their effect on popular superstition, but entirely dissimilar in method, were the astonishing pretensions of Doctor Walford Bodie, who appeared on the halls at the beginning of the present century. The doctor, who was originally intended for the Church, was born in Aberdeen in 1865. It is related of him in a short biography that he did not find in the prospect of an ecclesiastical career a sufficient solvent for his desire to achieve the greatest good of the greatest number, and was drawn into the study of medicine with this end in view. His unconventional studies and the realization that he possessed abnormal powers of personal magnetism led him to the practice of hypnotism together with the application of the more occult properties of electrical contact administered to subjects while under hypnotic suggestion. Armed with the theory and practice of these methods, he arrived on the music hall stage—that of the Britannia Theatre in Hoxton, to be precise—in 1903; there he endeavoured to establish his claim to powers which included the cure of paralysis by means of electric massage. Invaluable assistance in his hypnotic demonstrations was given him by his sister, known as Miss Marie Walford. Mental telepathy was also demonstrated—their brains having been discovered to be "in constant communication." Miss Walford died in 1906, but not before her distinguished brother had, with her help, established a considerable reputation and had thereby been enabled to set up an electrical drug company and three dental establishments. Later the doctor met with some reverses which may be attributed to a certain dissatisfaction expressed by patients suffering from the more obscure forms of paralysis and similar complaints. The

extent, however, of the public faith in his powers may perhaps be gauged by a personal anecdote which he published at Christmas 1906, and to which he gave the title of *The Hypnotized Ring;* in this he described the dangerous effects upon a lady of a ring, charged with hypnotic suggestion, which he (the doctor) was only able to combat by the execution of his will-power, which caused the ring to crumble into dust !

The work of music hall conjurors was in the latter period still under the influence of the elaborate methods of the mid-Victorian illusionist, Professor Anderson, " The Wizard of the North," of whom some mention has already been made. Setting aside for the moment such performances as that of the great prestidigitator, Blitz (who impressed the youthful Henry James), Bartolomeo Bosco, and Charles Bertram, the card manipulator, we find the Anderson tradition represented again at the beginning of the twentieth century in the illusions of the " Great Lafayette," of Chung Ling Soo, and of Oswald Williams. In all the cases, but particularly in the first, Anderson's use of animals as confederates was adopted. To Lafayette the " vanishing " of menageries of lions and tigers was a pedestrian matter. He was by birth a German, of amiable personality and of an irrepressible exhibibitionism which led him to paint the façade of his Brixton house in rainbow colours and to gild the area railings. He adored the animals he trained, and his adoration found expression in the regal magnificence with which he surrounded his favourite dog, a present from Houdini. His menagerie involved a travelling cortège of many trucks and vans, and his stage effects were carried out upon a scale of Babylonian magnificence. His end was tragic and characteristic. A fire broke out at one of his performances, and he died in an effort to save the life of his beloved dog.

Chung Ling Soo was an American whose stage methods resembled those of Lafayette, but in a consistently Oriental setting. The important English music hall conjurors who did not rely upon illusions were, at the end of our period, headed by David Devant, an artist of great charm.

The eternal tale of miscellaneous entertainments is continually retold. In no material direction are the ancient forms lacking in the Edwardian music hall. It is almost impossible to put forward a claim for novelty at any time—what occurs is merely a continual process of adaptation. Let us rapidly outline some of the more important forms which have not as yet been mentioned.

None is more static than ventriloquism, represented in the 'seventies and 'eighties by Lieutenant Cole, who invented some famous catch-phrases such as " Blow it out, Cole," and who introduced figures moved by electricity. He established the

convention of naval and military characters for this type of performance, which was continued in the work of Arthur Prince and Coram. Another distinguished ventriloquist is Fred Russell, who takes a place in music hall history as one of the founders and secretary of the Variety Artists' Federation. His amusing entertainment was based upon traditional lines.

The encroaching regulations of the London County Council tended to eliminate the child performer in miscellaneous entertainment, but up to the end of our period there still figured a number of juvenile stars and many "troupes." Prominent among them was the Fothergill Family—especially popular at the Metropolitan Hall. One comes across many other names, now lost in obscurity, such as Tiny Arnold, Little Griff, The Little Wonder, Baby Sparks, Mrs. Hana and Child and the like, while important features of music hall programmes in the early years of the twentieth century were the recurrent batches of Haley's Juveniles, trained to an almost maddening precision in the art of tap-dancing. At the end of the period came the dancing of Little June, later famous in revue and musical comedy, who fascinated audiences at the Empire of years ago.

A reference to dancing should involve some emphasis of the important relation between this art and the music-halls. The production of ballet was, of course, hampered in its dramatic aspect by the working of the 1843 Act. But the interference of the Act with the development of the ballet of action was never a really effective one, and, on the whole, one may say that the typically English—that is to say, democratic—approach to ballet and to dancing as a whole was fully represented in the music hall. Indeed, the decay of the opera ballet at Covent Garden may be to a large extent attributed to the predominance of the ballets at the Alhambra and the Empire. The movement had been stimulated by Morton at the Canterbury, who, with Frederick Strange and, later, Hollingshead, had worked for a literal revival of the conditions of the saloon theatre. With this attempt had been perpetuated the peep-show element of scenic display inherited from the earlier pantomime. The productions of this type at the Alhambra have already been touched on. These were reflected in the 'seventies by performances at the Royal, Holborn, such as that described in newspaper advertisements as containing "The Fairy Fountain and the Cascade of Gems, introducing Apollo, the God of Music, and the Crystal Grotto of the Naïades." Here the object of ballet production is chiefly centred only upon scenic display. After the obtaining of a music hall licence at the Empire in 1887, the production of ballet began to take on an aspect of greater importance under the direction of Katti Lannar; and as the study of this art in its æsthetic aspect is hardly the

province of such a book as this, it is sufficient to indicate that a remarkable advance was achieved by the inclusion, in 1900, of Adeline Genée, who flourished somehow in spite of the squalor and turmoil of her surroundings. Her first appearance in a leading part was made when she danced in the place of Mlle. Gattenburg in the ballet of *Round the Town*. At a much later date, Sir Alfred Butt created at the Palace a milieu for Anna Pavlova, and for Maud Allan, whose sensational Salome Dance was sufficiently in the music hall tradition.

Such æsthetic tendencies were not confined to the Palace, for by this time Sir Oswald Stoll had, at the Coliseum, achieved a revolution which paved the way for appearances of such artists as Sara Bernhardt, Yvette Guilbert and Raymonde Collignon. The advent of the last-named, a singer whose delicate work demands the conditions of intimacy, was a strange moment in the history of the music hall.

The poses plastiques by no means came to an end after the elimination of Saville House and the doubtful gaffs of Leicester Square. They remained, or rather reappeared, to form a part of the new æstheticism. It is said that when Charles Morton, towards the end of his career, took over the management of the Palace Theatre, he was troubled by the legacy of a family of these " poseurs " which had been left on his hands by his predecessor, Augustus Harris. His doubts as to their propriety were, however, allayed by the friendly assurances of the Prince of Wales. Since then, a number of such exhibitions, presented with much solemnity, have formed an element of music hall programmes, more particularly at the same house under the subsequent management of Sir Alfred Butt.

Another ancient form, that of the Protean Actor, remained throughout the later period. In the 'fifties this art had become especially associated with extra-theatrical entertainment, in that form which Albert Smith irreverently described as " the ducking business," for the artist at that time did not leave the stage, but sank behind a table in order to effect his quick changes. Such entertainments were related to the musical sketch, which grew out of the earlier comic lecture. These in turn owed their inspiration to the theatrical art of Dibdin and the elder Mathews ; and a liaison between the two was brought to the music hall by Frederick Maccabe, who was also to be seen in a one-man entertainment to which he gave the name of *Begone, Dull Care*. Maccabe was originally an accompanist at the concert rooms and he used the piano in introducing his character sketches. As an actor he had gathered experience in stock companies at Manchester and elsewhere. His rapid portrayal of varying types is said to have been brilliantly executed, but the material left us by

him in a book which embodies some of these studies is not enlightening. He added a ventriloquial element to his entertainment and wrote a short work on this subject also.

A number of foreign exponents of this protean art succeeded Maccabe, the most important of whom was Ugo Biondi, who was imitated with great success by Arthur Roberts, in burlesque. Within memory are the admirable one-man sketches of R. A. Roberts, whose most popular appearance was made in the pocket melodrama of *Dick Turpin*. This was an amazingly effective piece of work ending in the famous quick-change of the artist's envelopment, in the character of Turpin, by an angry crowd, and his immediate reappearance from the other side of the stage in another character.

In the related method of the one-man pianistic entertainment or "musical sketch," a number of well-known artists made appearances on the music hall stage. In extra-music-hall work the tradition of John Parry and Albert Smith was represented by Corney Grain (whose reputation, as we have already noted, was established at the German Reed Entertainments) and George Grossmith, later famous as the creator of a number of the Gilbert and Sullivan parts. Then there was Mel B. Spur at the Egyptian Hall, with Maskelyne and Cook. He was quite representative of the older type of entertainer who was prepared to make sudden transitions from "lively to severe." His performance embodied a monologue of great sentimentality, called *What is a Gentleman?* to which he supplied an accompaniment on the zither.

These influences combined to produce one Edwardian music hall star of major importance, Barclay Gammon. Gammon's transition to the environment in which he achieved fame was made after a long period of semi-professionalism, in which, while yet a clerk in the City, he entertained at dinners and at similar functions. His first appearance as a whole-time artist was made at the St. George's Hall under the management of Maskelyne and Devant. Thence, his fame growing rapidly, he made those triumphant appearances, the crown of his career, at the Palace Theatre, under Sir Alfred Butt. Describing himself as a "Society Clown," he sang at his piano perched upon a music-stool always on the point of collapse, made jokes, gave satirical opinions upon the events of the day and commented unsparingly upon his own prodigious girth; the whole in the breathless manner and rather asthmatical voice, the management of which was the secret of his style. One may imagine that all this was very little removed from the methods of Corney Grain; Gammon is thus an interesting figure as creating a revival of mid-Victorian entertainment into the period immediately before the War.

Gammon was not alone in the application of the one-man show to the music hall. There was a large number of rather less representative figures, among whom Nelson Jackson, achieved considerable success. It is to this type of performer that both Harry Pelissier, the creator of " The Follies," and his fellow comedian, Lewis Sydney, originally belonged. The latter, before the famous concert-party came into existence, was seen in a " curtain-raiser " entertainment at the Royalty Theatre. Here he performed his burlesque of a melodrama, an old-time musical sketch in the true John Parry manner, and both he and Pelissier included work of this kind in the earlier programmes of " The Follies," who made their first important impression as a music hall item at the Palace and the Tivoli.

The peep-show and, later, the panorama were as elements of miscellaneous entertainment in the music hall, eventually eliminated by the cinema which, in England, found here its chief fostering place. A reflection of Victorian earnestness may perhaps be discerned in the early devotion of this art in these surroundings to material of a semi-educational character. Perhaps the cinema may also be cited as a reason for the comparative absence of the marionette from latter-day programmes, though this absence is to some extent due to the fact that the larger houses were unsuitable for them. Still, they have found a place throughout the music hall period. To an extraordinary degree, indeed, the forms which satisfied the pleasure seekers among our remote ancestors survived.

At all times, however, the first place has been held by those forms which give the most direct expression to personality ; and of these the comic singer has, on the whole, been uppermost. In the nineteenth century, with the expansion of public-house singing, it entered upon its triumphant period and its complete predominance is reflected by the economic relation in which the comedian or comedienne stood to other performers. It is true that, at the height of some especial popularity, such artists as Blondin or Houdini could command very high payment in the music hall, but by the 'nineties such cases had become exceptional, and it is remarked by Rendle and others how completely a slump in the market the silent acts had become in the days of Dan Leno and the great comic singers.

The situation remained static for over a quarter of a century, producing in the public mind an identification of the music hall with the art of the comedian and that identification has remained. Indeed, one may go further and say that the London music hall is, for the majority, an identification with the association of houses known as the " Syndicate Halls " in which this policy reached its height. In a word, the tavern concert eventually triumphed over

all other influences, dominating them until the end of the Edwardian period. No explanation is therefore needed for devoting the remainder of this study mainly to aspects of the prevailing type.

Among women serio-comics who paved the way for Marie Lloyd, the greatest was undoubtedly Jenny Hill, known the world by the ingenuity of her agent, H. J. Didcott, as "The Electric Spark." There is always difficulty in placing values upon an artist from written record, but this conclusion is formed from a practically unanimous judgment among those who saw her; only once have I been able to discover a hint of dissent among the critics of her work. In the time sense she was midway between Annie Adams and Marie Lloyd, that is to say, her background (had she felt its influence) was that of a theatrical convention and of a super imposed gentility, with its "ladies' versions" and the rest. Her breakaway to raciness and originality must be attributed to her own original and vital nature. There must be added to this an intense instinct of class-consciousness which nearly always appears in the material of her work. A hint has already been given of Jenny Hill's humble origin and of her painful youth Like her younger contemporary, Bessie Bellwood, she was born into the life of the London slums—somewhere between Paddington and Marylebone. It is said that her father attended at a cabstand in the neighbourhood of the hall (the house in Marylebone High Street which had been converted by Sam Collins from the "Rose of Normandy") owned by her first employer, Botting, who was also concerned with an artificial flower factory. As a young girl working in this factory in the early 'sixties, she must have shown considerable aptitude for singing, as she was transferred, under articles (possibly with Botting's assistance), to the already-mentioned Bradford tavern sing-song. Apparently she kept the document which for some years bound her a prisoner to the place and it has been described as an iniquitous one. The *Era* for January 4, 1896 (the writer no doubt reporting from first-hand information), says: "She had to be up with the lark to clean the bars—she and a companion in misery. Often they had no breakfast and by noon they had to be dressed and in the singing-room to provide harmony for the early-afternoon drinkers.' There is no doubt that these early privations, as in the case of Dan Leno, shortened her life. What poignancy they gave to her melodramatic studies of suffering and ill-usage can only be guessed at. When she was free of her five years' bondage she was already sufficiently advanced in local reputation to achieve an engagement at a hall in Birmingham at £4 a week. This was presumably a single week's work, for she is said to have remarked of this engagement: "I put the money in a little tin

box and buried it at the bottom of my trunk—all but a sovereign which was to take me and my mother to Nottingham. When we got there the first thing I heard was that the hall where I was engaged was closed. I had to open the box in the Station Yard and find that poor £3 I had hidden away with such care. We wanted it to pay our fare to London."

Her arrival in London may be dated in 1868 or 1869. Her task in finding work was not an easy one, and it was remarkable that she did not starve to death. About this time she married an acrobat and for a period acted as an assistant at his performances. Then there was a child to look after. The situation finally became desperate, and in a moment of tragic courage she succeeded in arresting the attention of Didcott, the agent. He sent the distressed girl around to Loibl, of the Pavilion, with a note explaining that he was only doing so in order to get rid of her. The result was, however, that she was at once made use of by the manager as an extra turn, to supply the absence of George Leybourne, who was detained at another house. The incident may be concluded in her own words : " They sent me on, and my little song—a parody on *Old Brown's Daughter*—got a round of applause. Mr. Loibl said, ' Now, little woman, you must go on again.' I said, ' I can't, sir,' ' Why not?' says he, quite cross. I said, ' I can't tell you, sir.' I was fainting from sheer hunger. Well, Leybourne arrived, and he had to lead me on to acknowledge the applause before he could get silence for his song. Then Mr. Loibl took me and gave me a glass of port and a long engagement. He also gave me the agent's letter as a memento."[1]

One does not find an extensive repertoire of music hall songs associated solely with Jenny Hill's name, though the sketches with which she surrounded her singing gave individuality to her later performances. There are no signs of anything in the nature of a famous song until the later 'seventies, when E. V. Page wrote *'Arry* for her. This song successfully exploited Jenny Hill's vein of cockney banter, and it was probably the prototype of Bessie Bellwood's equally celebrated *Wot Cheer 'Ria*. Neither the words nor the tune of *'Arry* (both by Page) commend themselves especially to posterity. The gist of it has become over-familiarized by repetition—that of the coster swell in his holiday togs. Her performance of it must have been a miracle of comedy to have secured the song such a vogue. Of far more interest are two later songs written for her by Marie Lloyd's composer and librettist, George Lebrunn and Harrington. These are *The City Waif* and

[1]Jerome K. Jerome, in *Variety Patter*, gives a circumstantial account of the legend that during this early London period Jenny Hill appeared as a performer on the Zithere under the name of Signora Ballatino, and won her popularity from the audience of a hall in South-East London by quelling the attempt at interruption made by an intoxicated coal-heaver in the gallery.

Masks and Faces. The date of the songs is about 1887, at which time the romantic treatment of street life had recently received a post-Dickensian impetus from George R. Sims' *The Lights of London.* *The City Waif* is an interesting link between the departed "Spare me a copper" school of the Christy Ministrels and the dawning of a more robust age. The humour and the resilience of the street Arab are depicted in the first verse of the song; then comes a pathetic picture of the poor refugee from the country who has "seen better days." This is followed by a sympathetic account of how Sal Brown, who is delicately indicated as being a woman of easy virtue, spent her last penny on effecting a cure of the singer's starving and crippled sister. This breathes the very spirit of poor Jo's "'e wos very good to me, 'e wos." The last three verses of this six-act potted melodrama are devoted to domestic incidents in which a heightened class-consciousness colours the expression. The first tells of the death of a man turned out of home for defaulting in the rent, and the second an attack outside a "caffy" upon a "swell" by the father of the girl he has betrayed. A part of this verse deserves quotation:

> "Just then a gent comes from the Caffy
> With a lady all jools and lace
> And the shabby cove turns in a moment
> And meets the pair face to face.
> My Father! My child! You villain!
> The shabby chap 'oarsely cries,
> 'I've found you—my child's betrayer!'
> Then straight at his throat he flies."

The last incident is a terrific affair: a fire in which a child is saved from burning by the City Waif. And the Waif, having performed feats of almost incredible endurance, quite fails in his simplicity to understand why he has been called a hero.

Masks and Faces is upon the same lines and ends with the hair-raising murder of an elderly miser. I have been to some pains about these songs, for without such a reference the sécret of Jenny Hill's appeal would not suggest itself. It was from first to last a democratic appeal based on an intimacy with the poorest members of her audience. It was this predominating quality, rather than any lack of adaptability, which prevented this great instinctive actress from achieving an outstanding success on the legitimate stage when, in 1878, she appeared under Hollingshead in H. J. Byron's burlesque, *Jack the Giant Killer* at the Gaiety Theatre. In pantomime, however, she was popular as a principal boy.

In 1889 she appeared at the Grecian in a revival of Baldwin Buckstone's *Good for Nothing*, but only with moderate success. Hollingshead, who had a passion for transplanting the concert-room artists, realized the limitation of Jenny Hill's art and, following the general assumption that success is more worthily won by an appeal to the educated rather than to the uneducated classes, he regretted its cause while acknowledging her supremacy ; "Jenny Hill," he says in his reminiscences, "was without exception one of the greatest (*sic*) female geniuses who ever appeared on the music hall platform. Her sense of character—low life, of course—and her dramatic power of conjuring up solid pictures of men and women who never appeared bodily on the stage, would have delighted the elder Mathews. If education and early opportunity had been given to her in her youth the world would have had an actress who would have lived in stage history."

Allied to Jenny Hill only in her use of the native cockney was the boisterous Bessie Bellwood, about whose expansive personality Arthur Roberts and other commentators have left an appreciative record. The methods of this artist, delightful as the effects were, need not detain us. Here no claim can be made for genius, only for a superabundant vitality. The song by which her name is still remembered is the *Wot Cheer 'Ria* mentioned above, the tune of which she herself composed. The date of the song is 1887, and it arrived aptly as a continuance of the earlier type of Jenny Hill song at a moment when the latter was making a change in style. Bessie Bellwood was not affected by the somewhat missionary spirit which inspired the later work of *The Vital Spark*—she was content throughout with a purely humorous exposition of cockney life. This, in spite of the fact that she was of Irish birth—(her actual name was Elizabeth Ann Katherine Mahony)—she knew intimately from the days when she was a factory hand in the New Cut. From an early beginning as a singer, with performances of Irish ballads at the more obscure taverns, she made her first success at the Winchester under Preece. Thence she came to the West End and achieved a popularity both as an artist and as an outstanding personality of Bohemian life which was unshaken until her rather early death in 1896, which occurred within a few months of her return from a successful tour in the Colonies. The best known of Bessie Bellwood's songs, in addition to *Wot Cheer 'Ria*, were, perhaps, *Aubrey Plantagenet* and *Has anyone seen Mary Ann*, *The Barmaid*, *It's All Right if you Love the Girl*, *The Pro's Coachman* and *Woa Emma*, a song which appears, in another version, to have originated with George Leybourne.

Such was the work which heralded the perfected art of the

music hall comedienne as achieved by Marie Lloyd. Bessie Bellwood may be regarded as an artist belonging to a transitional period. Among her immediate predecessors are to be found singers such as Mrs. F. R. Phillips, a stately person, whose ladies' versions of Sam Collins' *No Irish Need Apply* and of Harry Sidney's *The Shadows on the Wall* were widely popular. A tendency to transition may be noted in certain of the songs of Annie Adams, who indeed may be cited as an early instance of the male impersonator in the modern music hall sense. Though she was stolid and stentorian, there are traces of raciness in one or two of her songs. Her *Oranges, Apples and Bills of the Play*, which she was singing in the early 'sixties, is quite a jolly song, and affords, in its pleasant pictorial cover by Concannen, a hint of a survival in the Victorian theatre, of Restoration manners. Some of her songs were the work of G. W. Hunt and of E. V. Page; the former contributing *Johnnie the Engine Driver*. *Gaslight Green*, another of her songs, has a promising title but there is little else to be said for it. Other titles were *Upon the Grand Parade*, *When the Band begins to Play* and *Goodbye, I'm going to March Away*, and one of the most popular was *Houp-La*. Another purveyor of "ladies' versions" was Louie Sherrington, of whom it may be recorded that in the late 'sixties she was upholding the Leybourne vogue with *Up in a Balloon, Girls*, that she was beautiful, and that she is said to have excelled in a ballad called *Wait Till the Moonlight Falls on the Waters*.

A definitive music hall quality is not perceptible in the work of these earlier artists—their slavish imitations of the male comedians alternating with burletta sentimentality: this came later with the work of such singers as Katie Lawrence, who survived into the twentieth century to make a tour of the cinemas. She especially calls for remembrance as the creator of one of the two most genuinely popular music hall song survivals, the charming *Daisy Bell, or a Bicycle made for Two*. Both words and music were the work of Harry Dacre and it is dated 1892.

These artists are fairly representative of the measure of high and low comedy among women singers before the predominance of the eccentric comedian. In this direction as in others the women followed suit. An early instance of emulation is to be found in Ada Lundberg, of whom Louie Freear, in so far as her work was connected with the music hall, was a direct successor. As one of the founders of a school which included such artists as Nellie Wallace and Lily Morris, she was a significant figure, though little memory of her survives. She was born in 1850 at Bristol, one year before Jenny Hill and in the early 'sixties was already making professional appearances. Indeed, one learns that she ran away from home at the age of eleven to join a circus,

and that she subsequently appeared in performances of the "Poses Plastiques." A song in which she made an early success was called *My First Young Man*, and in this she appears to have anticipated a favourite character of Marie Lloyd, that of the "baby romp." A later song, whose popularity probably influenced London engagements, was called *Betsy Barlow*. In 1875 she performed at the Marylebone Music Hall and at the Middlesex, and in the following year she appeared for the first time at the London Pavilion. From that moment she was a popular figure in the London halls, and after the formation of the Syndicate she played under contract for them until her death in 1899. In 1893 she visited America. Her greatest effect was made in a song in the character of a down-at-heel "slavey," "a cross," says the *Era*, "between Dickens' Marchioness and the Belinda of H. J. Byron's *Our Boys*." In the same disguise she sang a song called *Tooraladdie*. In a further song called *I'm All Right up till Now* she impersonated a drunken woman ; this had a vogue which lasted from the 'seventies until her death. Others which she popularized were *Such a Nice Gal Too*, *All through Sticking to a Soldier*, and *That's a Bit of Comfort to a Poor Old Maid ;* whose titles are sufficiently indicative of their content. She contributed to the vogue for Irish songs, it is said, with particular excellence.

After her came the vital and diminutive Louie Freear, who frequently performed to the vast radio audiences of the B.B.C. Owing to her remarkable success in George Dance's comic opera, *The Chinese Honeymoon*, produced in 1901 at the Strand Theatre, her work became primarily connected with the legitimate stage. Her range has been a wide one. Though the characters she was identified with were of the Ada Lundberg type, Herbert Beerbohm Tree, with happy inspiration, engaged her for the part of Puck in his production of *Midsummer Night's Dream*. In this she achieved another outstanding success.

The music hall has not been over-rich in eccentric comediennes though there are other distinguished examples, among them Vesta Victoria. Vesta Victoria was the daughter of a well-known negro comedian, Joe Lawrence, whose brother, Lawrence Barclay, wrote some celebrated music-hall songs. She is the creator of four songs at least which are in the very first comic rank. These are *Our Lodger's Such a Nice Young Man*, by Fred Murray and Lawrence Barclay, *It's All Right in the Summer Time*, *Daddy Wouldn't Buy me a Bow-Wow*, and Frank Godfrey and Charles Collins' *Now we have to call him Father*.

Male impersonation was brought a step nearer to realism by Bessie Bonehill, an artist with a meticulous sense of costume. She was a native of West Bromwich and, as a girl, became locally famous as a clog-dancer. Her first important London appear-

ances occurred in 1874 at the Metropolitan, Royal, and Oxford halls. Here she sang a patriotic song, the work of Clement Scott, called *Here Stands a Post.* This was a contribution to the fervour from which *Waiting for the Signal* was evolved. She was breezy, dapper and personable, with a vein of sentiment represented by her *Playmates of Mine.*

Such artists as Bessie Bonehill paved the way for the triumph of Vesta Tilley. The position achieved by this artist had an unique quality, for she brought to a well-worn type of work a new note, that of boyishness and refinement. Her style was mischievous, and with her boyish figure, set off by perfectly-cut male clothes, her effects were produced with a minimum suggestion of her own sex. The individuality of her style was so marked that for many years she was held by the public to be the creator of this type of entertainment. Many of her songs were famous—one or two of them achieved such general acceptance that their phrases passed into the language. Among these was E. W. Rogers' *Following in Father's Footsteps*, one of a brilliant series of songs, which included *The Midnight Son*, written for her by that author. These are dated about 1905, the period of her best work. It was then that she was singing the most famous, perhaps, of all her songs, *Jolly Good Luck to the Girl who Loves a Soldier*, the work of F. W. Leigh and Kenneth Lyle. Her first marked success among the many studies of fashionable young man was *Algy the Piccadilly Johnnie* by H. B. Norris (*c.* 1900). A delightful song of this type which she sang a year or so before the war was *Monty from Monte Carlo.* In the 'nineties she sang a number of songs by George Dance, of which *Angels Without Wings* was particularly successful.

The brilliant work of Vesta Tilley rather outshone that of two of her younger contemporaries, Hetty King and Ella Shields. The former is unforgettably associated with the magnificent *All the Nice Girls Love a Sailor*, and with a number of excellent songs portraying the " man-about-town," such as *Follow the Tramlines* and *I'm Afraid to come home in the Dark.* As for Ella Shields, it is perhaps not an exaggeration to say that in her admirable *Burlington Bertie from Bow* she brought to perfection, on individual lines, the art of male impersonation, preserving even more successfully than Vesta Tilley the exact balance between illusion and make-believe which can render the method a delightful one.

Bessie Wentworth, in a short career ending with her death in 1902, popularized the school of women coon singers, to which May Yohe and May Henderson belonged. One of her best songs, *Looking for a Coon like Me,* was written by Le Brunn and Harrington.

In returning to male singers there remain important instances

of artists whose fame preceded that of Dan Leno. There was, for instance, W. B. Fair, who is to be remembered for his creation of T. S. Lonsdale's *Tommy Make Room for Your Uncle*, a song which annoyed Robert Browning. His work is not otherwise significant. He was a vigorous and competent comic vocalist, popular as a chairman. His connection with the last years of the Winchester led to a financial collapse, and when he died he had been for some years in the employ of Oswald Stoll as the doorkeeper of the London Coliseum.

William Randall was a singer of the 'seventies and 'eighties whose portrait figured extensively on the comic songs published with pictorial covers. He was a handsome man of short stature, whose work was of the *buffo* variety and resembled that of Harry Sidney. But his best-known song, *The Charming Young Widow I met in the Train*, though facetious, cannot be described as funny.

In the crowd of blacked-up comedians (many artists were in their early years associated with this work, among them James Fawn, Tom Maclagan, Little Tich, Herbert Campbell, and even Edward Terry), a notable figure was Harry Hunter, in his nonage a City clerk who in spare hours sang at smoking concerts. Hunter was completely loyal to the minstrel movement ; from 1873 he entered into a partnership with the Mohawks, and it was he who, between the years 1890 and 1894, conducted the last combined seasons of the Mohawk and Moore and Burgess companies. At the latter end of his career he was seen on the music halls. The portraits of Hunter showing a bland and rather sleepy face with side-whiskers and heavy moustache, reveal the personality of the old-time humorist. It is one of those faces which seem inimical to humour ; yet it is an even greater stretch of the imagination to disentangle the suggestion of that quality from the countenances of the earlier funny men, such as Albert Smith or Arthur Sketchley, which were apt to be wreathed in the full beard.

Harry Hunter was born in 1841 and he died in 1906 ; his career furnishes a good example of the translation of the minstrel methods (he was a " cornerman ") to the music-halls. He was a prolific author and composer of songs, some of which have an historic quality especially his early *I Saw Esau Kissing Kate*, *Over the Garden Wall* (first performed at the Agricultural Hall in Islington), *His Name was Joshu-a* and *Look at the Price of Coal*. For twenty years Hunter was a partner in the music-publishing firm of Francis, Day and Hunter.

Some comedians may find mention by reason of particular songs which they made famous : George Beauchamp, for example, who created *Get Your Hair Cut*, almost as popular a catch-phrase as the earlier *How's Your Poor Feet*, which originated with the Scotch

comedian, Tom Maclagan. The former song was introduced by Beauchamp in 1891 at Sebrights in the Hackney Road. Victor Liston, self-designated " The Robson of the Music-Halls," made a great impression with Fred Albert's song, *Shabby Genteel* (" Too proud to beg, too honest to steal."). The song is reported to have charmed the Prince of Wales. A number of songs were admired by this distinguished *habitué* of the music halls, among them *Pal o' Mine*, sung by the great Vance ; in the case of *Shabby Genteel* he is said to have taken the Duke and Duchess of Sutherland to Evans's in its declining days especially to hear it.

Henri Clark, at first popular as a negro minstrel, made his reputation with Fred Albert's *The Mad Butcher*, which also appears in Albert's own repertory. Henri Clark became the manager of the Metropolitan Music Hall under Poole. Fred French, who kept alive those methods of melodrama which reappeared later in the work of Charles Godfrey, had, in addition, two popular songs based on nonsense rhymes, *Hanky Panky* and *Sago Fum*, together with a burlesque called *The Wreck off London Bridge*.

Harry Liston is to be remembered by the song, *Nobody's Child*, which made fun of the theme of a play of that name by Watts Phillips. He also succeeded with *The Tin Pot Band* and a song called *Ginger Ginger*. He was a boisterous comedian who first came into favour at the Oxford Hall under Charles Morton. He devoted the latter years of a very long career to the presentation of a concert-party revue called " Merry Moments " in which he toured the provinces till shortly before his death about thirty years ago.

Harry Rickards was a late example of the lion comique who, after a financial crash, made his way to Australia and built up a large fortune as a promoter of music halls there. He was bull-necked in appearance and had a waxed moustache, and though not held to be a singer of particular importance, his name is associated with several well-known songs, such as *Captain Jinks of the Horse Marines* and *Oxford Joe*. Another well-known song, *Cerulea was Beautiful*, was written for him by G. W. Hunt. He also sang a *Mugby Junction* song of Dickensian inspiration, and the *The Alpine Hat*, another contribution by the versatile Hunt. His most typical appearances, however, were made in songs with a political or national flavour. There was the egregious *That's the sort of Man we want in England here to-day*, composed by Vincent Davies and written by John S. Haydon, and the satirical *In England* by Harrington and Le Brunn, dated 1888, which reflected the unpopularity at that time of Queen Victoria, caused by her prolonged retirement from public life. After a somewhat familiar reference to the monarch as " the nicest plumpest little Queen in all the world," there comes the pointed refrain :

"In England, in England,
In England the ruler of the Sea,
We sing 'God save the Queen,'
Though she's very seldom seen ;
In England the Land of the Free."

James Fawn was a comedian of greater distinction than Rickards. As has been already noted, his music hall work was associated with "inebriate" songs—such things as E. V. Page's *Only One* and *It must have been the Lobster.* But earlier he had made some reputation in old comedy and in pantomime ballet at the suburban theatres.

It has been stated that the coster comedian, following the tendency towards specialization, became a separate entity in music hall singing. It is doubtful, however, if the distinction was fully achieved before the appearance of Albert Chevalier. Immediately before his appearance the path had been inundated by some singers to whom the cockney idiom was native. Teddy Mosedale, Hyram Travers and Walter Laburnum predated by a few years Gus Elen, Albert Chevalier and Alec Hurley. They were each, in their way, almost exclusively identified with coster songs, but of the three, Hyram Travers, with his complete command of back-slang, was the most faithful to type.

Walter Laburnum bore a strong resemblance to George Leybourne and was for some years associated with songs of the Leybourne character (these included one on the subject of cod-liver oil). Charles Coborn, too, alternated songs of a coster type, such as *'E's all right when you know 'im*, with those in his more familiar vein. The real vogue, however, was created by Chevalier and continued by Gus Elen.

Charles Godfrey, who is to be ranked among the most important of music hall singers, made a strange alliance between the descriptive songs, which, as we have seen, he elaborated into "scenas," and the drinking song of the ultra-boisterous kind. Such were his *Hi-Tiddle-I-Ti* by George Le Brunn. *Regent Street,* based by Richard Morton on a melody by Nevin, and *The Rickety, Rackety Crew.* These, though intensely popular, were, however, subordinate to the melodramatic song-sketches in which he revelled. Here is another case of the complete identification of a form with an artist who exploits it with conspicuous success. The *Era* for April 7, 1900, states in set terms that Charles Godfrey invented the descriptive song ; and the claim is upheld by Godfrey himself in an article published in 1894. This claim, if strictly examined, is fantastic, though the variant employed by Godfrey, with its use of tableau and elaborate scenic effect, was certainly an individual one. The compelling personality of the

artist had the effect of putting his work in a separate category. Godfrey was born about 1857 in Southwark and, according to a biographical note by Wal Pink, who wrote for him, made his first stage appearance, after a short period as a waiter at the Surrey Theatre, at a hall in the Kennington Park Road. Another more detailed account states that he appeared at the Bower Saloon and the Victoria Theatre, and on tour, during which period he appeared in abbreviated versions of *Hamlet* and *Sweeny Todd* on a single evening. An article in the *Era* places his arrival on the music hall stage in the late 'seventies; in which case his experience as a legitimate actor was very brief. The same writer states that as an actor he adopted the name of Paul Lacey and that he approached music hall work on the advice of Alfred Rayner, the Shakespearean actor. Chance Newton reports that he was a "general utility man" at the Whitechapel Pavilion. According to Godfrey's own account, he made his first essay in dramatic monologue by staging at Lusby's Music Hall a descriptive song called *Poor Old Benjamin the Workhouse Man*. This is forgotten by the commentators who all tell us that *On Guard* came first. It was certainly the most famous of his songs. This miniature melodrama of a Crimean veteran, originally presented in one scene was later elaborated by the addition of a second, placed at the gates of a workhouse. Chance Newton describes it vividly and says, "I have seen him move the patrons of the 'halls' to volcanic excitement and to thunders of applause." This was especially the case when he came to the part where the now starving old tramp warrior applied for a night's shelter at the workhouse casual ward. "'Be off, you tramp!' exclaimed the harsh janitor. 'You are not wanted here.' 'No,' thunders the tattered veteran, 'I am not wanted here, but at Balaclava I was wanted there!'" This scene, with its indictment of a graceless government, was subsequently omitted, or rather curtailed, though perhaps only in the West End of London. This curtailment was at the request of "several officers of the Household Brigade," who pointed out to Sam Adams, the manager of the London Pavilion, the possibility of its creating an unfavourable effect upon recruiting. For this type of song Godfrey often relied upon Le Brunn and Harrington. *On Guard*, however, so the *Era* tells us, was written by a South London hatter. Sometimes Godfrey was his own composer, as in the case of the early *Seventh Royal Fusiliers*, the words of which were by Wal Pink. Following this, he produced a number of patriotic and historical scenes, among them *The Bridge*, *Balaclava*, *Nelson*, *The Last Shot* and *Inkerman*. Meanwhile his output of comic songs continued; early successes in the comic vein were *Oh, Ain't it Peculiar* and *The Girl in the Pinafore Dress*. The most popular of

all was probably *Hi-Tiddle-I-Ti*, which occasioned many imitations. The growing æstheticism of the 'eighties was burlesqued by Godfrey, first in *The Masher King* and later in the borrowed *Flippity Flop Young Man*. The latter theme was imitated in a number of consequent songs.

There is every reason to regard Godfrey as belonging to a traditional line of performers, for in his work in bringing to the music hall the element of popular drama, he adopted a method which was precisely that of the quasi-dramatic saloon theatre. The form persisted in a number of directions and was continually attempted during the period of the disallowance of the dramatic sketch as a feature of music hall programmes. The most consistent use of the sketch in monologue form of recent years is to be found in the work of Fred Barnes ; and the song comedies of Wilkie Bard are related to instances.

The song of rustic comedy, ancient in origin, died a hard death on the music halls ; there are constant recurrences up to the end of our period. George Bastow, about 1906, was singing *Varmer Giles* to the tune of *Villikins and his Dinah*, and the traditional quality of the song was no barrier to its success. Another broadly characterized study, *The Galloping Major*, was equally popular ; in this case the song can be referred back to the work of Vance and Leybourne.

A fairly representative selection of singers has now been considered ; the temptation remains to make further mention of many who, for one reason or another, have left some mark on music hall history. There are so many delightful moments in the long story, so many phrases and glints of character and manners which have become part of the background of everyday life, that it is difficult to imagine a concrete image of the popular life of the country emerging without such a focus as the Music Hall provides. A thousand things recall the illuminating details which are at the core of the understanding of social conditions, indeed, one may often learn more in a flash from one song than from three books. They spring at random into one's mind—the forgotten genius (A. G. Mills) who wrote *Why did I leave my little back room in Bloomsbury* for Alf. Chester, Edward Marshall's singing of *The Last Man in Town*, Tom Costello's *At Trinity Church I met my Doom*, T. W. Barrett's *The Nobleman's Son*, Morny Cash's *I Live in Trafalgar Square*, Florrie Ford's *They're all single by the Seaside*, Charles Whittle's *Let's all go down the Strand*, Lily Burnand's *Two Little Girls in Blue*, Kate Carney's *When the Summer Comes Again*, George Lashwood's *In the Twi-twi-light*, and many another song of the kind, T. W. Barrett's *He's got 'em on*, J. W. Rowley's *My Sarah Ann* (with the somersault dance to follow)—all these artists and many, many more have made their contribution with

at least one song to this tremendous picture of life.

It would be easy to multiply this assemblage, but there is space only for a very brief glance at a group of singers who are still in the minds of contemporary audiences. One of them affords an instance of a surviving type, Harry Champion, the last of the comedians who have relied upon the subject of food for humorous material. His early songs, *I Like Pickled Onions* and *Boiled Beef and Carrots* relate themselves to the work of John Labern. The same theme reappeared later in Sam Cowell's *Bacon and Greens*, which Mr. Coborn erroneously mentions as the first of its kind. Probably the delight in food is by no means dead ; Ernie Mayne, in his songs about mince pies and other delicacies, took up the tale at a somewhat later date than Champion, but the latter survived him.

An artist who contrasted sharply with most of the comedians of his time was T. E. Dunville, in whose work there was a measure of comic genius. His work had two characteristics of significance: an extremely specialized style and the adoption of a costume which he rigidly adhered to whatever the character he was portraying. With George Robey he was an influence in establishing this method of presenting eccentric comedy. Dunville has left an autobiography which reveals that he was born in 1868 and that he was the son of a Coventry tailor. At the age of sixteen he began life on the stage as an acrobat. While engaged in this work, a comic tendency was revealed, but it was not until five years later that began to follow his true bent. During that time he worked in an acrobatic partnership known as "The Merry Men." This was the outcome of some amateur busking undertaken as a boy with two friends who called themselves "The Three Spires," in compliment to the chief architectural feature of their native town. The late troupe work led to pantomime engagements, and from these to an engagement in America in alfresco entertainment on a spectacular scale with fireworks, known as "The Fall of Pompeii." In 1889 he made his first individual appearances on the music hall stage, at the Middlesex, Gatti's in Villiers Street, and the Foresters. Shortly afterwards he was lucky in the choice of a song called *Lively on and Lively off*, which became the success of the season. This was followed by a song in which the staccato style, always afterwards adopted by him, came into play. This was the well-known *And the Verdict Was*, each chorus of which consisted of four terse lines, such as :

"Little boy,
Pair of skates,
Broken ice,
Heaven's gates."

With this he sang another equally successful song called *Bunka-doodle-ido*. Henceforward, Dunville appeared ostensibly in many characters—as policeman, postman, tax-collector and the like ; but the same galvanic style and fantastic costume served them all. He was indeed king of the comedians who adopted a "trade-mark" costume. The need for such a trade-mark among the jostling crowd of funny men was the outcome of later music-hall specialization, the original adoption of an emphasized appearance resulting, probably, from the large and brilliantly-lighted auditorium for the new type of music hall. The effect of this competitive grotesqueness was to turn the comedian once again into a clown in complete reaction from the "dress coat" school which had been ousted by the genius of Dan Leno. The new clown was a native, homely, but humanized being. His clothes, in some instances (those of Dan Leno among them), retained some semblance of normal costume, but in Dunville's case there was no element of realism. He wore a long, one-piece dress of black material which emphasized his height ; and this was relieved by a large white Puritan collar. A kind of Dutch-doll wig completed the design.

Other artists who adopted similar methods were George Robey, Wilkie Bard, Jack Pleasants and Mark Sheridan, and indeed, a fair percentage of the total number of comedians. T. E. Dunville was, I think, on the whole, one of the greatest of them, though Jack Pleasants was also an interesting example of the stylized method. He wore a costume suggestive of the charity boy who had outgrown his clothes, and in this absurd garb he raised a chorus of simple joy in such songs as *I'm Twenty-one To-day* and *Jack's Come Home To-day*. Mark Sheridan wore a pair of exaggerated bell-bottomed trousers and a strange top hat. He was an immensely able singer of chorus songs. His *I Do Like to be beside the Sea-side*, bracing as a week-end at Skegness, is still one of the best remembered of pre-war tunes, and there was another song of his, though outside the limits of our period, which is to be remembered for its association with an historic moment —Bennett Scott's exceedingly stirring *Here we are, Here we are again*, which Sheridan sang in the late autumn of 1914 at the Oxford Music Hall. The first war fever was, of course, at the summit, and Sheridan's singing of this song created a whirlwind enthusiasm in the audience. It was at once taken up by the troops and became (though it is interesting to note that it did not survive the whole war period) one of the most famous of their music hall repertory. Sheridan was but in externals an eccentric, a clown. The humanity in the appeal of a song such as *Here we are again* was reflected in others.

It is not by the more extreme forms of eccentricity that the

public remembers the music hall spirit : that spirit was in essence that of normal humanity, and though conveyed through a medium of burlesque, made an appeal to the emotion which was unhampered by distortion. Without this achievement, it is safe to say that the music hall period would not have been really memorable : no amount of mechanism, of stage tricks and comic " business " by themselves, would have placed upon it the mark of a moment in history of importance to people's lives. It was the genius of Dan Leno and the greater among his contemporaries which created this moment. These men, and the great women singers, such as Marie Lloyd, Vesta Tilley or Ella Shields, lifted the Music Hall into the higher realms of comedy, and by the observation of truth in its most everyday form, established a unity between the artist and the audience. This unity was the goal of the Music Hall, and in its day that goal was achieved.

A NOTE ON MUSIC HALL MANAGERS (TO THE YEAR 1935).

THE existence of the Music Hall must, in the end, be attributed to the tavern-keeper. Without such a focus it is doubtful whether its art would ever have achieved stability, for the tavern men of the early nineteenth century, who added to their other qualifications a knowledge of musical entertainment, recreated it on lines which led, as we have seen, to an astonishing development.

The tavern had at all times in the past been a centre of the entertainment industry. The further back one goes into time, the more obvious it appears the importance of this connection. All writers on theatrical history have emphasized the convenience of the inn yard in providing an auditorium for the presentation of plays, though that function has, I think, been given too great an emphasis from the æsthetic angle, for the gallery of the inn has assumed in the mind of commentators an importance greater than its undoubted usefulness as a scenic background. The reasons for its choice were in fact social and economic—the conditions which made the tavern the centre of all communal life.

But for lack of convenient space the plays would have found their way inside the tavern walls, and in numbers of unrecorded cases, no doubt did so. Two instances of tavern theatres in the early nineteenth century which are remarked on in Edward Stirling's volume of theatrical reminiscences, *Old Drury Lane*, suggest that this may have indeed been the case.[1]

In the non-dramatic field there is no need at this point to stress the connection of the tavern with entertainment, but as evidence of the very elaborate arrangements made by the innkeepers of earlier times for the housing of performances, one may quote here Ned Ward's visit to the Mitre in Wapping, as described by him in *The London Spy* ; " as soon as we came to the sign of the Spiritual Helmet . . . we no sooner entered the House, but we heard *Fidlers* and *Hoitboys* together with a *Hum-Drum Organ* . . . Having heard of the Beauty and Contrivance of the *Publick Music Room*, as well as other parts of the house, very highly commended, we agreed first to take a view of that which was likely to be most remarkable. In order to which we ascended the *Grades*, and were usher'd into a most stately Apartment, dedicated purely to the lovers of *Musick*, *Painting*, *Dancing*, and t'other thing too. No *Gilding*, *Carving*, *Colouring*, or good *Contrivance*, was here wanting to illustrate the Beauty of this most noble Academy . . . The room, by its compact Order and

[1](*a*) The Brown Bear.

" The ' Brown Bear ' in Goodman's Fields next opened its claws to grasp my slender means. A Jew, one Ikey Solomons . . . the landlord of The Bear, fitted up a dirty Club Room with a few paltry scenes and a ragged green baize curtain, and illuminated the floor with half a dozen oil lamps."

(*b*) The Red Cow at Chiswick.

" The brothers Strickland were lesses of a large Odd-Fellows Lodge Room called a ' Theatre.' . . . On the door a bill announced a London Company for ten nights only, to act at the ' Cow.' First night Sheridan's famous play of ' Pizarro ' ; Pit only one shilling, Boxes two shillings, sixpence standing places. Seats booked at the ' Cow ' from 10 to 4 daily, schools and children half price."

costly Improvements, looks so far above the Use it's now converted to, that the Seats are more like Pews than Boxes ; and the upper end, being divided by a Rail, looks more like a *Chancel* than a *Musick Box* ; that I could not but imagine it was built for a Fanatick *Meeting House*, but that they have for ever destroy'd the Sanctity of the Place by putting an Organ in it ; round which hung a great many pretty *Whimsical pictures*."

An unbroken procession of innkeepers of this type persisted right up to those latter days at the beginning of the twentieth century when the London music hall was revolutionized by the northern syndicates organized by Richard Thornton, Edward Moss, Oswald Stoll and others, all of whom had been at one time connected with a tavern concert room. The ground they conquered had been prepared many years before by men such as Rouse and Lane. To these pioneers may be added the names of some of their immediate successors, among them Edwin Winder, who became the proprietor of the Mogul in the early 'sixties. His tenancy of this tavern was a short one : in 1866 he sold it to H. J. Lake, who conducted the house thereafter for some years. On leaving the Mogul, Winder purchased the Metropolitan Music Hall, recently developed from the White Lion Tavern by a Mr. J. Meacock. The first programme presented by the new management included the Great Vance, M. and Mlle. D'Auban, John and Emma Ward (here separately announced), and Mdme. Losebini, with her daughter, " Miss Constance."

J. J. Poole is a less shadowy figure and one of many instances of a growth to power among the lieutenants of music hall proprietors. Poole was by profession a musician, the conductor of a provincial theatre orchestra. His first London post was that of manager and musical director of the Metropolitan Music Hall with which he was connected throughout his career, first under Winder, then his successor, George Speedy, and finally under Walter Gooch, a director of the Alhambra. In 1874 Poole acquired a proprietary interest in the South London Music Hall in succession to Edwin Villiers, who in that year took over the management of the London Pavilion. His vigorous policy at both these houses was evidenced by the number of artists to whom he gave a London reputation. The creation of the " Lion Comique " was in some measure the work of this manager—the phrase was actually his invention. Among the many artists whom he brought from the provinces, the most important was Vance. Poole died in 1882.

J. L. Graydon is memorable for his long and successful conduct of the Mogul. He was in 1861 a cellarman at Weston's in Holborn, and was connected with that manager when he attempted to establish a miniature Vauxhall Gardens at Highgate. In 1871 he became H. G. Lake's manager at the Mogul. The house was rebuilt in the following year, and soon afterwards Graydon purchased the hall and remained in control there for over twenty years. It was in 1891, shortly before his retirement, when some rebuilding of the house took place, that Graydon renamed the hall, " The Middlesex."

Harry Hart, born in 1828, enjoyed the longest recorded career among the music hall managers. He belonged to a theatrical family, (is it safe to assume that he was the brother of the man who assisted Renton Nicholson in his Judge and Jury performances?). The music halls which came under the control of this energetic Hebrew included the Raglan in Theobalds Road, and the renamed Salmon Hall in Union Street, Borough ; the Montpelier in Walworth ; the Marylebone, in succession to Oswald Stoll, who first converted the old theatre into a music hall ; the Sun at Knightsbridge and the Bedford in Camden Town. He had further activities at Margate and Ramsgate. His policy at the Lord Raglan (to give its full name) which he acquired in 1860, was a reflection of the methods of the first Canterbury. An amusing account of this hall, as it appeared to Edmund Yates, occurs in a number of a short-lived journal called *The Train*, in 1858. This

contains a vivid little picture of the proprietor of the Raglan and may be quoted here ; in this article the hall is called the Lord Somerset, but the identification with the Raglan is unquestionable :

"Over the side of a tavern are two enormous red lamps, on which, in white letters, are inscribed 'The Lord Somerset Music Hall.' Round the entrance are some half-a-dozen children, peering wistfully up the corridor and dancing fantastically before the looking-glass door which shuts out the glories beyond.

"'Here's some swells ! Now we shall see the hinside.' We pass the looking-glass door and find ourselves in front of a bar, at which a Jewish gentleman in a velvet waistcoat and much Mosaic jewellery is regaling. 'Take your tickets, gents,' says he in an authoritative manner. 'Sixpence the body of the 'all, ninepence the gallery, which is more select.' . . . We ascend the staircase to the left. Passing through a swing door, we enter a broad gallery, furnished with narrow tables and Windsor chairs ; and below us lies a large Salle, similarly furnished and thronged with people." The writer adds further that "A few, very few, of the frail sisterhood are present," and that for the most part the auditorium is filled with tradespeople—the men smoking churchwarden pipes. There is, moreover, no yelling ; no more than questionable chaff. The Opera Chorus performs the *Miserere* from *Il Travatore* with the assistance of a grand piano and a harmonium. The conductor is an ex-opera singer. Mr. Boss (e g., W. G. Ross) is announced and sings his "Hamlet" song in a costume divided equally between chain-mail and the traditional sables. Later, the piano and the harmonium are heard in Weber's "Surprise."

This description completely conveys the homely atmosphere with its increasing admixture of "flash" characteristics which one imagines to be fairly representative of a second-class music-hall of the period. After a variety of activities Hart became the manager of the Argyll Rooms for Bignell, and held this position at the time of its transformation into the Trocadero Music Hall. His death occurred a comparatively few years ago.

The name of William Holland, next to E. T. Smith, perhaps the most versatile of theatrical managers, is indissolubly associated with the Canterbury and with pantomime at the Surrey Theatre. With the self-imposed title of "The People's Caterer," Holland, throughout his career, adopted an easy-going and democratic attitude to his public, well suited to his rotund and amiable physique. Apart from his managements at the Surrey, the Canterbury and the Royal, Holborn, he is to be remembered for the part he played in promoting the Albert Palace at Battersea and the North Woolwich Gardens—a later version of the Surrey Gardens—with their monster concert hall, scenic lake, wigwams, maze and zoo. At the latter end of his career he turned his attention to the brightening of Blackpool, with well-known results.

The personality of Sam Adams of the Trocadero has already been described in this book. It was in 1863 that he first came into management with the purchase of the Islington Philharmonic. He conducted the house for seven years, and then joined Sweazey, Weston's successor of the Royal, Holborn. He subsequently became the manager of the London Pavilion under Edwin Villiers, and in 1889 acquired the Trocadero.

The redoubtable Edwin Villiers, whom H. G. Hibbert found to be such an uninteresting comedian when acting at the Haymarket Theatre, was chiefly memorable for his building of the South London Music Hall in London Road, Walworth (in conjunction with a manager called Tindall) ; and his direction and reconstitution of the London Pavilion. He erected the South London in 1860. Its decoration was considered exceptionally chaste. The entrance hall was planned in the manner of a Roman villa. The auditorium, reconstructed from a Catholic chapel, enjoyed for a time the unusual feature of a chairman's throne and table placed in the centre of the floor. In 1869 the

house was completely burned down, but Villiers rebuilt it and sold it in 1874 to J. J. Poole.

George Adney Payne may be considered an important pioneer of the music hall movement, for it was he who went into partnership with the Crowder who was the proprietor of the Britannia before it came under the Lanes, which links him with the pre-Morton halls. With Crowder, in 1878 he transformed Lusby's Summer Garden into the Paragon Music Hall. In 1887 his company acquired the Canterbury and the two houses together held a paramount position among suburban music halls for a number of years. These later became merged in a syndicate which included the Oxford, Tivoli, London Pavilion, and Metropolitan, and a number of other suburban halls, such as the Empress, Brixton, the Chelsea Palace, the South London, and the halls at East Ham and Walthamstow. Subsequently, as we have already noted, the Oxford, Canterbury, and Paragon were sold, together with the Tivoli. Payne's career, begun at the Greenwich Parthenon, influenced in its course most of the important London music halls. His death, as the result of a motor accident, occurred at Tunbridge Wells in 1907.

The romantic invasion of London by the managers of the syndicates in the northern counties was carried out with overwhelming success and resulted in knighthoods for the men who were responsible for this achievement. Sir Oswald Stoll and Sir Edward Moss were its most prominent figures. Oswald Stoll was of Irish blood and was born in Melbourne. When his mother's second husband, Roderick Stoll, an entertainer and manager, died, Oswald, still a boy, assisted his mother in carrying on the stepfather's property, the Parthenon, at Liverpool. His business genius was first exerted in the conduct of a small music-hall agency, and he prospered so rapidly that at the age of twenty-three he had already acquired Levine's Music Hall in Cardiff, which he renamed the Cardiff Empire. He extended his activities to other western towns, when, coming into competition with the Moss and Thornton circuit, he achieved a working arrangement with them which eventually developed into the famous partnership. The descent on London by this firm began with the formation of the Finsbury Park and Stratford Empires. In 1901 the London Hippodrome was opened. Five years later Stoll retired from the combine and built the London Coliseum. After two or three years of uncertain existence, during which a policy of spectacular revue was found to be unprosperous, the enormous building achieved popularity as a variety theatre somewhat in the manner of the Alhambra, and for twenty-five years was conducted in this way with enormous success; a success based upon the complete absence of those questionable elements which had characterized the latter house.

During his management of the Coliseum, Stoll rebuilt the Middlesex Music Hall, embarking the house upon its career as a theatre. He linked the Coliseum with a large circuit of provincial music-halls, forming the largest of all music hall syndicates.

Oswald Stoll has throughout his career proved his vivacity and versatility as a manager in numerous ways, but in none more than the manner in which he terminated the career of the London Coliseum as a variety house in 1931 by the production of the elaborate German operette *White Horse Inn*, which was performed twice daily for over a year. The same success attended, for a time, a similar policy at the Alhambra, of which he had been for some years the lessee. Stoll, a septuagenarian, still retained a quality of imagination in his theatrical management. He was an exceptional man with gifts outside the main channels of his work. He was an economist and something of a philosopher; in 1904 he published a book with the title, *The Grand Survival; a theory of immortality by natural Law*. His great gift of managerial insight is exemplified by the bold manner in which he rescued the music hall for respectability. The psychological acumen of this move won him an immense fortune.

The personal history of Sir Edward Moss is equally romantic. He was born in Lancashire and was the son of an entertainer whom he assisted as a youth by performing humorous songs at the piano at his father's pitch at the Waverley Fair in Edinburgh. His first experience as a manager was under the elder Moss at the Lorne Music Hall in Greenock. At precisely the same age as Oswald Stoll he acquired a music hall of his own, the Gaiety in Edinburgh. He achieved little success in these early years; according to *The Era* for December 24th, 1924, he made "one plucky attempt after another to attract people with a purified entertainment, but in vain." Then came the association with Richard Thornton, the Tynesider, who lived to a great age and was affectionately known as "Old Dick Thornton." This partnership was eminently successful, and the Moss and Thornton unit pushed its way across country and into Wales, where, as has been stated, it came into contact with Oswald Stoll's ventures. Then followed the Moss and Stoll combination, whose later history we already know. Edward Moss was knighted in 1903 and retired from action in 1904, his rather early death following shortly after.

The name of Frank Allen is inseparably associated with the Moss-Stoll-Thornton firm. He was with Moss in his early ventures at the Waverley Market. In 1885 he was manager of Thornton's Varieties in South Shields. Later he became the director of the North Circuit of Moss and Stoll. He remained to become the managing director of those vast companies which at their height absorbed the talents of the actor-managers, Sir Herbert Beerbohm Tree and Sir George Alexander.

Connected with the Stoll combine was Alderman Captain Davies, who died at the age of ninety-two. In the 'seventies, Captain Davies, then the leading member of the Islington Fire Brigade, became the proprietor of Deacon's Music Hall at Islington. His activities included the management for many years of the music hall in Chatham, in partnership with Oswald Stoll.

Another northern manager who made a spectacular contribution to the outgrowth of the London music hall was Thomas Barrasford, who, shortly before the death of Sir Henry Irving, in 1905, converted the Lyceum Theatre, for many years associated with that famous actor, into a music-hall. The house, enormously enlarged, and organized on a system of twice-nightly performances, did not prosper, and was abandoned by Barrasford after two years. Its opening performances had included scenes from Verdi's *Rigoletto*, together with Taylor's elephants and "La Wilma, a lady artist in sand and smoke." Before this, the scene of Barrasford's operations had been Jarrow, and by 1904 he had built up an extensive music hall following in the north of England. His characteristics as a manager were an enthusiastic advocacy of cheap prices, an active participation in the development of the cinema, and the creation of a number of halls, conducted in the English manner, on the Continent.

There remain those giants of modern music hall organization outside the Moss and Stoll companies whose knightly names, constituting an almost Arthurian cycle, include those of Sir Walter Gibbons, Sir Alfred Butt, Sir Walter de Frece, Sir Harry Day and Sir George Dance. In the great music hall booms preceding the European War, Walter Gibbons appeared on the scene as the youngest and most vigorous of the men who challenged the supremacy of Moss and Stoll. He was at first associated with George Adney Payne and later married his daughter. The London Theatres of Variety Syndicate was in part his creation. This was headed by the London Palladium built on the site of Hengler's Circus and opened in September 1910, its first bill including Sir John Martin Harvey in a one-act play. Gibbons who was knighted for his services in connection with the War, died in October, 1933.

Sir Alfred Butt, who was more famous as a theatre manager than as

a music-hall manager, began his career under Charles Morton at the Palace Theatre, whence he arrived from Harrods, where he had been engaged on accountancy work. He subsequently became director of the Palace, where he built up a brilliant record of management. His policy included the introduction of important continental and American artists, such as Gaby Deslys, Regine Fleury, Yvette Gilbert and Grace La Rue—the latter the creator of the immortal song *You Made Me Love You.* His revues, *The Passing Show* of 1914 and 1915, are still remembered as the highest expression of that art in the English idiom. His knighthood, a political one, occurred in 1918.

Sir Walter De Frece, the husband of Vesta Tilly, came of a long theatrical line. As the chairman of a syndicate known as the Variety Theatres Controlling Company, he was concerned with the direction of a number of halls in the south of England. One of his chief characteristics was a talent for song-writing. Many of these songs are famous. The majority, including *Jolly Good Luck to the Girl Who Loves a Soldier*, were performed by his wife. He also wrote Dan Leno's celebrated *Waiter Song*. Like Sir Alfred Butt, his interests in later life diverged to Conservative politics which eventually occupied his entire time.

Sir Harry Day was also a politician, on the Labour side. He was a Member of Parliament during Ramsay MacDonald's first premiership. The music hall chiefly identified with his management is the Bedford in Camden Town, which was relinquished to become a cinema. Sir Harry is of Polish origin.

Sir George Dance, a prolific song-writer and the author of *Come Where the Booze is Cheaper*, *Angels without Wings* (sung by Vesta Tilly), and *His Lordship Winked at the Counsel* (sung by Harry Rickards), made a fortune with his musical comedy *The Chinese Honeymoon*, which established the reputation of Louie Freear. His music hall interests were of a varied kind ; his most consistent undertakings being the management of innumerable tours of musical comedies. An important use made by Sir George Dance of the fortune thus acquired was the considerable assistance which he gave towards the stabilization of the Old Vic as a permanent Shakespearean repertory theatre.

Mr. Charles Gulliver, one of the founders of the Variety Artists' Federation, was at first the secretary and later the managing director of the London Theatres of Variety, Limited. In 1928, a reorganization of this company took place, Gulliver retaining some of the halls owned by the syndicate, including the Holborn Empire. Since then, this hall, together with the Palladium, became the property of the Gaumont British Company.

NOTE ON "VICTORIAN" ENTERTAINMENT BETWEEN THE WARS

By the end of the European war of 1914 the Music Hall was already half dead, robbed by events of its genuine psychological and social background. But in the relaxed atmosphere of the first post-war years—that well-remembered decade of " let's-have-fun-at-all-costs-and-be-madly-sophisticated-about-it "—some elements of entertainment connected with the Music Hall reappeared in the form of *pastiche*. This, as can be understood, occurred first among a small coterie, but the taste grew, and penetrated later into some London theatres.

Elsa Lanchester and I were, perhaps, mainly responsible for this: in the winter of 1920, we founded a small cabaret club, which we called (the name being supplied by Sylvia Townsend Warner) " The Cave of Harmony." Cabaret itself was an innovation, certainly in such a form as we gave it; and it was here that Elsa Lanchester first delighted her friendly audience with such things as "Please Sell No More Drink to My Father" and " Dark Times Come Again No More," which are still remembered by some Bloomsbury die-hards. Helen Rowe and Philip Godfrey were there, too, to give us " The Little Band of Gold " and " The Old Dun Cow "; while my contributions ranged from Ethiopian Songs, by the way of " More Work for the Undertaker " to Harry Champion's " I Like Pickled Onions "—performances as popular with my friends as they were distasteful to Mr. St. John Ervine. In 1927, " The Cave of Harmony " came to an end, but not before the outside world had seen " Riverside Nights " at the Lyric Theatre, Hammersmith, in which Elsa Lanchester and I repeated these antics, with a background designed by John Armstrong.

Meanwhile, revivals of " Old Music Hall " shows cropped up at the Garrick Theatre and at Collins' in Islington, together with various " Victorian " features in the Cochran Revues. Mr. Herbert Farjeon's first revue, called " Pic-Nic," which I produced at the Arts Theatre Club, also contained 19th century backgrounds. Then there was a pause. It seemed that this game had been played out. But it was destined for another innings; for at the end of 1937 I was approached by the late Peter Ridgeway for a " period " cabaret at his " Player's Theatre " in Covent Garden. He suggested a programme similar to that of " The Cave of Harmony," and reminded me that his premises were adjacent to the original " Evan's late Joys." The result (in which I had the collaboration of W. L. Hanchant) was the first programme along those lines which are now familiar to many Londoners who have found their way to the " Players." The details of this 1937 programme, which unwittingly brought about this obstinate state of affairs, are to be found in the published record known as " Late Joys."

APPENDIX A

EIGHTEENTH CENTURY COMIC SONGS

I

LAUGHING AND CRYING SONG

Comic Song performed by Vernon at Vauxhall

(*From a collection dated* 1766)

[This song is a somewhat isolated instance of the use of a tavern song at the Vauxhall type of concert. It anticipates the movement towards comic singing, which found full expression there in the nineteenth century.]

When I wake with painful brow
Ere the cock begins to crow
Tossing, tumbling in my bed,
Aching heart and aching head,
Pond'ring over human ills,
Cruel bailiffs, taylor's bills
Flush and Pam thrown up at Loo
When these sorrows strike my view,
  I cry . . .

And to stop the gushing tear
Wipe it with the pillow—
But when the sporting evening comes,
Routs, ridottos, balls and drums,
Casinos here, sestinos there,
Mirth and pastime everywhere,
Seated by a sprightly lass,
Smiling with the smiling glass,
Where these pleasures are my lot,
Taylors, bailiffs are forgot,
  I laugh . . .

Careless what may then befall
Thus I shake my sides at all,
Then again when I peruse
O'er my tea the morning news
Dismal tales of plunder'd houses,
Wanton wives and cuckold spouses,
When I read of money lent
At sixteen and a half per cent.
  I cry . . .

But, if ere the muffin's gone,
Simp'ring enters honest John,
Sir, Miss Lucy's at the door,
Waiting in a chaise and four,
Instant vanish all my cares,
Swift I scamper down the stairs,
  And laugh . . .

So may this indulgent throng,
Who now smiling grace my song,
Never more cry Oh ! oh ! la !
But join with me in Ha ! ha ! ha !

II

THE CHIMNEY SWEEP

By George Alexander Stevens

(*From* The Choice Spirit's Chaplet)

[A song of the tavern concerts]

In various shapes I've oft been known
To please your ears and eyes ;
Nor I the only man in town,
That wears the black disguise.
  Sweep ! Sweep ! Sweep !—Soot ho !

In spite of mocks or flouts or fleers,
A truth I must impart :
No chimney half so foul appears
As doth the human heart.

The learned lawyers could I win
To give their briefs to me,
From foul duress and many a sin
My brush should set them free.

Observe the doctors as they roll,
To shape from all degrees,
Much sweeping wants each sooty soul
All clogg'd with filthy fees.

Behold yon priest so neat and trim
That vicious reverend beau—
There's no such thing as charming him,
The Devil and I know.

The statesman with that brow severe,
Had been of will forgot—
His conscience is as ermine clear
And therefore needs me not.

III

THE BROWN JUG

By Francis Fawkes (1720-1777)

[The song is reprinted in the *New Universal Songster*, an early nineteenth-century collectior, but no tune is indicated.]

Dear Tom, this brown jug that now foams with mild ale,
(In which I will drink to sweet Nan of the Vale),
Was once Toby Philpot, a thirsty old soul
As e'er drank a bottle or fathom'd a bowl ;
In boosing about 'twas his praise to excel,
And among jolly topers he bore off the bell.

It chanced as in dog-days he sat at his ease
In his flow'r-woven arbour as gay as you please,
With a friend, a pipe puffing sorrows away
And with honest old Stingo was soaking his clay ?
His breath—door of life on a sudden were shut,
And he died full as big as a Dorchester butt.

His body, when long in the ground it had lain,
And time into clay had resolved it again
A potter found out in its covert so snug
And with part of fat Toby he form'd this brown jug :
Now sacred to friendship and mirth and mild ale—
So here's to my lovely sweet Nan of the Vale !

APPENDIX B

EARLY NINETEENTH-CENTURY COMIC SONGS

I

From THE COUNTRY CLUB

By Thomas Dibdin

[This song was introduced by Grimaldi at a benefit performance of *Mother Goose* held at Drury Lane in 1807, and continues the tradition of the eighteenth-century songs of convivial occasions. (See Appendix A.)]

Now we're all met here together,
In spite of wind and weather,
To moisten well our clay,
Before we think of jigging,
Let's take a cheerful noggin,
Where's the waiter? Ring away!

Bring the glees and catches,
The tobacco, pipes, and matches,
And plenty of brown stout.
Get the glasses e're we start 'em,
Let's proceed, *secundum artem*,
Let the clerk the names read out.

(*Spoken*). Gentlemen of the Quizzical Society: please answer to your names; Farmer Scriggins! "Why, I be here!" Dr. Horse Leech! "Here!" Parson Paunch! etc. At last; are you all assembled? "All! all! all!"

So here's to Master Wiggins!
So here's to Master Figgins!
etc.
So put the beer about!

II

I NEVER SAYS NOTHING TO NOBODY

By Thomas Hudson

From the seventh part of a collection of songs published annually by Hudson from 1818 *to* 1831)

What a shocking world this is for scandal,
The people get worse every day;
Everything serves for a handle
To take folks' good name away.

In backbiting vile, each so labours
The sad faults of others to showbody,
I could tell enough of my neighbours,
But I never says nothing to nobody.

'Tis a snug little house I reside in ;
And the people who're living next door
Are smothered completely such pride in
As I never met with before :
But outside the door they don't roam,
A large sum of money they owe body,
Folks call, but can't find them at home—
But I never says nothing to nobody.

The butcher so greasy and fat,
When out, he does nothing but boast :
Struts, as he cocks on his hat,
As if supreme, rules the roast :
Talks of his wealth and his riches.
Consequence always does show body,
His ugly old wife wears the breeches.
But I never says nothing to nobody.

The baker lives quite in great style,
His wife is, oh Lord ! such a fright.
New dresses she's got a great pile.
They sleep out of town every night,
Country cottage, completely in state,
Determined not to be a low body,
He's been pulled up three times for short weight,
But I never says nothing to nobody.

The publican thriving in trade,
With sorrow is now looking down,
His sweet little, pretty bar-maid
Has a little one just brought to town.
He's not to be seen much about,
His wife is a deuce of a shrewd body,
The beadles are on the look-out.
But I never says nothing to nobody.

A Methodist parson of fame
I see very often go by,
His heart is fill'd full of love's flame,
He visits a girl on the sly.
Altho' this daily I see,
And surely he's but a so - so body ;
Of course, as 'tis nothing to me,
I never says nothing to nobody.

The new married couple so happy,
Seem both the quintessence of love,
He calls her before every sappy
My darling, my duck, and my dove.

In private there's nothing but strife ;
Quarrelling, fighting, o'er flow body,
In short, quite a cat and dog life,
But I never says nothing to nobody.

I could tell, if I lik'd, such a tale,
Of neighbours all around, great and small,
That surely, I think, without fail,
Would really astonish you all.
But here now my short ditty ends,
I don't want to hurt high or low body,
I wish to keep in with my friends,
So I never says nothing to nobody.

III

From IF I HAD A DONKEY

By Jacob Beuler

[The composition of this song, which has persisted in popular memory until the present day, was occasioned by Theodore Martin's Prevention cf Cruelty to Animals Act. It was sung to the tune of *The White Cockade.*]

If I had a donkey what wouldn't go,
D'ye think I'd wallop him ? No, no, no :
By gentle means I'd try, d'ye see,
Because I hate all cruelty.
If all had been like me, in fact,
There'd ha' been no occ. for Martin's Act :
Dumb animals to prevent getting cracked
On the head—

For, if I had a donkey wot wouldn't go
I never would wallop him, no, no, no ;
I'd give him some hay and cry gee, wo,
And come up Neddy.

IV

From THE MAN THAT COULDN'T GET WARM

By Jacob Beuler

All you who're fond, in spite of price,
Of pastries, creams, and jellies nice,
Be cautious how you take to ice,
Whenever you're over-warm.
A merchant who from India came,
And Shiver and Shakey was his name,
A pastry-cook's did once entice
To take a cooling, luscious ice.
The weather, hot enough to kill,
Kept tempting him to eat until
It gave his corpus such a chill,
He never again felt warm.

Shiver and Shakey, O, O, O,
Criminey, Crikey, isn't it cold !
Woo, woo, woo, oo, oo ;
Behold the man that couldn't get warm.

V
HOT CODLINGS

[Grimaldi's best-remembered song. The words are probably by Thomas Dibdin ; the music is by John Whitaker.]

A little old woman her living she got
By selling hot codlings hot, hot, hot ;
And this little old woman who codlings sold
Though her codlings were hot, she felt herself cold,
So to keep herself warm she thought it no sin
To fetch for herself a quartern of——
Ri tol iddy iddy, ri tol iddy iddy ri tol lay.

This little old woman set off in a trot
To fetch her a quartern of hot ! hot ! hot !
Powder into her pan put and in it round stones,
Says the little old woman, " these apples have bones.'
The powder the pan in her face did send
Which sent the old woman on her latter——
Ri tol, etc.

The little old woman then up she got
All in a fury, hot ! hot ! hot !
Says she, " such boys, sure, never were known,
They never will let an old woman alone."
Now here is a moral, round let it buzz,
If you mean to sell codlings never get——
Ri tol, etc.

APPENDIX C

THE COMIC-NARRATIVE BALLAD

ALONZO THE BRAVE, OR THE SPECTRE AND BRIDEGROOM

This version, at any rate, is by J. B. Howe

[Published in the *Musical Bouquet* and attributed there to Hugo Camp "delineator of the Entertainment entitled *Hugo St. Leon ; Stars of the Social Spheres*," about 1850.]

Air : *Long, Long Ago.*
In days of old, a warrior bold, encas'd from helm to heel,
In armour of *wrought iron*, was known the hero of Castille.

Air : *Nae luck.*
But tho' his heart was *stirling coin*, I'm much griev'd to declare,
'Twas *paid* in *change* for goods received, to Imogene the Fair.

Air : *Come to Me.*
And on the green as twilight's gloom deep'ning shadows threw,
They swore to love till Nature's self should wear an azure hue ;
" But ah ! My love," Alonzo cried, " to Palestine I go,
And will you love me there as now, when I'm at Jericho ?
Some other tongue may talk of love, and your sweet smile will then,
And you will grant to other lips, the freedom of the *press*."

Air : *Oh Summer Night.*
Adone, Alonzo, do not go on so,
How can you wrong so,
The true heart that's beating for thee,
(spoken) *Hear my vow.*
If ever, ever, another should sever
My lover from thee, tho' that never can be,
I hope to crush my pride
Thy ghost may to me glide
And bear me off as bride.
(*Spoken*) " Down to the Charnel," she cried.
(Trumpet Call). Hark to the distant horn, announcing the departure of Alonzo's regiments with his *bags*, but, as he facetiously observed to Imogene—without his *baggage*. " Ciascun Lo Dice " (march dying away in the distance).

Air : *Auld Robin Gray.*
He had not been gone a twelvemonth so 'tis said,
When the Celtic Telegraph reported he was dead,
The maiden she shed tears, and of grief was like to die,
And she wore the darkest weeds for this bright flower of Chivalry.

Air : *Rosin the Beau.*

Fair Imogene wept for our hero
And disdained the first Lords of the land,
Until Baron Jo Faliero,
Came courting, and who could withstand ?
This jewel-bedizened old beau—oh ! oh !
Had gold-mines, acres of land,
Some shares too in every suspension
And he offered for Imogene's hand.

(Marriage bells to be played during the recital of the following lines.)

The Baron is accepted, and on the point of being united to his Belle, as the Marriage Bells clearly indicate. It is, however, my pleasing duty to assure you that Imogene is not *rebel* to her faith, but an unwilling victim to the very *apparent* avarice of a *pair* of *parents.* (*Crash*). Ah ! she has fainted from excess of emotion, but they pick her up without *one sort of ceremony*, and unceremoniously proceed with the other.

Meanwhile a multiplicity of guests are hastening to the wedding feast—Supper at Nine—Carriages ordered at three.

Air : *Haste to the Wedding.*

No sort of ill dreading, all haste to the wedding,
Prepared to do justice to everything nice,
There was turkey and chine and the raciest wine,
And gay flags of all nations with every device.
There was hock and Lafitte and Champagne quite a treat,
And the finest of Rhenish and Burgundy, too,
And round, round, they danced I'll be bound,
Until all were as tired as the Wandering Jew.

(Varsoviana)

Then the Varsovienne they danced now and then, and round (waltz) in the waltz they go, so, so, so.

(Polka)

And the polka's done with so much fun
That the old folks joined in, every one.
Now while dancing with the tide, the Baron, his lovely bride
Rose a form with ghostly stride and danced the polka by their side.

(Polka played, ghost-dancing to a few bars, in as *spirited* a style as possible.)

(Spoken) Permit me to call your attention to the fact that the spectre danced to the Corsican Ghost Melody, which imperceptibly adapted itself to the *Bridal* polka.

When lo ! in the very height of the festivities the clock struck two.
Now do the lights burn blue, as the lights always do.

(Dog howling)

Bow, wow, wow, wow. Wherefore are the dogs all howling ?
Some strange guest on Imogene from his visor dark is scowling.
Out of the way ! he comes to supper, really I'll no longer stop here !
Out of the way ! He comes to supper, out of the way, friends, out of the way.

(Spoken) Please observe that, the lights being extinguished, guests are going *out* also, in a *little* confusion.

The guests are all gone in the greatest dismay, and the spectre accosts Imogene in this way :
" Behold your Alonzo ! " (Shriek.) That shriek means to show,
That false Imogene recognizes her beau.

Air : *Corsican Ghost Melody.*
Whose rais'd vizor doth disclose,
The spot where should have grown his nose.

Air : *Down Among the Dead Men.*
" You ask'd that to punish your falsehood and pride
My ghost should here sit at thy side,
Should claim thee for my bride to go
Where we carouse in the shades below.
And since a perjur'd maid you be
Down unto the dead men, down, down down, down,
Down unto the dead men come with me."

Then slowly his arms round the lady he wound
To sink with his prey thro' the wide yawning ground,
When his mask falling off, on a sudden she found,
'Twas Alonzo alive who laid claim to his bride.

" Oh ! I've not been dead at all, Imogene,
But I'll wed you after all, Imogene :
Now the guests are all away, if you will not say me nay,
I will fly with you away, Imogene."

She acceded with delight, we are told, told, told,
And the Baron in a fright, being old, old, old,
Trembled o'er the river brink, and thus perished in a sink.
(Spoken) Observe him going to the bottom.
And the father touched no farthing of his gold, gold, gold.

Air : *Sprig of Shilaleh.*
Like the young Lochinvar 'tis reported he bore her,
Away on his steed 'ere the dawn of Aurora
And as all believ'd they had sunk to the tomb,
He was called the original " Spectre Bridegroom " ! ! !

APPENDIX D

W. G. ROSS AND SAM HALL

[The supposition that Ross's *Sam Hall* was related to an existing ballad, is borne out by the discovery, by Mr. W. L. Hanchant, of a version which refers to Jack Hall, a chimney sweep. I am also indebted to Mr. Hanchant for a ballad-sheet version of *Sam Hall*, which appeared at the time when Ross was singing it at the Cider Cellars. No authentic contemporary publication of the song appears to be extant, but the ballad-sheet version, reprinted here, may be presumed to be a near approximation.]*

* When I revived this song at the Players' Club in December 1937, it was found to have retained all its old fire and fury. Mr. Philip Godfrey performed it and gave the lyric its full melodramatic force. The audience inclined at first to a spirit of mild burlesque, were hushed to silence by the words, " He'll tell me wot to do, damn his eyes."

I

JACK THE CHIMNEY SWEEP

My name it is Jack All,
Chimney Sweep, chimney sweep.
My name it is Jack All, chimney sweep ;
My name it is Jack All, and I rob both great and small
And my life must pay for all, when I die,
When I die
And my life must pay for all, when I die.

I furnished all my rooms
Every one, every one
I furnished all my rooms, every one,
I furnished all my rooms with black brushes and black brooms
Besides the chimney pot, which I stole,
etc.

I sold candles short of weight,
That's no joke, that's no joke ;
I sold candles short of weight, that's no joke,
I sold candles short of weight and they . . . by the sly,
All rogues must have their right, so must I
etc.

O they told me in the jail
Where I lay, where I lay
O they told me in the jail where I lay
They told me in the jail that I should drink more brown ale
But I swore I'd never fail till I die,
etc.

O they told me in the hole
Where I lay, where I lay
O they told me in the hole where I lay
They told me in the hole that the candles that I stole.
Was to light me to the hole where I lay,
etc.

A-going up Holborn Hill
In a cart, in a cart,
Going up Holborn Hill in a cart,
Going up Holborn Hill at St. Giles' had my fill
And at Tyburn made my will, that went hard
etc.

Now I must leave the cart,
Toll the bell, toll the bell ;
Now I must leave the cart, toll the bell,
Now I must leave the cart, sorrowful broken heart
And the best of friends must part, so farewell
etc.

II

SAM HALL, CHIMNEY SWEEP

A version given by A. L. Hayward in " Green Room Recollection ."

Oh, my name it is Sam Hall,
Chimney sweep ! chimney sweep !
Oh, my name it is Sam Hall,
Chimney sweep !
My name it is Sam Hall,
I have robb'd both great and small.
And now I pay for all,
D—n my eyes.

My master taught me flam,
Taught me flam,
My master taught me flam,
Though he know'd it all for bam
And now I must go hang—
D—n my eyes.

I goes up Holborn Hill in a cart,
In a cart,
I goes up Holborn Hill in a cart,
At St. Giles takes my gill,
And at Tyburn makes my will,
D—n my eyes.

Then the sheriff he will come,
He will come,
Then the sheriff he will come,
And he'll look so gallows glum,
And he'll talk of kingdom come,
Bl—t his eyes.

Then the hangman will come too,
  Will come too,
Then the hangman will come too,
With all his bl—y crew,
And he'll tell me what to do
  Bl—t his eyes.

And now I goes upstairs,
  Goes upstairs,
And now I goes upstairs,
Here's an end to all my cares,
So tip up all your prayers,
  Bl—t your eyes.

APPENDIX E

SONGS OF THE MINSTREL TROUPES

" Ring the Bell softly, there's crape on the Door."

Words by Dexter Smith. Music by E. L. Catlin.

The literature of sentimental songs manufactured for the minstrel troupes is an enormous one. The following titles are representative : " Father, Pray with me To-night," words and music by C. A. White ; " Make me a Jacket of Pa's old Coat," words by Grace Carleton, music by Eva Clinton ; " Send for Mother, Birdie's Dying," words by George Cooper, music by Eastburn ; " The Old Man ain't what he Used to Be," words and music by C. A. White ; " Close the Shutter, Willie's Dead," words by James Stewart ; " Put my little Shoes away," words and music by Mrs. C. E. Pratt ; " Please give me a Penny," by W. Siebert, to music arranged by T. Westrop ; " Ring the Bell Softly," words by Dexter Smith to music by E. L. Catlin, was written in 1876.

Some one has gone from this strange world of ours,
No more to gather it's thorns with it's flowers,
No more to linger where sunbeams must fade,
Where, on all beauty, Death's fingers are laid ;
Weary with mingling Life's bitter and sweet,
Weary with parting and never to meet,
Some one has gone to the bright golden shore,
Ring the bell softly—there's crape on the door.

Some one is resting from sorrow and sin,
Happy where earth's conflicts enter not in,
Joyous as birds, when the morning is bright,
When the sweet sunbeams have brought us their light.
Weary with sowing and never to reap,
Weary with labour and welcoming sleep,
Some one's departed to Heaven's glad shore,
Ring the bell softly—there's crape on the door.

Angels are anxiously longing to meet,
One who walks with them in Heaven's bright street,
Loved ones have whispered that some one is blest ;
Free from earth's trials, and taking sweet rest,
Yes ! There is one more in angelic bliss,
One less to cherish, and one less to kiss,
One more departed to Heaven's bright shore,
Ring the bell softly—there's crape on the door.

APPENDIX F

RICE'S JIM CROW

[The following version, dated 1837, is from what is described as the author zed edition. The music is given as arranged by J. Blewitt and as sung in *The Flight to America*, one of the burlettas in which Rice appeared.]

I came from ole Kentucky
A long time ago
Where I first learn to wheel about
And jump Jim Crow,
Wheel about, turn about and do jes so,
Eb'ry time I wheel about, I jump Jim Crow.
I us'd to take him fiddle,
Eb'ry morn and afternoon
And charm the old Buzzard
And dance to the Racoon.
etc.

I landed first at Liverpool
Dat place of ships and docks,
I strutted down Lord Street
And as'd the price of stocks,
etc.

I paid my fare den up to town
On de coach to cut a dash,
De axletree soon gave way
And spilt us wid a smash,
etc.

I lighted den upon my head
All in de nassy dirt,
Dey all thought dat I war dead
But I laughed and wasn't hurt,
etc.

Dis head you know am putty tick,
Cause dere it made a hole,
On de dam macadmis road
Much bigger dan a
etc.

When I got into Lunnon
Dey took me for a savage,
But I war putty well behaved
So I gazed with Massa Davidge,
etc.

Den Johnny Jim Crow's 'bout de street
More like a raven rader,
Pray good people don't mistake
Indeed I'm not dare fader,
etc.

Dem urchins what sing my song
Had better mind dar looks,
For anyhow dey can't be crows,
You see d'ar only rooks,
etc.

[1]There was a conscious imitation of the crudities of broadside and ballad-sheet songs in the treatment and subject of such songs as *Villikins*, *Lord Lovel*, *Sam Hall*, though the broadsheet itself, for the most part, did no more than reproduce the popular songs and verses of the moment. A circular movement.

SONG INDEX

Please note that most page numbers shown in the Song and General Indexes (which are facsimile reproductions of the original 1946 indexes) are incorrect, being 1 too great—e.g. page 212 should read page 211.

NB. See note at top of page 243, regarding page numbers in the indexes.

NB. See note at top of page 243, regarding page numbers in the indexes.

NB. See note at top of page 243, regarding page numbers in the indexes.

NB. See note at top of page 243, regarding page numbers in the indexes.

NB. See note at top of page 243, regarding page numbers in the indexes.

GENERAL INDEX

NB. See note at top of page 243, regarding page numbers in the indexes.

NB. See note at top of page 243, regarding page numbers in the indexes.

NB. See note at top of page 243, regarding page numbers in the indexes.

NB. See note at top of page 243, regarding page numbers in the indexes.

NB. See note at top of page 243, regarding page numbers in the indexes.

NB. See note at top of page 243, regarding page numbers in the indexes.

BOOKS, ETC., REFERRED TO

A'Beckett, Gilbert .. .. Recollections of a Humorist
Green Room Recollections
London at the End of the Century
Ainsworth, Harrison .. .. Jack Shepherd
Anderson, J. H. .. .. .. Professor Anderson's Note Book
The New Universal Conjuror
Angelo, Henry .. .. .. Reminiscences
Anonymous .. .. A Description of Bartholomew Fair and the Funny Folks There
British Museum .. .. .. Actors by Gaslight. (1838)
History and Origin of Bartholomew Fair
Jim Crow's Vagaries
Noctural London. (1838)
The Book of Revelations of Jim Crow
The Dagonizing of Bartholomew Fair.
Variety Stars
Ashton, J. .. .. Social Life Under the Regency

Baker, H. B. .. .. .. The London Stage
Ballantine, William .. .. Extracts from a Barrister's Life
Banks, C. Linnaeus .. .. Life of Blondin
Baring-Gould, S. .. .. .. English Minstrelsie
Barnum, P. T. .. .. .. Autobiography
Baskervill, C. R. .. .. The Elizabethan Jig
Beerbohm, Max .. .. .. The Works of Max Beerbohm
Behn, Aphra .. .. .. The Emperor of the Moon
Blackmantle, Bernard .. .. New London Spy
Metropolitan Sketches
Booth, J. B. .. .. .. Old " Pink'un " Days
Boulton, W. B. .. .. .. The Amusements of Old London
" Boz " .. .. Sketches
Brayley, E. W. .. .. .. Historical and Descriptive Account of the London Theatres
Broadbent, R. J. .. .. .. History of Pantomime
Burnand, F. C. .. .. .. Memoirs
Bussey, Findlater .. .. Sixty Years of Journalism

Central Vigilance Committee First Annual Report, 1884
Chambers, Sir Edmund .. .. The Mediaeval Stage
Chancellor, Beresford .. .. The Pleasure Haunts of London
Chant, Laura Ormiston .. Why We Attacked the Empire
Chevalier, Albert .. .. A Record of Himself
Before I Forget
Chirgwin, George H. .. .. Life and Reminiscences

CIBBER, COLLEY .. .. .. An Apology for the Life of—
CLARKE, MARMADUKE .. .. The Royal Panoptikon of Science and Art
COBORN, CHARLES .. .. The Man who Broke the Bank at Monte Carlo
COLLINS, JOHN .. .. .. An Evening Brush
COLMAN, GEORGE (the younger) .. Broad Grins
COMPANION TO THE ROYAL SURREY ZOOLOGICAL GARDENS
COOK, DUTTON .. .. .. A Book of the Play
COOKE, GEORGE FREDERICK .. Diaries

DE CASTRO, JOHN .. .. .. Memoirs
DESMOND, SHAW .. .. .. London Nights of Long Ago
DIBDIN, CHARLES .. .. .. Professional Life
DIBDIN, THOMAS .. .. .. Memoirs
Mother Goose
DISHER, WILLSON .. .. .. Clowns and Pantomimes
DONALDSON, W. A. .. .. .. Fifty Years of an Actor's Life
DUNVILLE, T. E. .. .. .. Autobiography

EGAN, PIERCE .. .. .. The Life of an Actor
ELIOT, T. S. .. .. .. The Sacred Wood
Collected Essays
ELLIS, HAVELOCK .. .. .. Autobiography

FIELDING, HENRY .. .. .. Don Quixote in England
FITZGERALD, ADAIR .. .. Stories of Famous Songs
FITZGERALD, EDWARD .. .. Life of Garrick
FITZGERALD, PERCY .. .. Music Hall Land
FROST, J. .. .. Forty Years' Recollections
Lives of the Conjurors
Old Showman
FULLER, J. .. .. The Worthies of England

GEARY, W. N. M. .. .. The Law of the Music Halls
GOLDSMITH, OLIVER .. .. The Vicar of Wakefield
GRANT, JAMES .. .. .. Sketches in London
Travels in Town

HADDON, ARCHIBALD .. .. The Story of the Music Hall
HALLIWELL, J. O.—PHILIPS .. Tarleton's Jests
HAYWARD, A. L. .. .. .. The Days of Dickens
HAZLITT, WILLIAM .. .. Essays
HIBBERT, H. G. .. .. .. Fifty Years of a Londoner's Life
HOLCROFT, THOMAS .. .. Memoirs
HOLLINGSHEAD, J. .. .. .. The Story of Leicester Square
Memoirs
HOUDINI, H. .. .. .. A Magician Among the Spirits
His Life Story
HUDSON, THOMAS .. .. .. Song Books

ILLUSTRATED GUIDE BOOK TO OLYMPIA

JAMES, HENRY .. .. .. " A Small Boy and Others
JENKINS, EDWARD .. .. .. " The Devil's Chain "
JERROLD, DOUGLAS .. .. " Cakes and Ale "
JERROLD, WALTER .. .. .. A Century of Parody.

Jonson, Ben .. .. .. Bartholomew Fair

Killock, H. .. .. .. Houdini : His Life Story
Kirkman, Francis .. .. The Wits : or Sport upon Sport
Knight, ... London
Knowles, R. G. .. .. .. A Modern Columbus

Lawrence, W. J. .. .. .. Studies of the Elizabethan Stage
Pre-Restoration Stage Studies
Shakespeare's Workshop
Leno, Dan .. .. Hys Book
Le Roux, Hughes .. .. Acrobats and Mountebanks
Lewis, M. G. .. .. .. Abellino : or the Bravo of Venice
Rugantino
Ley, J. T. .. .. The Dickens Circle
Lillo, George .. .. .. The London Apprentice
Little Tich .. .. .. Little Tich
Lucas, E. V. .. .. .. A Wanderer in London

Maccabe, Frederick .. .. Autobiography
The Art of Ventriloquism
Mackay, Charles .. .. Fifty Years' Recollections
Mckechnie, Samuel .. .. Entertainment Through the Ages
Mahew, Henry .. .. .. London Labour and the London Poor
Mantzius, Karl .. .. .. European Drama
Mathers, John .. .. .. History of John De Castro
Miles, H. D. .. .. .. The Life of Grimaldi
Miller, David Pierce .. .. The Life of a Showman
Morley, Professor .. .. Old London Fairs
Morton, Charles .. .. Pamphlet on the Canterbury Music Hall

Nash, John ("Jolly") .. .. Stories and Anecdotes
The Merriest Man Alive
Nelson, John .. .. .. History of Islington
Newton, Chance .. .. .. Idols of the Halls
Sixty Years' Stage Service
Nichols .. .. History of Lambeth
Nicholson, Renton .. .. The Autobiography of a Fast Man
Nicholson's *Noctes*
Nicholson, Watson .. .. The Struggle for a Free Stage

O'Keefe, John .. .. .. Recollections
Oulton, W. C. .. .. .. History of the Theatres of London
Oxberry, William .. .. Dramatic Biography
The Dramatic Mirror
The Theatrical Banquet

Pearce, Charles E. .. .. Sims Reeves
Pearl, Cora .. .. .. The Memoirs of Cora Pearl
Philobiblion Society .. .. Ancient Ballads and Broadsides
Planche, J. R. .. .. .. Recollections and Reflections

Randall, Harry .. .. .. An Old Time Comedian
Raymond, E. T. .. .. .. Life of William Elliston
Rendle, T. Macdonald .. .. Swings and Round-a-bouts

Reynolds, Harry .. .. Minstrel Memories
Richardson, John .. .. Reminiscences of the Last Fifty Years
Ritchie, Ewing .. .. .. The Night Side of London
Roberts, Arthur .. .. .. Fifty Years of Spoof
Robey, George .. .. .. My Life up to Now
Russell, G. W. .. .. .. Collections and Recollections
Russell, Henry .. .. .. Cheer, boys, Cheer !
Russell, W G. E .. .. A Pocket full of Sixpences

Sala, George Augustus .. .. Robson
Gaslight and Daylight
Twice round the clock
Things I have seen
Sanger, George .. .. .. Seventy Years a Showman
Scott, Clement .. .. .. The Drama of Yesterday and To-day
The Diaries of E L. Blanchard
Old Days in Bohemian London
Sherson, Erroll .. .. .. London's Lost Theatres
Sims, George R. .. .. .. My Life
Sloman, Charles .. .. .. The Fitful Fancies of an Improvisatore
Smith, Albert .. .. .. The Ascent of Mount Blanc. (Handbook)
Wild Oats and Dead Leaves
Smith, J. T. .. .. .. A Book for a Rainy Day
Soldene, Emily .. .. .. My Life
South London Gardens. Mr. E. Holmes' Collection
Stevens, G. A. .. .. .. The Choice Spirits' Feast
The Adventure of a Specialist
Stirling, Edward .. .. Old Drury Lane
Stow, J. .. .. The Annales of England
Strutt .. .. Sports and Pastimes
Stuart, C. D.—Park, A. J. .. The Variety Stage

Thackeray, William Makepeace The Newcomes
Pendennis
Timbs, John .. .. .. Curiosities of London
Thurmond, John .. .. .. The Necromancer

Wagner, J. L. T. .. .. The Pantomimes and All About Them
Walford, E. .. .. .. Fairs, Past and Present
Old and New London
Wallett, W. G. .. .. .. Public Life of the Queen's Jester
Ward, Ned .. .. .. A Walk to Smithfield
Wheatley, H. B. .. .. .. London : past and present
White, William .. .. .. Illustrated Handbook of the Alhambra
Booklet on the Alhambra
Wild, Samuel .. .. .. The Authentic History of Old Wild's
Williams, Michael .. .. Some London Theatres
Williamson, David .. .. The German Reeds and Corney Grain
World's Guide to London. (1862)
Wroth, Warwick .. .. 18th Century Pleasure Gardens
Cremorne and the Later London Gardens

Yates, Edmund .. .. .. Reminiscences
My Haunts and their Frequenters

PERIODICALS, ETC.

Advertisements, etc., Relating to Bartholomew Fair. 1687-1849.
" The Atlantic Monthly," November 1867
Aaron Hill : " The Prompter "
Cremorne Gardens. A Collection of Programmes. (British Museum)
Earls Court Exhibition, etc. (British Museum)
" The Encore "
" The Entertainment Gazette "
" The Era "
" The Era Almanack "
Greenwood, T. : A Collection of Bills relating to Sadler's Wells
" Harleian Miscellany "
" Household Words "
" The Idler " (19th Century Magazine)
Jerome K. Jerome : Variety Patter. (Article)
" The King " (British Museum)
" The Music Hall Critic "
" The New Universal Songster "
" Pantomime Annual "
" Paul Pry "
Programme of Royal Polytechnic Institute. (British Museum)
" Mr. Punch's Victorian Era "
Scott, Clement : " Prudes on the Prowl " (*Daily Telegraph*)
" South Atlantic Quarterly "
" The Stage "
" The Stage Annual "
" The Train "—Article by Edmund Yates
" Variety Theatre Annual "
Variety " Who's Who "
" The Vaudeville Magazine," 1871
" The Vauxhall Observer "